ETHNIC CONFLICT IN WORLD POLITICS

DILEMMAS IN WORLD POLITICS

BOOKS IN THIS SERIES

Dilemmas of International Trade, Second Edition
Bruce E. Moon

Global Environmental Politics, Third Edition
Gareth Porter, Janet Brown, and Pamela S. Chasek

Humanitarian Challenges and Intervention, Second Edition
Thomas G. Weiss and Cindy Collins

The European Union: Dilemmas of Regional Integration
James A. Caporaso

The United Nations in the Post–Cold War Era, Second Edition
Karen A. Mingst and Margaret P. Karns

International Futures: Choices in the Face of Uncertainty, Third Edition
Barry B. Hughes

Global Gender Issues, Second Edition
Spike Peterson and Anne Sisson Runyon

International Human Rights, Second Edition
Jack Donnelly

Democracy and Democratization in a Changing World, Second Edition
Georg Sørensen

Revolution and Transition in East-Central Europe, Second Edition
David S. Mason

One Land, Two Peoples, Second Edition
Deborah Gerner

Dilemmas of Development Assistance
Sarah J. Tisch and Michael B. Wallace

East Asian Dynamism, Second Edition
Steven Chan

ETHNIC CONFLICT IN WORLD POLITICS

SECOND EDITION

■　　■　　■

Barbara Harff
U.S. Naval Academy

Ted Robert Gurr
University of Maryland at College Park

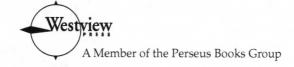
A Member of the Perseus Books Group

Copyright © 2004 by Westview Press, A Member of the Perseus Books Group

Published in the United States of America by Westview Press, A Member of the Perseus Books Group, 5500 Central Avenue, Boulder, Colorado 80301-2877, and in the United Kingdom by Westview Press, 12 Hid's Copse Road, Cumnor Hill, Oxford OX2 9JJ.

Find us on the World Wide Web at www.westviewpress.com

Westview Press books are available at special discounts for bulk purchases in the United States by corporations, institutions, and other organizations. For more information, please contact the Special Markets Department at the Perseus Books Group, 11 Cambridge Center, Cambridge, MA 02142, or call (617) 252-5298, (800) 255-1514 or email special.markets@perseusbooks.com.

Library of Congress Cataloging-in-Publication Data

Gurr, Ted Robert, 1936-
    Ethnic conflict in world politics / Ted Robert Gurr, Barbara Harff.—
2nd ed.
        p. cm.
    Includes bibliographical references and index.
        ISBN-13 978-0-8133-9840-2 (pbk. : alk. paper) — ISBN-13 978-0-8133-4107-1 (hard. :
alk. paper)
        ISBN-10 0-8133-9840-1 (pbk. : alk. paper) — ISBN-10 0-8133-4107-8 (hard. :
alk. paper)
        1. Ethnic conflict.   2. Ethnic relations.   3. Human rights.   4. World
politics—20th century.   5. World politics—21st century.   I. Harff,
Barbara, 1942-   II. Title.
D1056.G87   2003
323.1'09'049—dc21

                                                                        2003006627

Contents

Tables and Illustrations   ix

Acronyms   xi

Preface   xii

**1 Ethnopolitical Conflict and the Changing
    World Order**   1

    Defining and Mapping the World of Ethnic Groups, 3
    The Changing Global System and Ethnic Conflict, 5
    Contemporary Examples of Ethnopolitical Conflict, 11
    Conclusion, 17
    Discussion Questions, 18

2 The World of Ethnopolitical Groups   19

    The World Historical Background to
       Contemporary Ethnic Conflicts, 20
    Ethnonationalists, 23
    Indigenous Peoples, 25
    Ethnoclasses, 27
    Communal Contenders, 28
    Dominant Minorities, 29
    Conclusion, 30
    Religion and Ethnicity, 31
    Where We Go from Here, 32
    Discussion Questions, 33

3 The Pursuit of Autonomy: The Kurds and Miskitos   35

    The Kurds: A Nation Without a State, 35
    The Miskitos: An Indigenous Revolution Confronts a
       Socialist Revolution, 56
    Conclusion, 65
    Discussion Questions, 66

4 Protecting Group Rights in Plural Societies: The Chinese in Malaysia and Turks in Germany   67

The Chinese in Malaysia, 67
Turkish Immigrants in Germany, 81
The End of the Cold War and Immigration Pressures in
    Germany, 84
Minorities in Other Western European Societies, 90
Conclusion, 92
Discussion Questions, 93

5 A Framework for Analysis of Ethnopolitical Mobilization and Conflict   95

Approaches to Explaining Ethnopolitical Conflict, 95
Using Social Science Theories to Explain Ethnopolitical
    Conflict, 98
Explaining Ethnopolitical Mobilization and Conflict, 103
Concepts, Variables, and Indicators, 107
Overview of the Model, 112
Problems and Issues in Modeling Ethnic Conflict, 113
Conclusion, 115
Discussion Questions, 115

6 The Internal Processes of Ethnic Mobilization and Conflict: Four Cases   117

Conflict Processes: The Kurds in Iraq and Miskitos in
    Nicaragua, 117
Conflict Processes: Malaysian Chinese and Turks
    in Germany, 126
Conclusion, 133
Discussion Questions, 136

7 The International Dimensions of Ethnopolitical Conflict: Four Cases   139

The Emerging Ethnic Dimension in Global Politics, 139
Communal Identities and the Formation of New States, 141
The Theoretical Model Revisited, 142
The International Context of the Kurdish Conflict, 144
The Kurdish Situation in Spring 2003, 150
International Context of the Miskito Conflict, 151
The International Context of the Chinese Communist
    Insurgency in Malaya, 154
Malaysia from Independence to the Present, 158
The International Context of Minority Issues in Germany, 159

Conclusion, 161
Discussion Questions, 164

**8   Ethnic Groups in the International System: State
Sovereignty Versus Individual and Group Rights   165**

Legal Implications of Ethnic Diversity, 165
Theoretical Considerations: Individuals, Groups,
    and the State, 168
The Current Status of Groups in the International System, 170
The Case of Bosnia-Herzegovina: International Implications of
    Genocidal Communal Conflict, 173
The United Nations as Lawmaker, 174
The Legal Bases for International Action, 176
The Legality of Humanitarian Intervention, 177
Conclusion, 179
Discussion Questions, 180

**9   Responding to Ethnopolitical Challenges:
Five Principles of Emerging International Doctrine   181**

Five Principles for Managing Ethnopolitical Conflict, 182
The Future of Ethnopolitical Conflict, 191
Toward an Uncertain Future, 194
Discussion Questions, 195

Appendix   197
Notes   205
Suggested Readings and Research Sources   215
Glossary   221
About the Book and Authors   227
Index   229

Tables and Illustrations

Tables

3.1 Estimates of Kurdish population in Turkey, Iran, Iraq, and Syria, 2001

6.1 Summary of internal factors in ethnic mobilization for four groups

7.1 Summary of international factors in ethnic mobilization for four groups

Figures

1.1 Numbers and proportions of countries with ethnic wars, 1946 – 2001

1.2 Politically active ethnic groups by region, 2001

1.3 Strategies of political action used by ethnopolitical minorities in 1995, by world region

2.1 Types of politically active ethnic groups in 2001

4.1 The population of Malaysia, 2000

4.2 Foreign populations of thirteen European countries, 2000

5.1 Framework for explaining ethnopolitical violence

9.1 Global trends in numbers of democratic, autocratic, and transitional regimes, 1946–2001

9.2 Global trends in new, contained, and settled armed conflicts for self-determination, 1956–2000

Maps

3.1 Contiguous Kurdish-inhabited areas in the 1990s

3.2 Kurdish principalities of early modern times

3.3 Provisions of Treaty of Sèvres for an independent Kurdistan and
Armenia, 1921
3.4 Miskito settlements in the 1980s

4.1 Distribution of Chinese population in Malaya, 1957
4.2 Modern Malaysia

7.1 Kurdish autonomous region, 2003

Appendix: Serious and potential ethnopolitical conflicts in 2001

Photographs and Cartoons

Ethnic disputes explained.

Kurdish refugees who fled from Iraqi army attacks, April 1991.

Kurdish family in Sanandaj, Iran, 1991.

Children in a land at war, 2001. Kurdish boys playing with a toy weapon;
girl holding flag of the Kurdish Democratic Party (KDP).

Brooklyn Rivera in Puerto Cabezas, 2001.

Forum in Puerto Cabezas to protest commercial leasing of a community
pier, 2001.

Rama teacher on Rama Cay, 2001.

Chinese Malaysians' voter registrations are checked in Kuala Lumpur,
1999.

Chinese Malaysian children sit below Democratic Action Party posters,
2002.

Turks and others pray in front of a burned-out house in Solingen,
Germany.

Cem Oezdemir.

"Day of the Turks" parade, 2002.

Classroom at Sulaymaniyeh University, 2001, housed in a former Iraqi
prison.

United Nations notice.

Acronyms

ALPROMISU	Alianza para el Progreso de Miskitos y Sumos (Alliance for the Progress of Miskitos and Sumus)
CIA	Central Intelligence Agency
CPM	Communist Party of Malaya
CSCE	Conference on Security and Cooperation in Europe, renamed in the mid-1990s Organization on Security and Cooperation in Europe (OSCE)
DAP	Democratic Action Party (Malaysia)
ILO	International Labor Organization
KDP	Kurdish Democratic Party (Iraq)
KDPI	Kurdish Democratic Party of Iran
MCA	Malaysian Chinese Association
MISURA	Miskitos, Sumus, and Ramas
MISURASATA	Miskitos, Sumus, Ramas, and Sandinistas United
NATO	North Atlantic Treaty Organization
NDP	National Demokratische Partei, or National Democratic Party (Germany)
NEP	New Economic Policy
NGO	nongovernmental organization
OAU	Organization of African Unity
OSCE	*see* CSCE
PKK	Partiya Karkaren Kurdistan, or Kurdish Worker's Party (Turkey)
PUK	Patriotic Union of Kurdistan (Iraq)
UNITA	Unino Nacional para a Independencia Total de Angola (National Union for the Total Independence of Angola)
YATAMA	Yapti Tasbaya Masrika (Children of Mother Earth)

Preface

In 1994, when the first edition of *Ethnic Conflict in World Politics* was published, it seemed that the world was being overwhelmed by a tide of deadly ethnic conflicts. Book titles warned of "conflicts unending" and "pandemonium."[1] In 2002, more than a decade after the Cold War ended, less than a dozen ethnic wars are being waged compared with more than thirty in the early 1990s. International refugees in need of assistance have declined from about 25 million to 15 million. During the same period many new multiethnic democracies have been consolidated. International doctrine and practices for containing deadly ethnic conflict have evolved. The UN, regional organizations in Europe and Africa, and major powers have become more proactive in responding to ethnic quarrels. The net effect has been not to put an end to ethnic conflict but rather to contain some of its worst consequences and to channel the political energies of mobilized ethnic groups into conventional politics.

This edition points out the continuing challenges faced by multiethnic societies but gives closer attention to the evolution of more effective domestic and international policies for containing ethnic violence and repression. The challenge at the beginning of the twenty-first century is not whether the state system will disintegrate along ethnic or religious lines. Its capacity for adaptation and survival has been demonstrated by developments of the last decade. The question is how well civil societies, states, and the international system will respond to new ethnic and religious challenges.

The first chapter discusses the origins of ethnic conflict and traces some of its major implications for the international system. In Chapter 2, we identify the main types of politically active ethnic groups, discuss their grievances and political strategies, and summarize the historical processes that explain why they have been and continue to be important actors in domestic and international politics.

---

[1]Richard N. Haass, *Conflicts Unending: The United States and Regional Disputes* (New Haven, CT: Yale University Press, 1990); Daniel Moynihan, *Pandemonium: Ethnicity in International Politics* (Oxford: Oxford University Press, 1993.).

Chapters 3 and 4 sketch the historical background and conflicts of four peoples. The Kurds in the Middle East and the Miskito Indians of Central America, the subjects of Chapter 3, are examples of groups whose members have a strong sense of communal interest and identity they want to protect by gaining political independence or autonomy. We chose to analyze the Kurds for two reasons. First, their nationalist aspirations continue to be a major challenge to regional stability in the Middle East. Second, Iraqi attacks on the Kurds in 1991 led to a precedent-setting collective response: The United Nations authorized for the first time the use of force to establish a protected zone for victimized people in a sovereign state. Since that time, the Iraqi Kurds have developed an increasingly effective regional government and economy and, with international encouragement, have begun to bridge the factional rivalries that have crippled past efforts at Kurdish unity. The Miskitos are not nationalists, nor have they suffered to the extent of the Kurds. Like most indigenous peoples, the Miskitos are mainly concerned with protecting their traditional way of life, land, and resources. We selected them because unlike most other indigenous peoples, they rebelled against the Nicaraguan government in the 1970s, taking advantage of the U.S.-backed Contra war against the Sandinistas to secure greater autonomy. Autonomy during the 1990s did not bring them as many gains as they had hoped, mainly because of lack of development and renewed efforts by the impoverished Nicaraguan state to exploit natural resources supposedly under the control of the autonomous government.

The Chinese in Malaysia and the Turkish immigrants in Germany, described in Chapter 4, have been concerned mainly with protecting and improving their status in multiethnic societies. The low status and limited citizenship rights of Turks in Germany typify the situation of many immigrants from poorer countries to developed Western societies. During the last decade their status has significantly improved, as we show. We are particularly interested in the Chinese in Malaysia because despite a history of insurgency in the 1950s and victimization in racial rioting in the 1960s, they have secured a limited power-sharing role in a modernizing Asian state. But multiethnic democracy in Malaysia has a clouded future: increasingly autocratic leadership, growing Islamist sentiment, and economic uncertainty.

Chapter 5 begins with a review of some social science approaches to explaining communal conflict; we then propose a theoretical framework for analyzing the ways internal and international conditions lead ethnic groups into open conflict with states. This framework has been developed and used by the first author in undergraduate courses. It takes a scientific approach, one that emphasizes precision and objectivity, which some readers may not find congenial. In her experience it is pedagogically successful because it identifies for students the broad range of factors that need to be taken into account in case studies and helps overcome students' tendency to let preconceptions guide their selection and interpretation of evidence on value-laden topics.

The framework is used in Chapters 6 and 7 to compare the status and mobilization of the four groups and to assess some of the consequences of ethnic mobilization and international engagement. This leads us into a discussion of important policy issues such as how democracy affects ethnic conflict and whether countries' international economic and political status affects their treatment of minorities.

The eruption of new ethnic conflicts at the end of the Cold War and the persistence of old ones posed major legal, political, and humanitarian challenges to the international system. These challenges are identified in Chapter 1; international responses to them are the subjects of the last two chapters. The changing status of ethnic groups in international law and the evolving doctrine of humanitarian intervention are examined in Chapter 8. We argue in Chapter 9 that an increasingly effective set of national and international policies for containing conflict in ethnic conflicts emerged during the 1990s. These policies are largely responsible for the improving status of many ethnic groups and the diminution of ethnic wars.

The first author is principally responsible for Chapters 1 and 8, which are substantially new, and for revisions of chapters 5 and 7. The second author prepared the new concluding chapter 9, and revised Chapters 2, 3, and 6. Both authors worked on the revisions of Chapter 4. We have both read and commented extensively on one another's sections. This book is, in other words, a fully collaborative effort.

We acknowledge with thanks those who have contributed to this revision. Michael Johns, coordinator of the Minorities at Risk Project at the University of Maryland's Center for International Development and Conflict Management (CIDCM), prepared the appendix of current ethnic conflicts. Current and former doctoral students at the University of Maryland who helped us update source materials include Dr. Jonathan Fox, Dr. Pamela L. Martin, Deepa Khosla, and David Quinn. Michael Johns and Dr. Monty G. Marshall of CIDCM prepared the new figures. Barbara Harff thanks the U.S. Naval Academy for giving her a semester's sabbatical leave to pursue this project. We are especially thankful to Prof. Scott Pegg of Bilkent University for his detailed and helpful comments on the first edition.

Barbara Harff

Ted Robert Gurr

1

Ethnopolitical Conflict and the Changing World Order

Protracted conflicts over the rights and demands of ethnic and religious groups have caused more misery and loss of human life than has any other type of local, regional, and international conflict since the end of World War II. They are also the source of most of the world's refugees. In 2002 about two-thirds of the world's 15 million international refugees were fleeing from ethnopolitical conflict and repression. At least twice as many others have been internally displaced by force and famine. At the beginning of the new millennium millions of people in impoverished countries are in need of assistance, hundreds of thousands of desperate emigrants from conflict-ridden states are knocking at the doors of Western countries, and, to make things worse, donor fatigue among rich states threatens to perpetuate inequalities and misery.

Ethnopolitical conflicts are here to stay. Figure 1.1 shows that the number of countries with major ethnic wars increased steadily from a handful in the early 1950s to thirty-one countries in the early 1990s. We also know that between the mid-1950s and 1990 the magnitude of all ethnopolitical conflicts increased nearly fourfold—an astonishing increase in light of what was hoped for in the aftermath World War II.

The Holocaust should have enlightened us about what ethnic and religious hatred can do when used by unscrupulous leaders armed with exclusionary ideologies. Many people hoped that with the end of colonialism we could look forward to a better world in which nation-states would guarantee and protect the basic freedoms of their peoples. When the United Nations came into existence, were we wrong to believe that a new world order would emerge, one in which minimum standards of global justice would be observed and violators be punished? Is it still possible that a civil society will emerge in which citizens eschew narrow ethnic interests in favor of global issues?

Instead we have witnessed more genocides and mass slaughters, an increase in ethnic consciousness leading to deadly ethnic conflicts, and religious fanaticism justifying the killing of innocent civilians in faraway

1

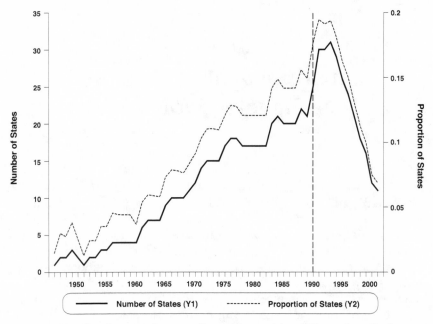

FIGURE 1.1   Numbers and proportions of countries with major ethnic wars, 1946–2001

lands. Some progress has been made to check ethnic wars since the mid-1990s, but we badly need more innovative ideas about how to fight the scourges that plague mankind. To top it off, the international political will to act has been waning in the wake of Somalia, Bosnia, Rwanda, Liberia, Burundi, the Democratic Republic of Congo, and other conflicts that need international attention. There is also the risk that, in the aftermath of the September 11 terrorist attacks on the World Trade Center in New York, the Western "war on terrorism" will divert international attention away from enduring problems.

So why write a book about ethnic conflict? This is what we hope for: If we understand the factors that contribute to the onset of ethnic conflicts, we may be able to suggest ways to stop escalation and find solutions by peaceful political means. We have ample evidence that deadly ethnic conflicts are not inevitable and can be contained or deterred, often without using force or the involvement of major powers. We hope that this book helps to further knowledge about ethnic conflicts and provides some guidelines about how to prevent, deter, or stop escalation.

DEFINING AND MAPPING THE WORLD OF ETHNIC GROUPS

Ethnic groups like the Kurds, Miskitos of Central America, and the Turks in Germany are "psychological communities" whose members share a persisting sense of common interest and identity that is based on some combination of shared historical experience and valued cultural traits—beliefs, language, ways of life, a common homeland. They are often called **identity groups.** A few, like the Koreans and the Icelanders, have their own internationally recognized state or states. Most, however, do not have such recognition, and they must protect their identity and interests within existing states.

Some religious groups resemble ethnic groups insofar as they have a strong sense of identity based on culture, belief, and a shared history of discrimination. Examples are Jews and the various sects of Shi'i Islam. Politically active religious groups, such as offshoots of the Muslim Brotherhood, are motivated by grievances similar to ethnic groups.

Many ethnic groups coexist amicably with others within the boundaries of established states. The Swedish minority in Finland, for example, has its own cultural and local political institutions, which are guaranteed by a 1921 international agreement between Sweden and Finland. For eighty years the Swedish minority has had no serious disputes with the Finnish people or government. Since the 1960s the Netherlands has welcomed many immigrants from the Third World with relatively little of the social tension or **discrimination** aimed at immigrants in Britain, France, and Germany. Even in these tolerant countries the explosive growth of asylum seekers has led to some antiforeign political movements and xenophobic attacks.

If peaceful relations prevail among peoples for a long time, their separate identities may eventually weaken. For example, Irish-Americans were a distinctive minority in mid-nineteenth-century North America because of their immigrant origins, their concentration in poor neighborhoods and low-status occupations, and the deep-rooted prejudice most Anglo-Americans had toward them. After a century of upward mobility and political incorporation, Irish descent has little political or economic significance in Canada or the United States, although many Irish-Americans still honor their cultural origins.

The ethnic groups whose status is of greatest concern in international politics today are those that are the targets of discrimination and that have organized to take political action to promote or defend their interests. A recent study, directed by the second author, surveys politically active national peoples and ethnic minorities throughout the world. As of 2001, the project has identified and profiled 275 sizable groups that have been targets of discrimination or are organized for political assertiveness or both.[1]

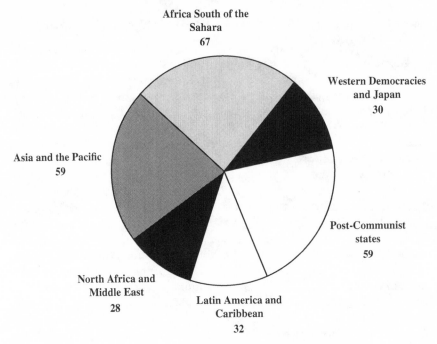

Africa South of the
Sahara
67

Western Democracies
and Japan
30

Asia and the Pacific
59

Post-Communist
states
59

North Africa and
Middle East
28

Latin America and
Caribbean
32

FIGURE 1.2   Politically active ethnic groups by region, 2001

Most larger countries have at least one such ethnic group, and in a few countries like South Africa and Bolivia, they comprise half or more of the population. Taken together the groups involve more than 1 billion people, or a sixth of the world's population. Figure 1.2 shows how these groups were distributed among the regions of the world in 2001. When the Soviet Union dissolved into fifteen independent republics at the end of 1991, the political demands of **ethnonationalists** like the Latvians, Ukrainians, and Armenians were met. Since then, however, at least thirty additional ethnic groups in the new republics have made new political demands.

The Minorities at Risk survey shows that about 80 percent of the politically active ethnic groups in the 1990s were disadvantaged because of historical or contemporary discrimination. Forty percent of these groups (111 out of 275) surveyed face discriminatory policies and practices harmful to their material well-being. For example, almost all indigenous peoples in the Americas have high infant mortality rates due in part to limited pre- and post-natal health care; Tamil youth in Sri Lanka have long been discriminated against by university admission policies that favor the majority Sinhalese. The survey also identified 135 minorities subjected to contemporary political discrimination. For example, Turkish governments have repeatedly banned and restricted political parties that sought to represent Kurdish interests; in Brazil people of African descent make up more than 40 percent of the country's population but hold less than 5 percent of seats in the national congress. Cultural restrictions also have been imposed on at least 116 minorities. Muslim girls attending French secondary schools have been expelled for wearing head scarves; principals of Hungarian-language schools in Slovakia have been dismissed for not speaking Slovak at Hungarian teachers' meetings. Such restrictions may seem petty but symbolically their effects can be a painful and enduring reminder that the dominant society disvalues a minority's culture.

Ethnic groups that are treated unequally resent and usually attempt to improve their condition. Three-quarters of the groups in the survey were politically active in the 1990s. They did not necessarily use violence, however. On the contrary, most ethnic groups with a political agenda use the strategies and tactics of interest groups and social movements, especially if they live in democratic states. Figure 1.3 shows the highest level of political action among minorities in 1995. One-quarter were politically inactive (some of them had a history of intense activism), half were mobilizing for or carrying out political action, and only one-quarter used violent strategies of small-scale rebellion (including terrorism) or large-scale rebellion. The latter include the most serious and enduring of all conflicts within states, including ethnic wars between Hutus and Tutsis in Burundi and Rwanda, civil wars by southerners in Sudan and Muslim Kashmiris in India, and wars of independence by Kurds in Turkey and Iraq and by Palestinians in Gaza and the West Bank.

Figure 1.3 also shows the relative frequency of different kinds of political action among world regions. The highest level of mobilization in 1995 was in Latin America—mainly among indigenous peoples. Ethnic rebellions were uncommon in Europe and the Americas and when they did occur were mainly terrorist campaigns. Rebellions were much more numerous in Africa, Asia, and the Middle East. The Appendix lists forty-six of the most serious contemporary ethnic conflicts, including some nonviolent conflicts that are potentially disruptive.

THE CHANGING GLOBAL SYSTEM AND ETHNIC CONFLICT

Ethnic conflict is not solely or even mainly a consequence of domestic politics. The potential for ethnic conflict, the issues at stake, and even the lines of **cleavage** between contending groups have been shaped and reshaped by international factors. In this section we introduce three general issues to which we return later, especially in Chapters 8 and 9—the tension between the state system and ethnic identities, the impact the end of

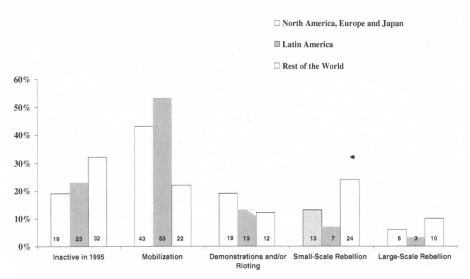

FIGURE 1.3 Strategies of political action used by ethnopolitical minorities in 1995

the Cold War has had on conflicts among nations and peoples, and the changing nature of international responses to ethnic conflict.

States or Peoples?

Historically, ethnic groups, nations, states, empires, and other forms of large-scale social organization—for example, Islam and Christendom—have coexisted, but since the seventeenth century the dominant form of social organization has been the **state system**—the organization of the world's people into a system of independent and territorial states, some of which controlled overseas colonial empires.

Despite attempts to change the existing world order by insisting that the state was obsolete, as Marxists proclaimed, the state remains the key actor in international relations. Key, because the state at the very minimum controls the principal means of coercion. Ethnic groups rarely are equal in terms of power, legitimacy, or economic resources. But it is wrong to suggest that the state is a single monolithic enterprise. Instead, we may want to think of the state as a recognized territorial entity in flux. It is one thing to think of England as an established state since the Middle Ages, yet Germany in something like its present form has existed only since 1870. The new states that emerged in the Middle East, Asia, and Africa following the demise of empires were often just creations of the former colonizers, endowed with neither historical nor cultural continuity, nor boundaries that recognized the living space of ethnic groups. Thus for example, we have states such as Burundi and Rwanda in both of which a Tutsi minority rules a Hutu majority, which led to major conflicts and postindependence genocidal killings in both countries.

Some would argue that certain states should have no independent existence, either because the notion of territory was not part of their people's culture or because they would be better off within the boundaries of established states. Indeed, one could ask how viable, necessary, or rational is the division of the Arabian peninsula into many sheikdoms, some of which have emerged as independent states only since the 1960s. But, what are the alternatives? In tribal communities, local loyalties were very well developed, but rarely extended beyond the narrow boundaries of family or clan, thus leaving local communities at the mercy of would-be conquerors and usurpers. Necessity may have been the force that unified some warring tribes, laws and coercion are the means that have kept them together.

We do not intend to cover in any comprehensive fashion the historical development of the state system but instead offer a brief glimpse into what led to its emergence and what factors may lead to the demise of some existing states.

On the one side, states act independently of their constituent parts, such as peoples and institutions. After all, we talk about the economic viability or capabilities of states, not of the people who reside within the state. Today most states control capital through either public ownership or state-owned enterprises. But some theorists still see the state as passive, reacting mainly to pressures emanating from society. Though scholars disagree on the extent of cooperation and conflict between the state and society, it is still a fact that the state is a legally recognized sovereign entity in international law, endowed with rights and obligations vis-à-vis other states, groups, and its own citizens. Whatever the reasons that gave birth to specific states, the nation-state is today the primary actor in international relations. It is the state that defines, provides, and controls the public good, through regulation and institutions. It is the state that enforces the rules through coercion and punishment.

Let us apply some of these arguments to the historical situation of the Kurds, whose situation is symptomatic of many other **ethnonationalists**. After the demise of the Ottoman Empire following World War I, they were the largest ethnic group within the former empire without a state of their own. Instead, Kurds came to live within five other states, the largest segment of them now citizens of the new Republic of Turkey. Ever since, the Turkish government has tried through incentives, coercion, discrimination, and punishment to undermine Kurdish ethnic consciousness, hoping to deter any attempts to secede. Here the state became omnipotent, using all means at its disposal to subdue Kurdish national aspirations.

An essential question is whether or not a people have rights to a territory on which they resided for many centuries. International law today
recognizes that it is inadmissible to acquire territory by waging an aggressive war, but the reality is somewhat different. International law, often invoked but seldom enforced, was used to bolster the legality of the Gulf
War in 1990, ostensibly to free Kuwait from Iraqi occupation, as well as
U.S. intervention in Panama and Vietnam. Israel, invoking its defensive
posture in the 1967 war, holds on to territory inhabited by Palestinians for
centuries. The Abkhaz in Georgia have technically won an independence
war, but are not recognized by the international community of nation-
states. What does this mean for the rights of groups vis-à-vis states? It
means that sometimes group rights are recognized by individual states
and the international community and sometimes, depending on various
power constellations, they are not. However, international law can provide the justification or the means to establish claims to specific territory.
Let us look briefly at the state as arbiter, problem-solving agent, or re-
stricter or denier of the rights of collectivities.

Indeed, few states are able to unite a multitude of **ethnies** into a harmo-
nious unit. Although long-established liberal democracies probably are
more successful than autocracies in doing so, problems persist. Recall the
situation of African-Americans prior to the Civil Rights movement and
current issues ranging from outright discrimination to disenfranchise-
ment. Consider that Native Americans are a people organized into a
number of self-governing segments or "nations" within the greater American nation yet are economically and politically dependent on the United
States.

One of the more heretical thoughts that comes to mind is whether the
institutionalized state has a future, given the many ethnic groups that
clamor for independence. The answer has to be yes, because what is it
that these ethnic groups demand? They seek the right to govern their own
territory, which they hope will become a sovereign, internationally recognized state. What this suggests is that the current international system
may fragment into hundreds of mini-states unless ethnic demands can be
satisfied within existing states. In fact more than a dozen ethnic wars
were settled in the 1990s by granting autonomy to ethnonationalists
within existing states. Successful settlements like these depend on the political system. Democracies are better able to accommodate ethnic demands than autocracies. But it is also true that in newly emerging democracies, ethnic demands may exceed the capacity of state structures, thus
leading to failure of existing states.

The ascendance and expansion of the state system has meant that
states are parties to most deadly conflicts: wars between states, civil wars
within states, and **genocides** and political mass murders by states. But

here we find a different phenomena at work. States wage war, but people decide to make war. Here the collective can triumph over state structures. The collective will as exemplified by prevailing ideologies and political movements within the state system have dramatically influenced ethnic conflict. In the 1920s and 1930s, anti-Semitic doctrines in Germany and other European countries promoted ethnic polarization. They competed with Communist doctrine in the Soviet Union, which emphasized the common interests of all Soviet peoples and minimized the significance of ethnic and nationalist identities. In the 1940s and 1950s anti-colonialism emerged as a major form of resistance against European domination in Asia and Africa. With the help of liberation ideologies, nationalists were able to unite diverse ethnic groups in their efforts to replace colonial rule by European powers with their own independent states. And they succeeded beyond what was expected. By the early 1960s almost all European-ruled colonial territories had gained independence and become members of the state system. But the success came at a cost as tribal and ethnic consciousness soon reemerged in a number of states. Congo immediately after its independence from Belgium in 1970 and Nigeria a decade later experienced major ethnic wars. More recently we have seen a new kind of resistance to the state system that has affected every world region except Latin America: It is an accelerating wave of self-determination movements.

But there are other trends. At times throughout the twentieth century, ethnic peoples have coalesced across boundaries to join in common causes—for example, by joining pan-Islamic, **pan-Arab,** and **indigenous peoples'** movements. In the Arab world such movements have been short-lived and have been characterized by constantly shifting coalitions. Despite paying lip service to equality of economic status, a shared religion, and the brotherhood of a common ancestry, Arabs have continued to fight fellow Arabs.

But rarely has a common ethnic or religious background been sufficient to cause peoples to subordinate the interests of states to a greater transnational identity or cause, even a limited one. This is especially true for peoples of countries with long-established boundaries who have developed identities beyond their immediate tribes and clans.

At present we witness two competing trends in human organization. At one extreme, we see a reemergence of xenophobia in long-established countries—for example, the increase in exclusive ethnic identity that motivates antiforeign excesses in Germany, France, and Great Britain. No less extreme are movements that demand ethnic purity in formerly heterogeneous federations, such as Serbian nationalism in the former Yugoslavia. At the other end of the continuum are oppressive leaders who defend existing boundaries at all costs, despite historically justified claims by national peoples, such as Palestinians in the Middle East and Kurds in Iraq, for internal autonomy or independence. Ironically, the new elites of former Asian and African colonies share with Saddam Hussein a willingness to fight to maintain existing boundaries and states, despite arbitrarily drawn borders that accommodated European interests but ignored demographic and cultural realities.

The End of the Cold War

The Cold War between the Soviet bloc and the U.S.-led Western alliance created, for better or worse, a sense of stability among most of the world population. Policymakers' calculations concerning conflict outcomes could be made with greater confidence in a more rigidly ordered world. The dissolution of the global system from a loose, bipolar world into an ethnically fragmented multipolar system left in its wake a greater sense of insecurity among the leaders of the established states. This is what U.S. President Bill Clinton alluded to when he told a journalist, "I even made a crack the other day . . . 'Gosh, I miss the Cold War.'" How does one deal with hostile warlords in Somalia and respond to ethnic and nationalist unrest in the Soviet successor states? Finding a workable framework for this new era and defining the role of the United States, Clinton added, "could take years."[2] By the end of the Clinton administration, no clear framework or consistent set of policies had emerged, though the administration had shifted toward more proactive engagement.

But events do not wait for policymakers to devise new frameworks. With the collapse of Soviet hegemony at the end of the Cold War, the citizens of the former Soviet Union and Eastern Europe were freed to act upon communal rivalries with a vengeance. The demise of communism in the former Soviet Union left a political and ideological vacuum that is only gradually being filled. It was ideology that bound historically hostile peoples together; now old rivalries have reemerged, and neighbors have again become antagonists fighting for power, status, and control of adjacent territories. Communist citizens' place in society was predictable, and their economic welfare was guaranteed at a basic level. Communism in its ideal form also instilled a sense of collective responsibility and solidarity that overcame more parochial identities. The transformation of socialist societies into predatory capitalist societies has led to a sense of alienation and isolation and an increased emphasis on narrow group interests and self-interests. This increased sense of isolation has been circumvented by a heightened ethnic awareness and, in some states, a growth in intolerance toward members of other groups.

A decade after the end of the Cold War, the ethnic landscape of postsocialist states is remarkably diverse. The Russian Federation has been widely and justly criticized for fighting a dirty war against rebels in the breakaway republic of Chechnya. But during the 1990s it also successfully negotiated autonomy agreements with Tatarstan, Bashkiria, and some forty other regions in the Russian Federation, thus defusing a number of potentially violent conflicts. A new sense of common interest and identity is being built among most of the peoples of Russia. In East Central Europe, the civil wars that broke up the Yugoslav Federation contrast sharply with Czechoslovakia where ethnic conflict between the Czech and Slovak republics ended peacefully in a "velvet divorce" in 1993. Nationalist governments in Romania and Slovakia cracked down on their restive Hungarian minorities in the early 1990s, but the nationalists were ousted in democratic elections in the late 1990s and Hungarian politicians joined new coalition governments. And the new democratic government of Bulgaria, whose Communist regime had persecuted the country's large Turkish Muslim minority, granted the Turks full cultural, economic, and political rights. The Roma (gypsies) are a worrisome exception to these trends toward ethnic tolerance. They are disliked and discriminated against throughout Europe, East and West.

CONTEMPORARY EXAMPLES OF ETHNOPOLITICAL CONFLICT

Since the 1960s increasing numbers of ethnic groups have begun to demand more rights and recognition, demands that are now recognized as the major source of domestic and international conflict in the post–Cold War world. The protagonists in the most intense ethnic conflicts want to establish their **autonomy** or independence, as is the case with many Kurds. Other ethnic conflicts arise from efforts by subordinate groups to improve their status within the existing boundaries of a state rather than to secede from it. For example, most black South Africans wanted—and gained—majority control of state power. Turkish and other recent immigrants to Germany are worried about their security, seek greater economic opportunities, and hope to become citizens. Native peoples in the Americas want to protect what is left of their traditional lands and cultures from the corrosive influences of modern society. Here we consider some implications of both kinds of ethnic conflict.

The **civil wars** accompanying the dissolution of Yugoslavia into five new states show that subject people's demands for autonomy often escalate into warfare. After Slovenia, Croatia, and Bosnia declared independence in summer 1991, Serbia—the dominant partner in the old Yugoslavian Federation—tried to reestablish its **hegemony** by promoting uprisings by Serbian **minorities** in the latter two states. These Serbs justified their actions by recounting Croat atrocities against Serbs during World War II. They devised brutal and often deadly policies called **ethnic cleansing,** which involved the murder or forced removal of Croatians, Bosnian Muslims, and other minorities from areas in which Serbs lived and prompted hundreds of thousands of refugees to flee to surrounding countries. In Serbia proper the government and local activists severely restricted the activities of Albanian and Hungarian minorities.

One of the longest modern civil wars was waged by the people of the Ethiopian province of Eritrea, who supported a war of independence that lasted from the early 1960s until 1991. The Eritrean nationalists received some diplomatic and military support from Middle Eastern states such as Egypt, whereas in the first decade of conflict the imperial Ethiopian government relied heavily on military assistance from the United States. Even the military-led **revolution** that overthrew Emperor Haile Selassie in 1974 did not end ethnic conflict. Instead, the new Marxist military leaders of Ethiopia sought and received support from the Soviet Union to enable them to continue the war against Eritrea. By the end of the 1970s many other ethnic groups in Ethiopia were stimulated into rebellion by the Eritrean example. An alliance was eventually formed among Eritreans, Tigreans, Oromo, and others that culminated in the rebels' triumphal capture of the Ethiopian capital, Addis Ababa, in May 1991.

Unlike the situation in Yugoslavia, there was no serious international effort to check the Ethiopian civil war. No major power recognized Eritrea as an independent state; international organizations regarded the conflict as an internal matter, and there was no media-inspired publicity of atrocities that might have prompted greater action. Only when famine threatened the region did the Ethiopian government allow humanitarian assistance but then prevented distribution of the aid in rebel-held areas.

Following thirty years of warfare, the moderate policies of the new revolutionary government allowed for a peaceful reconciliation. The government made and kept a commitment to hold referendums in 1993 to set up autonomous regional governments or, in the case of Eritrea, to allow full independence. The Eritrean referendum in April 1993 resulted in a 99.8 percent vote in favor of independence. Eritrean independence was accepted by the Ethiopian government, and the new state immediately received diplomatic recognition from the United States and many other countries.

But new sources of ethnic tension soon cropped up. Some Eritreans living in the Ethiopian capital were forced to leave the country, with retaliatory threats by Eritreans to expel Ethiopians. Political and economic tensions escalated until May 1998, when the two countries began a deadly two-year war over some scraps of disputed territory. The Eritrea-Ethiopia conflict, like that between Muslims and Hindus in the Indian subcontinent, shows that separation is not a perfect solution for ethnic tensions because it may lead to future conflicts within and between states.

Conflicts over group demands for better treatment within existing states and societies are seldom as deadly as the civil wars in Yugoslavia or Ethiopia; nor are they likely to have serious international repercussions. But they can be just as fateful for the people caught up in them, as the following example suggests. Kara (not her real name) is a woman in her late twenties who works as an assistant manager of a resort hotel on Turkey's Aegean coast. She was born and raised in Germany by parents who had emigrated there as "guest workers." After Kara's graduation from secondary school, her parents accepted money from the West German government to return to Turkey. Kara also had to return, and, like her parents, was prohibited from returning to Germany. Kara does not fear for her life or safety, but she is caught between two cultures: the German society in which she was raised and whose language she speaks fluently, and the Turkish society in which she must live and work. Her desk clerk, a man in his early twenties, has the same story and a similar problem: Turkish girls mock him as "the German" who speaks Turkish badly. Neither likes living in Turkey, and both have doubts about finding marriage partners.[3] Their lives would probably have been more satisfying, and their identities more secure, if they could have gained full citizenship and stayed in the country in which they grew up.

Enduring Conflicts, Changing International Responses

We cannot entirely blame the explosion of ethnic conflict in the early 1990s on the end of the Cold War. Figure 1.1 shows clearly that the extent of conflicts worldwide between ethnic groups and states increased steadily from 1950 to 1989, before the Cold War ended. Thus we need to identify other factors that contributed to that explosion. We begin with three Third World examples, which may offer some clues to why some ethnic conflicts were neither affected by nor indirect by-products of Cold War confrontations.

In the 1970s the newly independent African states of Uganda and Equatorial Guinea experienced intense ethnopolitical conflict that had little relationship to the tensions produced by the Cold War. Dictators Macias Nguma of Equatorial Guinea (1968–1979) and Idi Amin of Uganda (1971–1979) each sought to consolidate power by killing thousands of their ethnic and political rivals. These horrifying events elicited no substantive response from the United Nations and few condemnations from individual states. Amin and Macias were virtually free to kill people they defined as enemies, in part because their countries were of little consequence to either the United States or the Soviet Union.

The third case is Rwanda, in which during a genocide in 1994 800,000 to 1 million Tutsis and moderate Hutus perished. When Tutsi exiles of the Rwandan Patriotic Front launched a major invasion from bases in Uganda in 1993, Hutu armies and militias responded with counterattacks. Intermittent negotiations led to the Arusha Accords, but the mobilization of Hutu militias continued. In neighboring Burundi, massacres following a 1993 coup led to a massive exodus of some 342,000 refugees to Rwanda. Militant Rwandan Hutus sought to undermine the Arusha Accords. They probably arranged the downing of the aircraft that carried the presidents of Rwanda and Burundi, Juvenal Habyarimana and Cyprien Ntaryamira, back from peace talks in Tanzania on April 6, 1994. This signaled the beginning of a killing spree in which Belgian peacekeepers and the moderate Rwandan prime minister, Agathe Uwilingiyimana, were among the first to die. Ethnic Tutsis were the primary targets. In the next 100 days, some 800,000 people were killed by marauding Hutu militias, encouraged by their leadership and hate propaganda. In July 1994, Tutsi rebels seized the capital, declared victory, and named a Hutu president. At the end of July Tanzania recognized the new government and Western powers promised aid. But killings continued in Hutu-dominated refugee camps in Zaire.

What these three cases show is that despite warnings of impending disasters, especially in Rwanda, Western powers had little or no interest in intervening. UN peacekeepers in Rwanda were poorly armed and few in number, and their mandate was to remain impartial.

Could more have been done? This question is more fully answered in Chapter 9, but let us outline a few thoughts on the topic. We believe the international community has an obligation to protect the rights of minorities, beginning with protecting the most basic rights to life and security. For example, and from our point of view, the civil wars and ethnic killings in the breakaway states of the former Yugoslavia could have been preempted by early and active international mediation that would have led to guaranteed independence and security for all newly emerging states in the region and to commitments from all parties to protect the rights of each state's ethnic peoples. But the international community is only gradually acquiring the legal principles, political will, and foresight to respond effectively to such conflicts.

In the three cases described above, the consequences of colonialism were a major impediment to decisive action. Colonial subjects in Africa and Asia had few rights, and many ethnic groups were trapped within artificial boundaries imposed by the departing colonial powers. Faced with challenges from peoples of different cultures and kinships, most leaders of newly independent Third World countries opted to accept existing boundaries, insisting on absolute sovereignty and the inviolability of territorial borders. This insistence on the right to conduct internal affairs without outside interference gave unscrupulous dictators like Macias and Amin freedom to commit atrocities against their subjects in the name of "nation building." In Rwanda and Burundi, French favoritism, U.S. disinterest, and the UN's self-imposed limited mandate conspired to allow unscrupulous leaders to exploit ethnic tensions.

If the United Nations and the superpowers were indifferent to ethnic conflict and mass murder in peripheral states of the Third World, could regional organizations have responded? Many such deadly episodes occurred in the member states of the Organization of African Unity (OAU, founded in 1963) and the Organization of the Islamic Conference (which represents all states that have significant Muslim populations). But these organizations have usually been politically divided and have had few resources; thus, they have seldom responded to ethnic warfare and severe human rights violations in member states. The OAU, for example, was limited by its charter to mediating conflicts between African states, not within them. In 1981 and 1982, the OAU made its first effort at active peacekeeping when it sent a multinational force to help de-escalate a civil war between communal rivals in Chad; the effort was largely a failure. Partisan support for Rwandan rebels by Uganda did little to defuse the situation. After the Arusha Accords, the OAU verbally condemned international inaction, but had little more to offer than postconflict negotiations.

The impotence of Third World regional organizations combined with the reluctance of the superpowers during the Cold War era to interfere in the internal affairs of states that had little impact on global competition virtually ensured that most ethnic conflicts would remain domestic affairs, even if they led to gross violations of human rights. However, and despite Rwanda, we think that since 1991 the United Nations and the last remaining superpower, the United States, have taken more vigorous action against human rights violators and aggressive states.

No doubt the United Nations, established to create and preserve international peace, has had a mixed record as peacekeeper. A brief review of its record follows.

During the Cold War the UN played a significant peacekeeping role by separating combatants in communal conflicts in Congo, Cyprus, the Middle East, and Kashmir, but this occurred only because the superpowers agreed on the course of action. Since 1991, with encouragement from the U.S. government and other states, it has expanded its role. In Cambodia, for example, the United Nations mounted the biggest and most expensive peacekeeping operation in its history. Under a 1991 peace plan agreed to by warring Cambodian parties, an international force of 22,000 police and military and administrative personnel was stationed in the country to help establish order and oversee the transition to an elected civilian government. The effort was largely completed, and all military forces withdrawn, by October 1993.

The expanded role of the United States is illustrated by the dispatch of U.S. troops returning from the Gulf War to assist flood victims in Bangladesh in April and May 1991 and by the U.S.-led mobilization of reluctant states to intervene militarily in Iraq during the 1991 Gulf War in a renewed spirit of collective responsibility.

Regional organizations also have a mixed record. In the early 1990s the European Union, the world's second most powerful economic entity, was divided about whether and how to respond to escalating ethnic conflict in adjacent East Central Europe. The North Atlantic Treaty Organization (NATO) had the military means to intervene forcefully in European conflict situations, but both its European and North American members were very reluctant to use force to control the Bosnian conflict and ethnic cleansing in 1992–1995. The response in Kosovo in 1998–1999 was a somewhat different story—it was essentially proactive. Although U.S. pressure and promise of participation was probably instrumental in overcoming the lack of political will among the leaders of NATO's European members, international initiatives were not lacking. Some thirteen government and sixteen NGO efforts were made to halt crisis escalation. But the efforts were not sustained until violence occurred. From early 1998 to early 1999, attacks and counterattacks were a daily occurrence. Despite resolutions, mediation attempts, sanctions, and negotiated cease-fires, violence spiraled out of control. Only after NATO bombing in May of 1999 did Serbia under Milosevic withdraw its forces.

Regional organizations in the Third World are also taking a more active role in response to internal conflicts. Their leaders are involved in drafting and arguing for extensions to the human rights conventions that would allow for some exceptions to the rule of nonintervention. In the early 1990s, for example, the OAU established a new mechanism for conflict resolution and prevention that, in effect, redefined the OAU doctrine of noninterference in the affairs of member states. The OAU now monitors elections, makes periodic assessments of emerging conflict situations, and sends envoys to countries in which serious crises are brewing. For example in early 1993 the OAU sent a sixty-man observer mission to Rwanda to monitor a cease-fire between rival Hutu and the Tutsi armies, but it had neither political nor military clout.

Nongovernmental organizations (NGOs) such as Amnesty International, Human Rights Watch, and the International Crisis Group also play a role by calling attention to ethnic conflict and repression. Activists have lobbied their respective governments and the United Nations to take active roles in supporting humanitarian efforts, have denounced various interventions, and have reported human rights violations to international agencies.

CONCLUSION

We have shown that the "explosion" of ethnopolitical conflicts at the end of the Cold War was, in fact, a continuation of a trend that began as early as the 1960s. It is a manifestation of the enduring tension between states that want to consolidate and expand their power and ethnic groups that want to defend and promote their collective identity and interests. The breakup of the USSR and power shifts elsewhere within the state system have opened up opportunities for ethnic groups to pursue their interests. Coincidentally, the CNN-led explosion of global news coverage has increased public awareness of the human dimension of these conflicts and thus has contributed to pressures on policymakers to take constructive action.

Recent developments send encouraging signals to those who are concerned about checking the rise of ethnopolitical conflict and human rights abuses such as ethnic cleansing. For the first time since World War II, the United Nations has begun to realize the vision of its founders: New leadership in the UN, notably Boutros Boutros-Ghali, past secretary-general, and Kofi Annan, the current secretary-general, have tried to change the role of the UN from reactive to proactive in its role as peacekeeper, intervenor, arbiter, and mediator in communal and regional conflicts. A consensus is emerging that the United Nations should establish minimum standards of global security through collective decision making. Of course, the UN's ability to work for world security is directly dependent upon its ability to influence the outcome of emerging ethnic or nationalistic conflicts. However, the continuing caution apparent among most member states over enhancing UN military capabilities signals those who stir up ethnic hatred that they may face a minor roadblock rather than a major obstacle.

At the beginning of the new millenium we see some resemblance to the period following World War I, in which the collapse of the old order was followed by the birth of many new states, upsurges of ethnic violence and oppression, and the ascendancy of dictators and ideologies of exclusive nationalism. The pattern of conflicts in the Balkans, the Caucasus, the Middle East, and Central Africa fits this scenario and signifies the continuation of challenging times.

DISCUSSION QUESTIONS

1. States are defined in international politics as territories that have a population and an effective government whose sovereignty is recognized by other states. What general definition can you suggest for politically active ethnic groups?
2. How important was ethnic conflict in world politics prior to the end of the Cold War?
3. In what ways did the end of the Cold War contribute to increases in ethnic conflict?
4. Politically active religious groups, such as offshoots of the Muslim Brotherhood, are motivated by grievances similar to ethnic groups. Comment!

2

The World of
Ethnopolitical Groups

Four important types of politically active ethnic groups coexist with modern states: **ethnonationalists, indigenous peoples, ethnoclasses,** and **communal contenders.** The distinctions are important because they summarize a great deal of information about peoples' history, their status in society, and their political agendas. The first two types are peoples who once led a separate political existence and want independence or autonomy from the states that rule them today. Ethnonationalists like Kurds and Palestinians want to (re)establish their own states, while others like Albanians in Macedonia and Russians in Ukraine seek closer ties with their national homelands. Indigenous peoples like Native Americans are mainly concerned with protecting their traditional lands, resources, and culture within existing states. By contrast, ethnoclasses and communal contenders aim to improve their position in existing societies, not to change political boundaries. Ethnoclasses, like African-Americans and Turks in Germany, are descendants of slaves or immigrants who want to break out of the social and economic niches into which they were segregated by the dominant society. Communal contenders like the Druze in Lebanon and Chinese in Malaysia are among a number of culturally distinct groups that compete for a share of political power. The difference is that ethnoclasses live in **stratified societies**, in which ethnic groups are in a hierarchical or ranked relationship to each other. Communal contenders are members of **segmented societies**, in which roughly equal ethnic and religious groups compete for economic and political power.[1]

The numbers of each type of group are shown in Figure 2.1, based on a survey by the Minorities at Risk Project (see Chapter 1, note 1). Ethnonationalists are most numerous, with eighty-five. Communal contenders, found mainly in Africa, number sixty-eight. Ethnoclasses, most of which live in advanced industrial societies, number forty-three.

We begin with a sketch of global historical processes that set the stage for political activism by ethnic groups in contemporary states. Some of those processes continue today, including migration from poor to rich

19

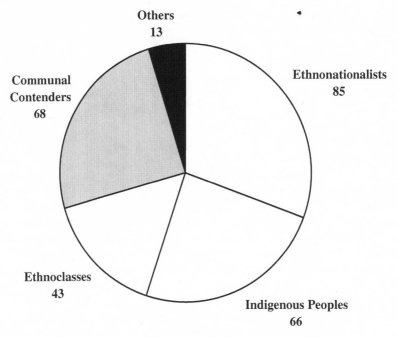

FIGURE 2.1 Types of politically active ethnic groups in 2001

countries and the corrosive effects of resource exploitation on traditional peoples. Then we discuss each of the four types in more detail, including the traits that define them, their typical grievances and political strategies, and the international dimensions of their activities. The last section considers some connections between religion and ethnic conflict.

THE WORLD HISTORICAL BACKGROUND TO CONTEMPORARY ETHNIC CONFLICTS

Contemporary conflicts between ethnic groups and states are a part of the heritage of large historical processes: imperial conquest, colonial rule, slavery, frontier settlement, and the international migration of labor. For example, every state that once established an empire did so at the expense of weaker and less fortunate peoples. Typically, European colonial rulers exercised direct influence over the social, cultural, and political lives of their dominions. The same was true of most other peoples who established empires by conquest, including the Han Chinese, the Ottoman Turks, and the Amharas of the Ethiopian highlands.

Local economies were undermined by colonial rule. Through the introduction of new economic systems that favored the dominant group, conquered peoples were forced into servitude, slavery, or dependency. Colonial rule also established hierarchies and rivalries among groups where few or none had previously existed. In colonial Nigeria, the British recruited clerks from the Christian Ibo of the southeast and soldiers from the Muslim northerners, laying the basis for group rivalries that continue to the present. Colonial rule did not create ethnic identities but often led to stratification or segmentation of colonized people along ethnic lines.

The sense of separate identity and grievances that result from imperial conquest and colonial rule can persist for many generations and provide the fuel for contemporary political movements. Burma, a former British colony, has been locked in ethnically based regional conflict since independence in the late 1940s. The conflict began during World War II, when nationalists within the Burman majority attacked the British colonial army, which was recruited largely from ethnic minorities such as the Karens, Chins, and Kachins. Thousands died in the ensuing struggles, laying the basis for enduring conflict between the minority peoples and the independent Burman state.

Societies that were ethnically divided and stratified in this way were fertile ground for conflict when newly formed Asian and African states won independence during the two decades following 1945. The new states were seldom ethnically homogeneous. They inherited borders that had been drawn to fit the political and administrative interests of the colonial powers. In some cases rival ethnic groups were merged into one new state; other groups were divided among several states by European-imposed borders. Nationalists contending for political power in the new states often played communal groups against one another, thus polarizing them. Rivalries in the Indian subcontinent between Muslim and Hindu politicians during the transition to independence led to partition in 1947 and the violent transfer of populations. It laid the foundation for a half-century of rivalry between Pakistan and India that continues today and recurring violence between Hindus and the Muslim minority that remained in India.

Another source of friction in colonial societies resulted from policies that encouraged immigration of outsiders to work newly established plantations or to engage in commercial activities for which the indigenous population lacked social capital. Most immigrants were not incorporated into the indigenous social structure but remained on the political and social margins. The British brought some 60,000 East Indians to their Fiji colony between 1879 and 1916 to work as indentured servants on sugarcane plantations. Native Fijian chiefs and political leaders have fought ever since to maintain control of Fijian politics, especially as East

Indians began to outnumber natives. Fiji became an independent democracy in 1970 and rivalries between the two groups are the country's main source of political conflict. When an Indian-led party won elections in 1987 the new prime minister's government was overthrown in a Fijian-led military coup, for example. Similar tensions among immigrants and indigenous peoples have bedeviled the politics of post-colonial Trinidad, Guyana, and Surinam in the Western Hemisphere, and Sri Lanka and Malaysia in Southeast Asia.

The previously mentioned policy of using immigrants and members of favored ethnic groups to staff colonial bureaucracies often gave them privileged status in the host country and also provoked discriminatory measures against their descendants after independence. The Chinese in Malaysia provide an example. They readily adopted Western education, language, and styles and, after independence, were resented by Malays for their privileged status and sometimes were victimized by nationalist movements and state authorities (their situation is described in detail in Chapter 4).

In the Americas and Australia, Europeans settled in large numbers, with devastating consequences for indigenous peoples. Some of the latter were agriculturalists; most were hunters. Organized into nations, tribal federations, or bands (particularly in Australia), they were on the losing side of competition with European settlers. The settlers' victories were accomplished through the slaughter, enslavement, forced **assimilation,** or forcible removal of indigenous peoples to reservations in remote and inhospitable areas. Thus, the migration of Europeans throughout the colonial period contributed to ethnic rebellions and mass slaughter and also to the displacement or genocide of indigenous peoples.

Another invidious European practice was to import Africans as slaves to provide labor for plantations in the Americas. In some societies the descendants of slaves were eventually incorporated into the dominant society: Examples are found in Brazil, parts of the Caribbean, and Canada. In the United States, however, slaves liberated by the Emancipation Proclamation of 1863 were rarely given the opportunity to achieve higher status. In the rigid class structure of Southern society following the Civil War, former slaves were free only of their chains.

In summary, each of the major historical processes left legacies of antagonisms and inequalities that fuel contemporary ethnic conflicts. Conquered peoples seek to regain their lost autonomy; indigenous peoples ask for restoration of their traditional lands and protection of their resources from exploitation; immigrant workers and the descendants of slaves demand full equality. Not all ethnic peoples with these kinds of heritages are pursuing political objectives today, yet most have done so in the past or have the potential to do so in the future. It is essential, when

Ethnic disputes explained. By Jeff Danziger in *The Christian Science Monitor*, June 15, 1992. © 1992 TCSPS. Reprinted by permission.

one is trying to understand the passion and persistence with which ethnic groups pursue their objectives, to analyze the general historical processes and the particular experiences that have shaped each people's sense of identity and their grievances.

ETHNONATIONALISTS

Ethnonationalists are relatively large and regionally concentrated ethnic groups that live within the boundaries of one state or of several adjacent states; their modern political movements are directed toward achieving greater autonomy or independent statehood. Most have historical traditions of autonomy or independence that are used to justify these contemporary demands. In some instances autonomy was lost centuries ago, as was the case of the Corsicans and Bretons in France,[2] but it still motivates modern political movements. More than 100 ethnonational groups—including some indigenous peoples—at some time since the 1950s have supported movements aimed at establishing greater political autonomy. Seventy of these groups have fought armed conflicts for national independence or for unification with kindred groups elsewhere, with twenty-two of these small wars being fought in 2003.[3]

Most people with nationalist aspirations live in the Third World, such as the southern Sudanese, the Kurds in the Middle East, and the Tibetans. They have fought some of the modern world's most persistent wars of self-determination, but only two new internationally recognized states have been born in the Third World in armed ethnonational conflict during the last forty years. They are Bangladesh (1971) and Eritrea (1993). Most other ethnically based wars of self-determination have either failed or ended in negotiated grants of greater autonomy within existing states.

Other ethnonationalists such as the Scots, Basques, Latvians, Albanians, and French-Canadians live in European and North American states. Their campaigns for greater autonomy have usually been pursued by nonviolent political means, although the terrorist campaigns of some Basque nationalists and Albanians in Kosovo and Macedonia suggest that many have the potential for violence. Most ethnonationalists in European societies have gained significant concessions in the past few decades; many won independence in 1991 as a result of the breakup of the USSR and Yugoslavia.

After 1991 two dozen new or revitalized ethnonationalist movements emerged within the boundaries of the Soviet and Yugoslav successor states. For example, 96,000 Muslim Abkhaz in the northwestern corner of the former Soviet republic of Georgia fought successfully, with unofficial Russian assistance, to establish their own state. In October 1993 they decisively defeated the Georgian army and expelled most Georgian civilians from Abkhazia. Since then the Abkhaz are effectively independent of Georgian authority, though no other state recognizes their claim to be a sovereign state. To the east of Abkhazia, 164,000 Ossetians in northern Georgia sought to be united in a new state with 402,000 Ossetians who live in an autonomous region in southern Russia.[4] The term **micronationalism** is sometimes used to describe the independence movements of numerically small groups like these, although there is no minimum size required for statehood. Fifty-six of the UN's 190 member states have populations less than 1.5 million, the smallest being the Pacific island state of Tuvalu with 11,000 inhabitants.

Ethnonationalists usually have some kind of organized leadership and occupy substantial territory. Like the Ossetians, the Basques—who live in adjoining areas of France and Spain—and the Kurds, whose traditional homeland includes parts of five different states, more than half of ethnonationalist peoples straddle recognized international boundaries. Thus, political conflicts over autonomy are likely to have international repercussions. Wars for national independence attract military and political support from nearby states, stimulate similar movements in adjoining countries, and are the main source of international refugees. As a result, major powers and international and regional organizations often try to contain nationalist wars by encouraging negotiations, delivering humanitarian assistance, and sometimes—especially when conflicts threaten regional security—sending peacekeeping forces.

INDIGENOUS PEOPLES

Indigenous peoples like Native Americans, New Zealand's Maori, and the Naga in India are also concerned about autonomy issues but differ from ethnonationalists in other respects. They are the descendants of the original inhabitants of conquered or colonized regions. Before their conquest, most indigenous peoples lived close to the land as subsistence farmers, herders, fisher folk, or hunters, and many still do. Until recently few had large-scale political organizations or a strong sense of collective identity or purpose. Instead, in most countries indigenous peoples were divided among many separate clans or tribes that only gradually developed a larger group identity. Loss of land to settlers, discrimination in daily life, and resource exploitation by more technologically advanced people have been major causes of their growing sense of common identity and purpose.

The best-known indigenous groups are the native peoples of the eighteen countries of mainland North and South America. In the aggregate, the 38 million Native Americans (our 1998 estimate) comprise only 5 percent of the population of the Western Hemisphere, but in Bolivia, Guatemala, and Peru they make up 40 percent or more of the population. In Bolivia, Peru, and Ecuador they have become major political actors, using the electoral process to gain direct representation in governments and to shape decisions about indigenous issues.

There are also many indigenous peoples in Asia. Half a dozen large and politically active indigenous tribes live in northeast India and the borderlands of Bangladesh, among them the Naga, Mizos, and Tripura. In Southeast Asia serious conflicts have developed over the political demands of indigenous peoples like the Cordillerans ("mountain people," a label provided by Europeans) in the Philippines, the Karen and Shan peoples of the Burman uplands, and the native Papuans of the western, Indonesian-controlled half of the island of New Guinea.

Because most of them live in peripheral regions of modern states, these peoples—along with the Scandinavian Saami (who are called Lapps by outsiders), the Australian Aborigines, the cattle-herding Masai of East Africa, and others—have been called "peoples of the frontier." Similar themes are expressed repeatedly by their contemporary leaders: They want to protect what remains of their ways of life from what their advocates call ethnocide—that is, the destruction of their culture—and they seek to regain as much control as possible over their lands and resources.

For centuries, traditional peoples resisted dominant groups through sporadic and uncoordinated uprisings and attempts to migrate to more remote regions. After the League of Nations was established in 1919, a number of North American tribes and the Maori of New Zealand began to petition it and other international bodies for recognition of their rights. Before the 1950s, however, only a handful of indigenous peoples secured significant political autonomy from Western-style governments. In New Zealand the Maori gained control of some traditional lands and obtained representation in the English settlers' parliament in 1867. As we describe in Chapter 3, the Miskito Indians of Nicaragua were recognized as constituting an autonomous state from 1860 to 1894. And the Kuna Indians of Panama gained local autonomy as the result of a rebellion in 1920.

By far the most important international development affecting indigenous peoples has been the global indigenous rights movement that took shape in the 1970s. The San Francisco–based International Indian Treaty Council (founded in 1974) and the World Council of Indigenous Peoples (1975) were the first of a growing number of influential nongovernmental bodies that provided a forum for discussions, publicity, and planning of joint action among representatives of indigenous peoples from all parts of the world. UN agencies also have established advisory groups concerned with indigenous issues. The most influential has been the UN Working Group on Indigenous Populations which since 1982 has convened frequent international meetings of indigenous representatives. It has prepared a Universal Declaration of Indigenous Rights, a step in the direction of gaining international legal recognition for groups that are typically not subject of **international law.** For an elaboration of the argument see Chapter 8.[5]

The indigenous people's movement has had great influence, first by encouraging political action by many previously passive local and regional groups, second by making forceful presentations to international bodies, most recently to the World Bank and the World Trade Organization. It has also directly or indirectly affected the policies of many governments toward indigenous peoples. National officials responsible for developing policies toward indigenous peoples meet with their local and international representatives with increasing frequency; their policy goals often change as a result. The indirect impact results from political actions inspired by the global movement, often in collaboration with environmental groups. The main weapons are protest: publicity campaigns directed toward the media and national parliaments, lawsuits against corporations extracting resources from indigenous lands, demonstrations, blockades of access roads, and land occupations. Their cumulative effect has been to soften public, corporate, and official resistance to indigenous demands in the countries in which they take place and to prompt similar protests, and obtain concessions, elsewhere.

Another kind of indirect effect is seen in the work of other international organizations. In the late 1980s, for example, the International Labor Organization (ILO) substantially revised its standards for the treatment of indigenous and tribal peoples. Member states of the ILO were asked to give greater attention to the collective rights and interests of these peoples and to grant them a voice in decision making about development plans that affected their homelands. The ILO is one of the oldest and arguably more progressive organizations within the framework of the United Nations. It has a built-in advantage in dealing with group issues because its membership includes both labor and corporate representatives in addition to governments. The Senate of Brazil, whose treatment of Amazonian peoples and their environment has attracted intense international scrutiny, finally ratified the ILO convention in June 2002, nine years after it was first introduced.[6]

ETHNOCLASSES

Ethnoclasses are ethnically or culturally distinct minorities who occupy distinct social strata and have specialized economic roles in the societies in which they now live. They are, in other words, ethnic groups who resemble classes. Most ethnoclasses in advanced industrial societies are descended from slaves or immigrants who did the hard and menial work scorned by the dominant groups. Examples include people of African descent in Britain and North America, the Turks in Germany, and Koreans in Japan. Upward mobility and policies of integration have eroded old ethnoclass barriers in Western Europe and North America but members of these and similar groups are still heavily concentrated in occupations at or near the bottom of the economic and social hierarchy.

In Third World societies ethnoclasses also have immigrant origins, but their members are more likely to be economically advantaged merchants and professionals who are subject to political restrictions. Examples include the Chinese minorities in most Southeast Asian countries and the Lebanese communities in postcolonial Africa.[7] There are at least fifty politically active ethnoclasses in the world today, and more are forming as a result of international migration from poor countries to wealthier ones.

Leaders who represent ethnoclasses seek to improve their status within an existing political system: They want greater economic opportunities, equal political rights, better public services. Some, such as the North African Muslims in France, the Koreans in Japan, and many African-Americans, are also concerned about protecting and promoting their peoples' cultural traditions. Unlike ethnonationalists, indigenous peoples, and communal contenders (discussed below), ethnoclasses are usually

widely dispersed within a larger population. Even if they live in particular urban neighborhoods or rural villages, they rarely have a single territorial base or traditions of separate nationhood. Therefore, ethnoclasses
seldom use the language or demands of nationalists; instead, they are
preoccupied with receiving more equitable or favorable treatment from
the larger society.

The formation of ethnoclasses continues to be shaped by international
factors. The transnational movement of immigrants and refugees fleeing
poverty and violence accelerated sharply in the 1990s and continued in
the early years of the twenty-first century. Most of these people are visible
minorities, which means that they are too easily singled out for special,
often discriminatory treatment in their host countries. Few are likely to
return to their homelands. In almost any town and village in western Germany, for example one can see—as the authors have on recent trips—people of African and Middle Eastern origin living side by side with native
Germans. Host countries often try to smooth their acceptance but, as their
numbers increase, the immigrants are the source of political contention
and the targets of occasional acts of violence.

COMMUNAL CONTENDERS

Communal contenders are ethnic groups whose main political aim is not
to gain autonomy or to break through discriminatory barriers but, rather,
to share political power. Communal contenders are the most prevalent
kind of ethnopolitical group in African states and also in some of the
more established states in the Middle East and Asia—like Lebanon, Pakistan, and Malaysia. The most close-to-home example for North Americans is Trinidad, where peoples of African and East Indian descent have
jockeyed for political power since independence. In Lebanon, for example, the main contenders historically have been Maronite Christians and
the Druze, a distinct Muslim sect. The Sunni Muslim community has
been a moderating force in the communal politics of Lebanon; since the
1970s the Shi'i Muslim minority has become a major political actor.

In Lebanon, as in other plural societies, the government's political
power has been based on coalitions among the leaders of major ethnic
groups. The balance of power between Christians and Muslims in the
coalition was spelled out in Lebanon's unwritten "National Pact," agreed
to in 1943. In most states, including Lebanon, such arrangements have
been informal and vulnerable to manipulation. Multiethnic coalitions are
usually dominated by an advantaged group—like the Punjabis in Pakistan
and the Malays in Malaysia—that uses a mix of concessions, co-optation,
and sometimes repression to maintain its position. Such arrangements

become unstable if and when one ethnic group's leader attempts to improve his or her relative position at the expense of others. If constitutional restraints and political guarantees are absent, and if other groups are unwilling to work out a new compromise, such conflicts can escalate into full-scale civil or revolutionary warfare. Recent examples of ethnic wars caused by the failure to establish or maintain multiethnic coalitions in societies have occurred in Lebanon, Sri Lanka, Sierra Leone, and Liberia. In some cases the ethnopolitical group that finds itself losing gives up hope of sharing power and shifts to a strategy of autonomy. This happened in Nigeria in 1967 when the Eastern Region, the home of most Ibos, proclaimed an independent Republic of Biafra and fought an unsuccessful war of secession.

War is not inevitable in such situations. By 1993 the white–dominated South African government had reluctantly but decisively accepted the right of other ethnic groups to participate in governance. The cooperation established between Nelson Mandela, the black nationalist leader, and the white establishment made it possible to establish a new multiracial political order and avoid widely feared civil war along ethnic lines.

Conflicts engaging communal contenders are highly susceptible to international involvement. During the Cold War era, the contenders sometimes became clients of the superpowers, as happened in Angola. The southern Ovimbundu people, represented by an organization called the National Union for the Total Independence of Angola (UNITA), relied on military and political assistance from the United States and South Africa during a fifteen-year war against a coalition of their ethnic rivals, led by the Mbundu people, who held power in the capital of Luanda. The Luanda government, in turn, was strongly supported by the Soviet and Cuban governments. Intense diplomatic efforts by the United Nations, the Organization of African Unity, and the United States throughout the 1980s attempted to defuse the conflict. An internationally brokered agreement among the rivals ended the fighting and led to a national election in 1992, but UNITA leaders rejected the results and were attacked by the government. By 1993 the country was again embroiled in a bitter and deadly civil war that did not wind down until 2002, following the death of UNITA founder Jonas Savimbi.

DOMINANT MINORITIES

We also should mention **dominant minorities,** a distinctive type of ethnoclass that has historically been more common than it is at present. Dominant minorities are culturally distinct ruling groups like the Afrikaaners of South Africa, before 1993, and the Tutsi overlords who have governed the Hutu peasants of Burundi. Such minorities have used the powers of the state to maintain political and economic advantages over subordinate majorities. Not all members of dominant minorities benefit equally. Some working-class white Afrikaaners, for example, continue to be resentful of blacks' demands for equality. Iraq provides another example. Until the U.S.-led invasion of 2003, its ruling elite was a small clique from the Sunni Muslim minority, most of whom came from Saddam Hussein's hometown of Tikrit.

CONCLUSION

One of the most widely shared values of the modern world, one that is ratified in numerous international agreements on human rights, is the principle that people of all ethnic and religious backgrounds within each society should enjoy equal economic and political opportunities. This principle has motivated political movements that work for greater equality among disadvantaged peoples throughout the world. It has pushed many governments to reduce discrimination against ethnoclasses and indigenous peoples and has contributed to the toppling of minority-dominated governments throughout the European colonized world, from Algeria to Zanzibar. It also brings international pressures, both political and economic, to bear on dominant groups. Thus, countervailing international factors are at work. On the one hand, migration is creating new ethnoclasses; on the other, advantaged groups are being pressured to incorporate them on an equal basis with other classes and citizens.

The distinctions among the four types of groups are not rigid because the status of ethnic groups and the strategies of their leaders can change over time. An ethnoclass may gain enough power and self-confidence that its leaders shift from seeking equal rights for its members to demanding collective participation in government. Some African-American leaders in the United States have moved in this direction. Or an ethnonational group whose leaders at one time fought a breakaway war of secession may later be persuaded to join a governing coalition with other communal groups. This is the vision many outsiders have for Iraq now that Saddam Hussein's regime is toppled—a democratic coalition or federation of Kurds, the Shi'i community, and the Sunni Arabs. This illustrates the two most promising long-term strategies for accommodating the interests of large ethnopolitical groups. One is to persuade their leaders that it is in their interest to accept a share of power in the governing elite. The other, which can be used in combination with power-sharing, is to grant communal groups regional autonomy within a federal political system.

RELIGION AND ETHNICITY

The categories of ethnonationalists, indigenous peoples, communal contenders, and ethnoclasses enable us to compare and contrast most, but not all, politically active communal groups in the contemporary world. Much attention has been given in the past two decades to the resurgence of religious-based conflict, especially conflicts involving Muslims, but not exclusively so. Religion also has been an important identifier in communal conflicts in other world regions. The Protestants and Catholics of Northern Ireland are examples of warring communal groups who define themselves mainly in terms of religious beliefs.

However, there are significant differences in strategies and objectives among religious groups roughly comparable to differences among ethnic groups. Some religious groups work peacefully within existing polities while others are more inclined to use violence. For example, extreme Orthodox Jews in Israel and fundamentalist Christians in the West want to control most or all aspects of civil affairs. Islamists in the Arab world such as the Muslim Brotherhood typically want to achieve a more just order, i.e. government based on Shari'ah, or Islamic law. Jihadists (typically named after martyrs) and movements such as Hammas have revolutionary objectives to eliminate the Israeli state, analogous to the collusion of Jewish Orthodoxy and Zionism that aspires to a Greater Israel purified of Arabs. Al-Qaeda is the most dangerous kind of movement because it calls for cleansing the entire Muslim world of nonbelievers and Western influence. At present it has no counterpart among Christians, Jews, or Hindus.

It is important to recognize that many contemporary religious conflicts in and around the margins of the Islamic world arise not from opposition to the West but from the reassertion of traditional Islamic values in opposition to the values and often corrupt practices of secular governments. Most such conflicts occur between people with the same ethnic background, as, for example, in Jordan, Egypt, and Algeria. So-called fundamentalism is only likely to fuel *ethnic* conflict when the split between traditional Islamic and secular values coincides with ethnic divisions, as is the case in Sudan, where an Arab, traditional Islamic government in the north has attempted to impose an Islamic system of law and government on non-Muslim Africans in the south.[8]

The general principle, exemplified by the situation in Sudan, is that religious differences create a special intensity in conflicts between peoples when a dominant group attempts to impose rules based on its religious beliefs on others. But research done using the Minorities at Risk data (see Chapter 1, note 1) show that differences of religion are seldom the only or the most important cause of ethnic conflict. Instead, religious differences usually combine with or reinforce ethnic conflicts that are based on nationality and class differences. For example, the Palestinians' conflict with Israel is first and foremost a nationalist one whose intensity is reinforced by religious differences. Similarly, Northern Ireland's Catholics are motivated in part by their subordinate class status and in part by a nationalistic desire to be united with the Republic of Ireland. A shared religion provides some of the social cement that holds these groups together.

Afghanistan under the rule of the Taliban helps illustrate the complex interplay of religion, ethnicity, and politics in the Islamic world. The Taliban were a Sunni Muslim sect motivated by a vision of a pure Islamic society. The Taliban's local supporters were limited mostly to the Pushtuns, the dominant majority in Afghanistan and a significant minority in western Pakistan, where the sect had its origins. It was opposed by Afghanistan's three other large communal groups: the Harzaris of central Afghanistan—Shi'i Muslims whom the Taliban branded as heretics—and the Tajiks and Uzbeks of northern Afghanistan. The Tajiks and Uzbeks practice a more relaxed form of Sunni Islam and are long-term rivals of the Pushtuns for influence in the central government. In brief, a traditional form of Islam provided the social cement for the Taliban's Pashtun-supported war to establish political control of Afghanistan, which was opposed by the Northern Alliance of three communal groups whose shared objectives were to protect their own territorial bases and thwart the Taliban/Pashtun threat. The U.S.-led campaign in 2001–2002 toppled the Taliban regime and curtailed the influence of militant Islam, but the communal and regional rivalries among the four groups remain. They will continue to drive Afghan politics for generations to come.

A contrasting case is Algeria, where Muslim radicals have indiscriminately attacked civilians in their quest to wrest power from the secular government. Ethnic divisions between Arabs and Berbers are largely irrelevant to this conflict.

WHERE WE GO FROM HERE

We have defined and discussed four major types of politically active ethnic groups in the contemporary world. In Chapters 3 and 4 we present historical accounts of four peoples, one of each of these four types, whose status has been deeply affected by the interaction of internal and international political forces. The claims of ethnonationalists, who want greater autonomy or independence, pose the greatest dilemma for states and the international system; they are the source of some of the most deadly and protracted conflicts of the last half-century. The history of the Kurdish people, detailed in Chapter 3, illustrates both the group type and the issues at stake. Communal contenders who seek a greater share of power in existing states usually pursue their objectives through conventional politics but sometimes become involved in revolutionary wars when their ambitions cannot be met through other means. The Chinese in Malaysia, whose history is surveyed in Chapter 4, provided the basis for a failed revolutionary movement in the 1950s; they now have a well-defined political and economic role within a multiethnic political system.

The other two important types of politically active ethnic groups are indigenous peoples and ethnoclasses, whose demands and actions are seldom a major threat to regional or international security. Nonetheless, their status is of serious concern to the international community: Most are more disadvantaged and suffer greater discrimination than any other groups in their societies, and domestic conflicts over their status often have important spillover effects that require attention from regional and international organizations. These dilemmas are illustrated in our case study of the indigenous Miskitos of Nicaragua in Chapter 3 and in the account of Turks in Germany in Chapter 4, a group that typifies the growing numbers of ethnoclasses in Western societies.

DISCUSSION QUESTIONS

1. Three of the four types of politically active ethnic groups exist in the contemporary United States and its dependencies. Identify at least one of each type, and explain the basis for your categorization.
2. Which of the four types of ethnic groups, and in what regions of the world, are most likely to become involved in protracted communal conflicts?
3. Which types of ethnic groups are most likely to be linked to specific territories, and which are less likely to have such linkages? What implications does the difference have for the groups' political objectives and the kinds of conflicts in which they become involved?
4. What kinds of historical justifications do ethnonationalists use for their demands for autonomy or independence?
5. Ethnoclasses in Western societies were established as a result of what historical processes?
6. How do religious differences between groups affect the nature and intensity of ethnic conflict?

3

The Pursuit of Autonomy:
The Kurds and Miskitos

Ethnic groups become involved in political conflict for many reasons that are specific to a particular time, place, and political setting. Two underlying factors, however, are present in all instances. First, people become more sharply aware of their common identity. This awareness may be intensified by attacks from other groups, by the appeals of their leaders, or by dramatic examples of political action undertaken by similar groups elsewhere. Second, people become increasingly resentful about their unequal status in comparison with other groups. The sense of resentment is usually based on inequalities and people's belief that they have been unjustly denied rights and opportunities. The theoretical importance of these two factors is examined as part of the **model** presented in the second half of Chapter 5. The sketches in the present chapter and in Chapter 4 provide the information needed to gain an understanding of the historical and political circumstances that have shaped the identities and status of four peoples.

THE KURDS: A NATION WITHOUT A STATE

"Before I was born my whole family—my mum, my brothers and my grandfather—were put in prison by the Iraqi government. They put my family in prison because my father was a peshmerga—a fighter for the Kurds. The prison was in the south of Iraq, far away from our city of Halabjah in Kurdistan. . . .

"I was born on the 19th [of] December 1976. My mother told me I was born in prison. . . . In 1979, when the government gave up hope of catching my father, they let us out of prison on bail. We returned to our village . . . four kilometers away from Halabjah.

"After a short time the government started to catch Kurdish families again and unfortunately they caught my grandfather and beat and tortured him so badly that half his body was paralysed. They tortured him to find out where my father was hiding. . . . My mother and brothers and I had to leave our house . . . to go to live in

the mountains of Kurdistan near where my father was. We had to move from place to place because the government kept shelling the area. When we got to school age at seven years my mother wanted to send us to school. There were no schools in the mountains so my mum had to send us to school in the Kurdish cities under the control of the Iraqi government. She put each of us three brothers in a different school and we had to change our names so the Iraqi government wouldn't know that we were the family of a peshmerga [literally, "those who face death"]. . . .

"In the summer holidays from school we lived with our parents in the mountains. . . . Sometimes when we were in the mountains we hid from the bombs that the Iraqi government dropped, in tunnels. We took medicines, food and towels because sometimes we had to stay for some time in the tunnels. We made the towels wet to protect us from burns from chemical weapons. . . .

"The government bulldozed our village and destroyed it in 1986. After the people had built it up, they came again in 1987 and destroyed it again. So my family had to move to the town of Halabjah. In March 1988 my brother and I were living in Halabjah with relatives. The Iraqi government destroyed Halabjah with chemical weapons. Over 5,000 Kurdish people were killed at Halabjah and thousands were injured. My brother and I were saved from death because a few hours before the bombing we had gone out of the town to a village. . . .

"We had to go with thousands of other people towards the border with Iran. I walked with my grandmother and brother. . . . When we got to Iran they took us to a camp and gave us a tent. At the camp we found our mother and grandfather. . . . While we were in the camp the Iraqi government started to get its agents to put poison in the food and water in the camp. Because of that my father decided to sell everything and borrowed money from friends and found a way for us to leave Iran.

"I arrived in London on 17th September 1989 with my mum, dad and brothers."[1]

This personal account illustrates vividly the human dimension of the long and bitter conflict between Kurds and the Iraqi government. Its statements about policies and actions of the Iraqi government are consistent with information reported by many other sources. In 1975, during a lull in intermittent warfare with the Kurds, the Iraqi government initiated a policy of destroying Kurdish villages near the Turkish and Iranian borders and forcibly resettling their inhabitants. At least fifty villages were destroyed and tens of thousands of Kurds were deported before the policy was reversed in 1976. In 1987 the policy was resumed on a much larger scale to discourage Kurds from supporting Iran during the last stages of the Iran-Iraq War: An estimated 3,000 villages and hamlets were razed, and half a million Kurds were deported to detention camps. The government especially targeted villages and families that supported the guerrilla fighters–the *peshmergas*. It also began to use mustard gas on civilian and combattant Kurds. Kurdish sources identify more than eighty such uses, the most deadly and best documented of which was the attack on the

Kurdish refugees who fled from Iraqi army attacks, April 1991. Photo by Salah Aziz, Badlisy Center for Kurdish Studies, Tallahassee, Florida.

town of Halabja on March 16, 1988. Also in 1988 the Iraqi government began an operation, code named "Al-Anfal," during which 182,000 Kurdish civilians were arrested; police documents and videotapes captured in 1991 showed that many, perhaps most, became victims of mass executions.[2]

The conflict between Kurds and the Baghdad government flared up again in the aftermath of the 1990–1991 Gulf War, when U.S. President George Bush called on Iraqis to resist the regime of Iraqi President Saddam Hussein. Kurdish leaders interpreted this as a promise of support, and in March 1991 they organized a widespread rebellion. No immediate U.S. support came and the rebellion was crushed by Iraqi forces within a month. But the plight of a million or more Kurdish refugees fleeing toward neighboring Turkey and Iran prompted UN Security Council Resolution 688 in April 1991 that condemned repression of the Kurds and required the Iraqi regime to allow humanitarian assistance to be provided them. Immediately thereafter a U.S.-led coalition of governments opposed to Saddam Hussein established a protected zone in northern Iraq. Coalition ground forces (withdrawn by mid-July) and long-term air cover from bases in Turkey made it possible to provide humanitarian assistance without risk of Iraqi government reprisals. A year later, in May 1992, representatives of the estimated 3.4 million Kurds in the region established the Kurdish Regional Government with a democratically elected parliament. (Another 2 million people of Kurdish descent live elsewhere in Iraq.) Kurdish authorities began to export oil from fields under their control and, from the mid-1990s until the 2003 toppling of the Saddam Hussein regime, have received a 13 percent share of the Iraqi government's proceeds from the UN-authorized sale of oil to finance food imports. The local Kurdish economy also benefits from cross-border trade with Turkey.

The 1991 rebellion of the Iraqi Kurds and the precedent-setting **humanitarian intervention** on their behalf by a UN-authorized international force must be understood within a larger historical and political context. We begin with a general overview and then focus in greater detail on the political status of Kurds in Turkey, Iran, and Iraq.[3]

The Kurdish People

The Kurds are a culturally distinct national group of 25 to 30 million people whose ancestors have lived for at least 2,000 years in a 400-mile arc of mountains and valleys that lie north and east of the Tigris-Euphrates River basin. Kurdistan, the term commonly used by outsiders since the nineteenth century to denote the region, is divided among contiguous areas of four Middle Eastern states: Turkey, Iran, Iraq, and Syria, as shown in Map 3.1. Estimates of the Kurdish population in the four countries vary widely; the 2001 figures shown in Table 3.1 are approximations, as explained in the note to the table. Another half-million Kurds are dispersed through the former republics of the USSR and more than 1 million have migrated to Western Europe. All estimates are controversial because some governments want to minimize the size of their Kurdish populations, whereas Kurdish leaders want to maximize them. The question of "how many Kurds" is also complicated by the fact that many Kurds have assimilated into non-Kurdish societies. The crucial question for Kurds, and other ethnic groups, is "Do you think of yourself as Kurdish?" but no such ethnic censuses have been taken in the four countries.

Many Kurds live beyond the boundaries shown in Map 3.1, as is evident from a comparison with Map 3.2. Map 3.2 shows that many Kurds, past and present, have lived beyond the periphery of Kurdistan in close association with Turks, Iranians, Azeris, Arabs, and others. This intermingling is partly a result of the Kurds' own expansion and migration and is partly a result of the resettlement policies of the governments and peoples with whom the Kurds have interacted for centuries.

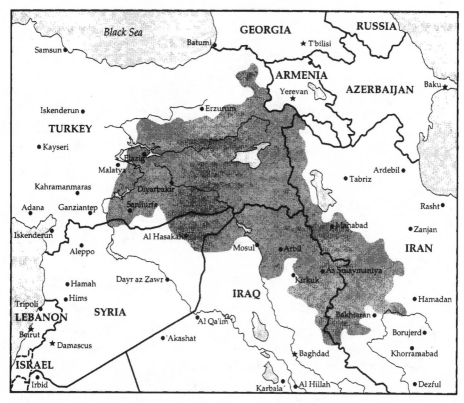

MAP 3.1 Contiguous Kurdish-inhabited areas in the 1990s. *Source:* Central Intelligence Agency.

The Cultural Basis of Kurdish Nationalism

The idea of a Kurdish nation is a twentieth-century construction built on the foundation of a common culture, including a contiguous homeland, a myth of common origin, a shared faith in Islam, similar languages, and a history of bitter conflict with outsiders. Kurds believe they are descended from the Medes, a people who were incorporated into the Persian Empire in the sixth century B.C. In fact, they are probably an amalgam of different peoples who gradually developed a common culture based on a life of seminomadic herding. Most Kurds speak one of two major dialects, both related to Iranian languages such as Farsi, but differences between them make communication difficult. Kurmanji is spoken by most Kurds in northernmost Iraq and Turkey, while Sorani is spoken elsewhere in Iraq and by most Iranian Kurds. Sorani is the only Kurdish dialect recognized by the Iraqi government. Records of the Kurds' history as a separate

Country	Population	As % of	
		Country's Population	Kurdistan's Population
Turkey	14,600,000	22	51
Iran	7,300,000	11	25
Iraq	5,400,000	23	19
Syria	1,500,000	9	5
Totals	28,800,000		100

Sources: Population estimates for 1991 in percentages and numbers are given by David McDowall, *The Kurds: A Nation Denied* (London: Minority Rights Group, 1992), p. 12, and by Mehrdad R. Izady, *The Kurds: A Concise Handbook* (Washington, D.C.: Taylor and Francis, 1992), p. 117. We used the average of their percentages—Izady gives somewhat higher percentages for Turkey and Iran—and applied them to 2001 estimates of the total populations of each of the four countries.

TABLE 3.1 Estimates of Kurdish population in Turkey, Iran, Iraq, and Syria, 2001

people date from their conversion to Islam in the ninth century A.D.; about three-fifths (estimates vary) are Sunni Muslims, one-tenth are Shi'is, and most others are Alevis and Yazidis.

Until the twentieth century, most Kurds were mountain-dwelling pastoralists who followed seasonal cycles of migration with their sheep to high summer pastures and then wintered in lower-lying villages. Like mountain clans and tribes elsewhere, they had a strong tradition of independence and of warfare and raids against outsiders. According to a folk saying, "Level the mountains, and in a day the Kurds would be no more." For more than 1,000 years, most Kurds resisted conquest by or assimilation with the three major peoples who surround them: the Turks to the northwest, the Persians to the east, and the Arabs to the south and southwest. However, local Kurdish leaders—*aghas, mirs, begs, shaikhs*—often accepted the authority and fought in the service of the rulers of surrounding states.[4] Some became generals and senior officials in the governments of their conquerors, a pattern that continues to the present.

The Historical Background to Kurdish Nationalism

Kurdish leaders for centuries have performed a balancing act between local and outside forces. They have fought for autonomy from external powers but also have fought one another in political rivalries that con-

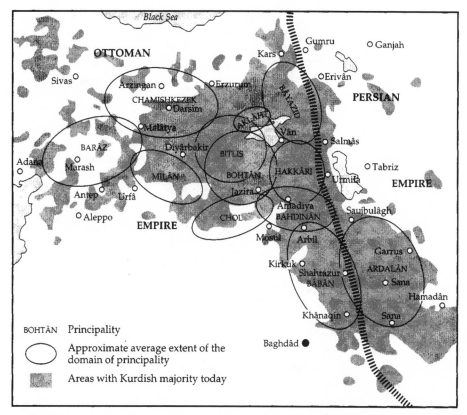

MAP 3.2 Kurdish principalities of early modern times. *Source:* Mehrad R. Izady, *The Kurds: A Concise Handbook* (Washington, DC: Taylor and Francis, 1992).

tinue to the present. From the sixteenth to the nineteenth centuries the Kurds occupied the borderlands between the Ottoman Empire, ruled from Constantinople (changed to Istanbul in 1930), and the Persian Empire, ruled from Isfahan and, after 1800, from Tehran. In the early sixteenth century, the Ottoman rulers concluded a pact with Kurdish chieftains that recognized sixteen autonomous Kurdish principalities and many smaller fiefdoms. Their hereditary rulers were confirmed in office and were granted privileges, but in exchange they were required to provide military support to the Ottoman rulers in time of war. The Persian rulers also had client Kurdish chiefs and tribes. By the nineteenth century, there were nine major Kurdish principalities and many lesser ones, two within the Persian sphere of influence and the rest within the Ottoman Empire. The approximate domains of the largest historical principalities are shown in Map 3.2. Beginning in the early nineteenth century, the pattern of indirect rule was disrupted when the Ottoman Empire forcibly moved to establish direct control over the Kurdish principalities for reasons that now would be called state-building. The northern areas of Kurdistan needed to be strengthened against the threat of Russian expansion; rebellious leaders in southern Kurdistan had to be checked. Moreover, in 1826 the Ottomans had decided to establish a "new army" along European lines, which meant they needed to recruit more foot soldiers and secure new tax revenues. The Kurdish areas of the empire were seen as a major untapped source for both resources.

Resistance to the tightening Ottoman rule led to more than fifty rebellions. Among these were five major revolts that, had they occurred in the twentieth century, would have been called wars of national independence. The Kurdish princes who led these wars, from Abdurrahman Pasha in 1806 to Shaikh Ubaydullah in 1880, mobilized up to 100,000 fighters, sustained their campaigns for as long as six years, and, in several instances, conquered and briefly held large sections of both Ottoman and Persian Kurdistan.

The Kurdish rebellions failed to stop the inexorable imposition of direct rule and the deconstruction of the autonomous principalities. Kurdish and Western scholars who have studied the Kurdish revolts attribute this failure to two factors. First, they were fought by traditional leaders of tribes and tribal federations who had no political organizations or programs that might attract and hold long-term support. And however widespread and enthusiastic immediate support for the leaders of the great revolts seemed to be, all leaders were envied and openly opposed by rival Kurdish leaders. In short they lacked centralized leadership and an ideology of nationalism. Second, Ottoman and Persian rulers quickly took advantage of tribal divisions among the Kurds; despite their own rivalries, the two empires cooperated with one another to defeat Kurdish armies, and both encouraged defectors, some of whom ended up fighting fellow Kurds.

Twentieth-Century Changes in Kurdish Society

One important source of change in Kurdish life and society during the past century has been an expanding number of Kurds whose interests and politics have diverged from those of traditional leaders. First, a small urban elite, relatives of traditional leaders, began to emerge in the nineteenth–century imperial capitals of the Ottoman Empire and Persia. They and their descendants were the Kurds most likely to become army officers, politicians, and officials in the governments of the ruling empires. These urban Kurds were also the first to articulate modern ideas of Kurdish nationalism. They were influenced especially by the nationalism of the Young Turks, who staged a constitutional revolution in Constantinople in 1908, and by the Western-inspired ideals of national self-determination that were in vogue at the end of World War I.

A second change involves the growth in the numbers of Kurds who live a settled existence in the valleys and plains. Some are farmers; others are concentrated in towns and growing cities like Diyarbakir in Turkey and Sulaymaniyeh and Kirkuk in Iraq. They include professionals and merchants as well as craftspeople and unskilled workers, and they provide much of the support for modern political movements.

A third source of change is the dispersion of a great many Kurds away from their homeland through voluntary or involuntary migration. Hundreds of thousands of Kurds were forcibly resettled in Turkey in the 1920s and 1930s and in Iraq during the 1970s and 1980s.[5] Similarly large numbers of Kurds have been displaced as refugees fleeing twentieth-century rebellions. Although some recently resettled Kurds and most refugees have eventually returned to their villages, many others have not. Some have swelled the populations of the Kurdish or mixed Kurdish towns and cities of Turkey, Iraq, and Iran; others live as an underclass minority among non-Kurds, especially in central Turkey.

Finally, since the 1950s, many Kurds have migrated far from their homeland in search of employment. Istanbul now contains more Kurds than any city in Kurdistan, and more than half a million others are in Western Europe, 90 percent of whom live in Germany's Turkish community.

This dispersion of Kurdish people has important political implications. The typical Kurd is now as likely to live in a modern town or city as in the mountains. Contemporary Kurdish leaders have wide international networks of communication and support. Their political movements are more likely to emphasize modern political objectives, such as regional autonomy and access to resources, than the defense of traditional privileges and ways of life. The mountain villages still provide most of the fierce *peshmerga* fighters who fascinate outsiders, but they represent a dwindling share of the total Kurdish population. Despite these changes, clan and tribal loyalties remain important for the vast majority of Kurds, in cities and the countryside, and continue to provide the basis of support for contending political movements. No overarching nationalist movement has emerged to link Kurds throughout their traditional homelands, nor is there a dominant Kurdish political movement in either Iraq or Turkey.

Kurdish Nationalism in the Twentieth Century

The idea of national identity tied to a territorial state was a European import to the Middle East. The Ottoman religious-social-political system was centered on the idea of community, especially the religious commu-

nity of Islam. However, separate Christian and Jewish religious communities—*millets*—had a recognized place within the larger Ottoman society.
Peoples like the Kurds, Armenians, Greeks, and Slavs who lived within
the empire had no such place. Ethnic consciousness was supposed to be
subordinated first to Islam and second to identification with the imperial
state, which was reinforced by the practice of co-opting local leaders into
the hierarchy of Ottoman rule—or, in the case of traditional Kurdish leaders, granting them autonomy on the condition that they remain loyal to
the empire. Viewed from this perspective, the rebellions in Kurdistan
were not *Kurdish* rebellions but were efforts by traditional leaders to extend or defend their privileges.

Before World War I the idea of a separate Kurdish state was of interest
only to a few urban intellectuals. During World War I the Ottoman Empire was defeated by the Allies, and the British occupied the lower Tigris-
Euphrates valley and southern Kurdistan. At first the British planned to
establish separate Kurdish and Armenian states, both to be carved out of
the defeated empire. U.S. President Woodrow Wilson was also sympathetic to the idea: His Fourteen Point Program for World Peace included
the statement that non-Turkish minorities of the Ottoman Empire should
be "assured of an absolute unmolested opportunity of autonomous development." In 1920 the representatives of fifteen Allied powers convinced the defeated Ottoman state to accept the Treaty of Sèvres, one of
whose provisions included the establishment of an independent Kurdistan, as shown in Map 3.3.[6]

The treaty was never implemented. Mustafa Kemal Ataturk, the reformer who founded the modern Turkish state, came to power committed
to creating a unitary nation-state that included northern Kurdistan. The
British and French became preoccupied with establishing their spheres of
influence in the former Ottoman territories of what is now Iraq and
Greater Syria. The British particularly wanted to ensure their control of
the Mosul oil fields, over which Turkey was also making claims. They
also found that the people of southern Kurdistan, which includes Mosul,
were divided as to whether they wanted to be part of an autonomous
Kurdish state or of the new Arab-Kurdish country of Iraq. So in 1923 the
Allies abandoned the Treaty of Sèvres and replaced it with the Treaty of
Lausanne, which recognized the state of Turkey within its modern
boundaries. As a result, Kurdistan, already divided between the Ottoman
and Persian Empires, was further divided among Turkey and the two
new Arab-dominated territories of Iraq and Syria, which were to be administered for an interim period by the British and the French, respectively. As a result, the Kurds never achieved the political statehood that
was restored to the Turks and granted to the Arabs. Kurdistan remains
the largest nation in the Middle East without its own state.[7]

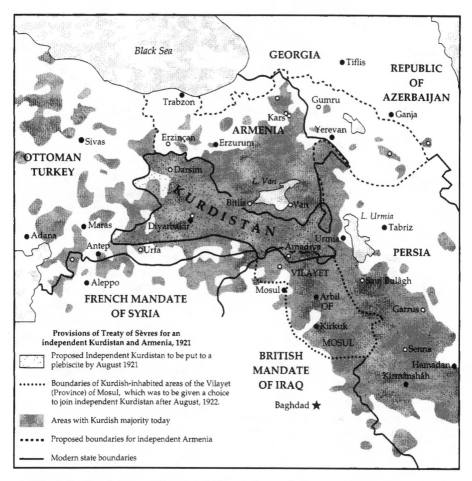

MAP 3.3 Provisions of Treaty of Sèvres for an independent Kurdistan and Armenia, 1921
Source: Mehrad R. Izady, *The Kurds: A Concise Handbook* (Washington, DC: Taylor and Francis, 1992).

After 1920 the history of Kurdish nationalism is mainly the history of three separate conflicts in which one or more Kurdish political movements have challenged the governments of Turkey, Iran, and Iraq.[8] These movements and their leaders have sometimes cooperated with and sheltered their kindred from adjoining regions; at other times they have been persuaded by outside powers to fight fellow Kurds. We review briefly the situation of Kurds in each of the three states at the beginning of the twenty-first century.

Kurds in Turkey

About half of all Kurds live in Turkey. At the beginning of the 1920s some Kurds were attracted to the Turkish nationalist ideal of establishing a state in which Turks and Kurds had equal standing. But from the Turkish point of view there was only one acceptable identity and that was Turkish: Kurds were encouraged to assimilate into Turkish society; their separate identity was rejected. When the last vestige of Ottoman rule, the Caliphate, was abolished in March 1924, "all public vestiges of separate Kurdish identity were crushed. Kurdish schools, associations, publications, religious fraternities and teaching foundations were all banned."[9]

From 1924 to 1990 the separate identity of Kurds was denied as part of the effort to establish a unitary Turkish nation and state. Kurds were referred to officially as Mountain Turks and were prohibited from teaching, writing, or publishing in Kurdish. Even public speech was forbidden. In the 1930s peasants marketing their produce were subject to a fine of five piasters for every word of Kurdish they spoke, even though few of them knew any Turkish.[10] From the mid-1920s to the late 1930s, the most serious rebellions in Kurdistan occurred in Turkey. These were suppressed harshly and with great loss of life; many thousands of Kurds—Kurdish sources say over 1 million—were deported from areas that supported the rebels. Young Kurds today speak of continuing discrimination: "I have lived with Turks for as long as I can remember. . . . When I was young, without even knowing what being Kurdish or Turkish was, we were looked down upon. They called us names I dare not repeat. . . . When it came to schools there was segregation everywhere between Kurds and Turks. The teachers would just make it obvious . . . we could never understand why they treated us in that way."[11]

Official policy in Turkey was directed not toward segregation but toward assimilation of Kurds and all other minority peoples in the country. In practice, many individuals have subordinated their Kurdish identity to that of the Turkish nation, and some have played an active role in political life. Following Turkey's first democratic elections in the 1950s, Kurds were able to take a more open political role. The pro-Kurdish People's Democratic Party (HADEP) and its successor, DEHAB, compete in national and local elections and have elected parliamentary deputies and mayors in the predominantly Kurdish southeast. But pro-Kurdish parties are suspected by conservatives and the military of secretly favoring separatism and as a result their officials are subject to raids and arrests, and some have been barred from party or public office.

The prohibitions against the public use of the Kurdish language and any reference to collective Kurdish interests continued to be enforced until 1990–1991, when, in response to international pressures and growing concern in Turkey about the spillover of rebellions in Iraqi Kurdistan, Turkish President Turgut Ozal made important symbolic gestures to Kurds. He spoke sympathetically about their plight, acknowledged meeting with Iraqi Kurdish leaders, tolerated public references to Kurds, and, in February 1991, introduced legislation that legalized public uses of Kurdish—although it did not allow publications in Kurdish. These accommodations, however, were strongly opposed by conservatives—including most of the military—and Kurds who exercised their rights risked harassment, arrests, and even murder at the hands of police.

Nonetheless, the cultural rights of Turkish Kurds are still tightly restricted. People may speak Kurdish in public and teach it in private, but public education in Kurdish continues to be banned. Kurds can and do celebrate the Kurdish New Year, in March, but celebrants are sometimes detained by police. Television stations broadcast in Kurdish but they cannot air messages that imply support for separatism. In February 2000 antiterrorism police arrested five people for singing Kurdish songs at a wedding because, while love songs are legal, Kurdish songs with political implications are not. The Turkish government is very eager to gain membership in the European Union (EU), and, in December 1999, the EU accepted Turkey's candidacy for membership. But one precondition of EU membership is that Turkey must bring its policies toward minorities more closely into line with European policies. In August 2002, the Turkish Parliament adopted measures to bring language policy in line with the European Union's standards on protection of minority rights (see Chapter 8). While many of Turkey's elite recognize that this means expanding Kurdish cultural and political rights, many conservatives and the military are not willing to make further concessions.

Political and cultural gains for Turkish Kurds also have been undermined by the activities of the militant Kurdish Worker's Party (PKK). Beginning in 1983 the PKK, with a training center in Lebanon's Bekka Valley and base areas in Iraqi Kurdistan, used guerrilla and terrorist tactics in the pursuit of an independent Kurdish state. It repeatedly attacked government forces and officials in Turkey's Kurdish provinces and also targeted moderate Turkish Kurds, for example destroying schools and killing some 200 teachers to "stop assimilation." Government statistics show that 4,302 civil servants, 5,018 soldiers, and 4,400 civilians were killed during the PKK campaign. The campaign provoked reprisal attacks by soldiers and police, many indiscriminately targeted against Kurds, and prompted the government to evacuate some 1,100 settlements and relocate about 1 million people to large cities.[12]

The PKK rebellion largely ended after the capture of its founder, Abdullah Öcalan, in February 1999. He called on his followers to halt their attacks and a number of fighters did in fact surrender, or crossed the Iraqi border to "safe areas." Turkish courts sentenced Öcalan to death but, in response to European pressure, have not executed him. The government was confident enough of its victory that in June 2002, it ended a fourteen-year-old state of emergency in most Kurdish provinces. The PKK rebellion had mixed effects. On the one hand it helped increase Turkish Kurds' awareness of their common identity and shared interests, and stimulated an increase in conventional political activity. On the other the rebellion created a backlash among Turkish nationalists, hardening their unwillingness to expand Kurdish cultural rights and political opportunities. They suspect that separatism underlies any expression of Kurdish interests. Nonetheless a great many observers, inside and outside Turkey, think that the long-term political solution to "the Kurdish problem" is to enable Kurds to participate effectively within the Turkish political system.[13]

There also was significant "spillover" of armed conflict into Iraq. During the 1990s, many PKK fighters sought to escape Turkish reprisals by moving across the border to autonomous Iraqi Kurdistan. This move helped internationalize the conflict because it prompted episodic ground and air attacks by Turkish forces—attacks that were sometimes indiscriminate, hitting Iraqi Kurdish villages as well as PKK camps. In October 1992, under pressure from both the PKK and the Turkish government, the autonomous government of Iraqi Kurdistan fought a month-long war with the PKK that aimed at neutralizing its sanctuaries. Turkish military operations in Iraqi Kurdistan continued throughout the decade, including a significant episode in April 2000.

Kurds in Iran

From the 1920s to 1979 the governments of the shahs of Iran, father and son, followed policies that encouraged Kurds to assimilate into the dominant society, although after 1960 limited publications and broadcasting in Kurdish were allowed. Pressures to assimilate do not seem to have been as consistent or as severe as they were in Turkey, in part because the shahs governed a multiethnic state that included the Turkic-speaking Azeris, the Arabs of Khuzistan, and the Baluchi, as well as the Kurds. Together these groups made up half of Iran's population. There were only two serious uprisings in Iranian Kurdistan during the 1920s and 1930s, both led by traditional Kurdish chiefs.

During World War II, northern Iran was occupied by the Soviets and southern Iran by the British to ensure that Iran did not join the Axis alliance. With Russian encouragement (but no military support), the Kurdish Republic of Mahabad was declared in January 1946. It was governed by a coalition of pro-Soviet Kurdish nationalists and a popular traditional leader from the town of Mahabad, Qazi Muhammad. It controlled less than half of Iranian Kurdistan; its government was opposed by many tribes in the re-

Kurdish family in Sanandaj, Iran, 1991. Photo by Salah Aziz, Badlisy Center for Kurdish Studies, Tallahassee, Florida.

gion; and it was defendable only because of the presence of Mustafa Barzani, the leader of Iraqi Kurds, who had fled to Mahabad in 1945 and was soon joined by 3,000 armed followers, as we discuss in the next section. The republic survived less than a year before it was conquered, without resistance, by the Iranian army. Its printing press was closed, the teaching of Kurdish was prohibited, and the leaders of the revolt were hanged in public in Mahabad's main square. Weak and short-lived though it was, the Mahabad Republic continues to be celebrated by Kurdish leaders as their closest approach to national independence prior to 1992.

In early 1979 some Kurds took advantage of the temporary weakness of the new Islamic government of the Ayatollah Khomeini and established control of Iranian Kurdistan. The same kind of leadership coalition emerged as had governed the Mahabad Republic: The left-linked Kurdish Democratic Party of Iran (KDPI) joined with a widely respected local religious leader, Shaikh Izzeddin Hosseini. And like Mahabad's leaders, they sought autonomy rather than outright independence. During 1979 a number of serious proposals for local autonomy were exchanged between the Tehran government and the KDPI, but no agreement was reached. From 1979 to 1984, the Kurds and the Tehran government alternated between negotiation and warfare. The government ordinarily held the towns, and the Kurdish fighters held most of the countryside. By early 1984, however, the Kurdish-controlled areas were virtually eliminated, despite some continued assistance from Iraq; since that time violent Kurdish resistance in Iran has taken the form of sporadic guerrilla actions. In 1989 the leader of the KDPI, Dr. Abdul-Rahman Qassemlou, still searching for accommodation with the government, was invited to meet in Vienna with Iranian representatives, where he was assassinated. Three years later his successor was assassinated in Berlin.

A few armed clashes were reported in the 1990s between Iranian forces and Iranian Kurdish rebels. Some of the latter were based in Iraq, prompting occasional Iranian air strikes and, in 1996, intervention by Iranian troops. Few Iranian Kurds now support rebellion. Rather their political energies are directed into conventional politics. Reformer Mohammad Khatami won more than 75 percent of the Kurdish vote when he was elected president in 1997 and twenty-two Kurds now serve in the Majlis (the Iranian national parliament). Elected on an independent ticket, the Kurdish parliamentarians are not allowed to form a pro-Kurdish party, but since the late 1990s they have repeatedly and loudly opposed Tehran's policies on several issues. One is the government's failure to protest Turkish reprisals against rebels of the PKK, some of whom have sheltered in Iran. A more important issue is the government's unwillingness to provide for Sunni mosques either in Iranian Kurdistan or in Tehran; since most Iranian Kurds are Sunni rather than Shi'i, this has become a contentious issue. Kurdish parliamentarians also have demanded that the government appoint more local officials who are Sunni Kurds. There are no indications that the government has retaliated against Kurdish politicians for their criticisms.[14]

The political status of Kurds in Iran makes an instructive contrast to Turkey. Both governments suppressed recent Kurdish rebellions by force, but overall Iranian policy is more tolerant of Kurdish aspirations and encourages teaching of the Kurdish language. A regime motivated by Islamic principles is less threatened by the assertion of minority rights and political participation than a regime motivated by the Turkish brand of exclusive nationalism.

Kurds in Iraq

The British who occupied the Basra-Baghdad-Mosul area in 1918 were generally sympathetic to Kurdish aspirations, as noted previously. Their initial plan was to establish an Arab state with one or more autonomous Kurdish provinces loosely attached to it. In 1919, to forestall Turkish efforts to take control of central Kurdistan, British forces encouraged

Shaikh Mahmud Barzanji, the Ottoman-appointed Kurdish governor of Sulaymaniya province, to run such a government. His authority was rejected by Kurds elsewhere in Iraq and by educated Kurds in Sulaymaniya. In 1923, after he proclaimed himself king of Kurdistan, the British suppressed his government.

Thereafter, the British sought to ensure that the Kurds would be incorporated into Arab Iraq with recognition of their separate cultural and political rights. Since the 1920s all Iraqi governments have accepted this principle. In 1954 Colonel Abdul Karim Qasim overthrew the monarchy and introduced a constitution that declared that Iraq was composed of two distinct nations, the Arabs and the Kurds. In the late 1950s Qasim's government offered concessions to the Kurds, as did the **Baathist** (Arab socialist) regime of Hasan Al-Bakr in the late 1960s. The Kurds' repeated rebellions after 1961 centered on disputes about implementation. Each time accommodation seemed within reach, escalating Kurdish demands and political distrust and maneuvering on both sides led to the breakdown of negotiations and the outbreak of fighting.

A key cultural issue that contributed to conflict was whether the Sorani dialect of Kurdish could be the language of instruction and government in Iraqi Kurdistan. During periods of accommodation, Baghdad governments have permitted it; at other times they have sharply restricted its use and have attempted to replace Kurdish with Arabic.

There have been two major political issues: One involves the extent of autonomy in Kurdish regions; the second is whether the regions should include places like Kirkuk and Mosul that have mixed Kurdish, Turkmen, and Arab populations. The minimalist position, taken by the most nationalistic Baghdad leaders, is that Kurds should have limited self-government only in narrowly drawn Kurdish areas. After 1974 the Baghdad government relocated Kurds and sponsored Arab settlement in mainly Kurdish areas, reducing still further the areas of Kurdish administration. The broadest demand, made by leaders of the Kurdish Democratic Party (the KDP, founded in 1946) and leaders of its principal rival, the Patriotic Union of Kurdistan (PUK, which split from the KDP in 1976), has been that a unitary government be established that has broad powers over all predominantly Kurdish areas. There were various subsidiary issues—for example, the number and role of Kurdish officials in the Baghdad government, the mix of Kurdish and Arab officials in autonomous regions, and whether a Kurdish administration should share in revenues from the Kirkuk oil fields. All of these issues surfaced again in the immediate aftermath of the U.S.-led invasion of Iraq in spring 2003, including the Kurdish seizure of Arab-settled villages from which they had been forcefully relocated in years past. The future stability of Iraq and the preservation of the Kurds' hard-won autonomy depend on how the issues are negotiated.

The first modern Kurdish rebellion occurred in 1943 under the leadership of Mustafa Barzani, the most influential twentieth-century Kurdish nationalist. Defeated in 1945, he retreated from his native district of Barzan, near the Turkish border, to Iranian Kurdistan; his role in defending the Mahabad Republic was discussed in the previous section. After the short-lived republic fell, Barzani took refuge in the USSR for twelve years. In 1958, the Iraqi monarchy was overthrown in a military-led revolution, and Barzani returned to lead KDP participation in the democratic reforms promised by the Qasim government.

By 1960 the government had backed away from its cultural and political concessions to the KDP and had begun to crack down on KDP activists. This pushed the party into armed rebellion, which continued episodically until 1976. Qasim's successors used all military means at their disposal in efforts to suppress these rebellions, beginning with heavy air attacks on Kurdish villages in September 1961. Barzani's KDP turned to outside support, which at various times was provided by the shah of Iran, the U.S. Central Intelligence Agency, and Israel.

Fighting was interrupted periodically by attempts to reach agreement on Kurdish demands. The leftist Baathist government that came to power in 1968 was willing at first to make significant concessions. In 1970 Barzani and the government negotiated a peace agreement that met many long-standing Kurdish demands. But in 1971 the agreement collapsed, in part because the KDP insisted that Kirkuk be included in the new Kurdish autonomous region and in part because an attempt was made on Barzani's life. By September 1973 Barzani had secured promises of substantial support from the shah of Iran and had resumed fighting. The next year a new round of negotiations collapsed, and the government implemented its own abridged version of the 1970 agreement. It established an autonomous region with its capital in Arbil; the region encompassed three provinces that contained about half of Iraq's Kurdish population and Kurdish-inhabited areas. Little information is available about the region's policies or administration. It is worth noting that the Kurdish Regional Government (KRG) established in northeastern Iraq in October 1992 under Allied protection, shown in Map 7.1 in Chapter 7, controls approximately the same area.

In 1975 the shah of Iran made a deal with the Iraqi government, which was represented by its vice president, Saddam Hussein. In return for Iraq giving up its claim to the Shatt-al-Arab waterway (the Tigris-Euphrates River estuary, which flows into the Gulf), the shah agreed to close the Iranian border to stop support for the Kurds. Barzani decided to stop the war, and again many of his followers fled as refugees to Iran. This was the worst defeat the Iraqi Kurds had suffered. Many of the refugees who returned to Iraq later that year were resettled away from the border zones.

In 1980, with Saddam Hussein now president, Iraq invaded Iran on Hussein's mistaken assessment that the revolutionary Iranian regime could be easily defeated and forced into concessions over the Shatt-al-Arab waterway and other boundary issues. The elder Barzani was now dead, and the KDP was led by his son Masoud. The PUK had split from the KDP in 1975, under the leadership of Jalal Talabani, who had rejected the elder Barzani's decision to stop fighting. During the next six years the PUK and the KDP fought both one another and the Iraqi government. At times the Kurds accepted help from the Iranians, negotiated cease-fires with Baghdad and with one another, and fought again.

By early 1987 PUK forces held large areas of Iraqi Kurdistan, but they were soon devastated by an overwhelming government campaign. An area encompassing more than a thousand villages was declared a killing zone by the Iraqi defense minister, who issued orders on June 20, 1987, that concluded with these two points:

- The corps commanders shall carry out sporadic bombardments using artillery, helicopters and aircraft, at all times of the day or night, in order to kill the largest number of persons present in those prohibited zones, keeping us informed of the results.
- All persons captured in those villages shall be detained and interrogated by the security services and those between the ages of 15 and 70 shall be executed after any useful information has been obtained from them.[15]

Tens of thousands of Kurds died in this episode of political mass murder. By August 1988 the PUK and the KDP had suffered not only a military defeat but had provoked the destruction of more than 3,000 Kurdish villages and the deportation of Kurds from most of their homelands. In response the Kurdish leaders suspended armed resistance, but they did not trust Saddam Hussein sufficiently to begin new negotiations. Matters remained suspended until Saddam Hussein's invasion of Kuwait in 1990, the coalition's assault in February 1991, and the March 1991 Kurdish uprising described at the outset of this section.[16]

The 1991 uprising and the Allies' intervention, which established a protected zone in northern Iraq, led to the establishment of the Kurdish Regional Government (KRG) by leaders of Barzani's KDP and Talibani's PUK. The KDP and PUK spent the next decade in fierce and sometimes violent conflict for control of the KRG, which is based in Arbil. The 1992 elections left them in a 50-50 deadlock for control of the KRG. The political differences between the two parties are in part a reflection of bitter rivalry between the two leaders, but have other

Children in a land at war, 2001. Kurdish boys playing with a toy weapon; girl holding flag of the Kurdish Democratic Party. Photos by Michael Rubin, reproduced by permission.

sources as well. Barzani, based in Salahuddin in the north, draws his support from a coalition of tribes and clans of Kurmanji-speakers. The region under his control is more prosperous, because the KDP taxes transborder trade with Turkey, and he has been politically more flexible—enough so that in 1996 he invited Iraqi government forces to assist the KDP's attack on Arbil, then controlled by the PUK. He justified what many condemned as a betrayal of Kurdish unity by the growing Iranian presence in PUK-controlled areas. Talibani, based in Sulaymaniya, draws support from Sorani-speaking Kurds, many of them of urban background. He sought to offset his relative lack of revenues by continuing to seek Iranian assistance.

Civil war within Kurdistan has ended and a delicate balance was reestablished in 1998 between the KDP and PUK under the terms of an agreement reached in Washington, D.C. Their external supporters, particularly the United States, pressured them to find common ground in maintaining regional autonomy. Cooperation has been reinforced by a 50-50 patronage system at every level of the Kurdish Regional Government administration that guarantees both parties' supporters a share of the pie. In September 2002 the leaders of the KDP and the PUK finally reactivated the unified parliament. Four of its sixty seats are held by women as are two of the twenty-five seats of the KRG's cabinet.[17] The future of the KRG's autonomy depends above all on the political institutions that are imposed or designed in postwar Iraq. Since the 1990s Kurdish leaders have emphasized that they are Iraqi as well as Kurds. In the aftermath of the 2003 war they have formulated a common aspiration for "a democratic, independent, unified, parliamentarian, federated Iraq." Sunni Arab leaders in the south might agree but many in the Shi'i majority have hopes of dominating a new Islamic republic. The overriding priority of the United States is a secular government in Baghdad that is strong enough to maintain the country's unity. A federal solution is likely, but the balance of powers among communal contenders and between center and periphery will be the subject of tense debate and negotiations.

It is important to point out that the population of northern Iraq is not homogenous. It also is home to the Turkmen, Iraq's third-largest minority, a people with historic links to Turkey. The oil-rich city of Kirkuk, for example, which lies at the southwestern edge of the Kurds' traditional homeland, has had many Turkmen residents since the time of the Ottoman Empire. The Turkish government has encouraged the formation of Turkmen political organizing that Turkey expects will have a role in a post-Hussein Iraqi government—and also help check Kurdish political aspirations. The international factors that will shape the future of Iraqi Kurds are analyzed more fully in Chapter 7.

THE MISKITOS: AN INDIGENOUS REVOLUTION
CONFRONTS A SOCIALIST REVOLUTION

In 1985, during peace negotiations between Miskito rebels and the government, Sandinista Comandante Luis Carron said, "Nicaragua is disposed to protect the culture of Nicaraguan Indian ethnic groups." Brooklyn Rivera, representing the Miskito's MISURASATA movement, replied, "Ethnic groups run restaurants. We have an army. We are a people. We want self-determination."

On September 18, 1989, former U.S. President Jimmy Carter spoke to 200 Miskito Indians packed into a church in Puerto Cabezas (its Miskito name is Bilwi), a ramshackle town on Nicaragua's Atlantic Coast that serves as the Miskitos' capital. He announced that he had reached a compromise with Tomás Borge, the interior minister of the revolutionary Sandinista government, that would allow the return of rebel Miskito leaders from exile and decisively end eight years of armed struggle. The unofficial mediation of President Carter and representatives of the world indigenous rights movement was the final step in sporadic peace talks about autonomy between the government and Miskito leaders that had begun in January 1988. Brooklyn Rivera soon returned to Nicaragua and later joined the government of Violetta Chamorro as minister-director of the Nicaraguan Institute for the Development of Autonomous Regions.[18]

The Miskito People

To understand why the Miskitos were at war and why international actors were involved in ending that war, we must begin with a brief look at Miskito society and history. About 150,000 Miskito Indians live in the humid tropical lowlands of eastern Nicaragua and Honduras, as shown in Map 3.4.[19] Their villages are the most heavily concentrated on the banks of the Coco River, the heart of their traditional homeland. Because of a decision of the International Court of Justice in the Hague, the Coco River has also been the international boundary between Nicaragua and Honduras since 1960. This decision resolved a long-standing dispute between the two countries but gave no consideration to the prior Miskito political claims to the entire area; thus, many Miskitos abandoned their villages on the northern, Honduran bank of the Coco River and moved to the southern bank.

The Miskitos share Nicaragua's Atlantic Coast region with much smaller numbers of Sumu and Rama Indians, about 30,000 Creoles and Garifuna of African origin, and Spanish-speaking **mestizos,** most of whom have migrated to the lowlands in recent decades from Nicaragua's densely settled Pacific and northcentral regions. The Miskitos and their Indian and Creole allies differ sharply from the dominant Spanish-speaking peoples of both countries. They speak indigenous languages and English, are

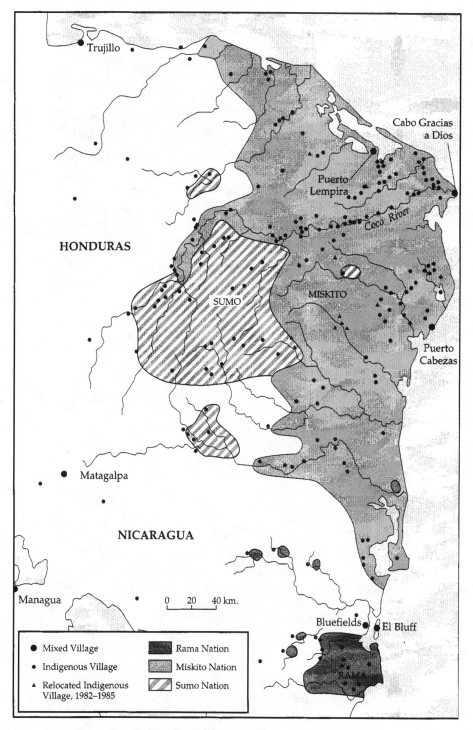

MAP 3.4   Miskito settlements in the 1980s. *Source:* Dunbar Ortiz, *The Miskito Indians of Nicaragua* (London: Minority Rights Group, 1988).

Brooklyn Rivera in Puerto Cabezas, 2001. Photo by Mark Pitsch and Robert Ritzenthaler, reproduced by permission.

mostly Moravian Protestants rather than Roman Catholics, and have closer cultural and economic ties to the English-speaking Caribbean and North America than to their nominal rulers, whom they refer to dismissively as "Spaniards."

The Miskitos have been more successful than most indigenous peoples in the Americas in defending their political and cultural domains against outsiders. The historical sketch that follows shows that the Miskitos' participation in the U.S.-sponsored "**Contra**" war against Nicaragua's Sandinista government during the early and mid-1980s was merely the latest and best publicized instance of Miskito resistance to outsiders' attempts at political domination.

The Rise and Fall of the Miskito Kingdom

In Miskito legend their people are descended from a migrant warrior named Miskut who founded a settlement on a coastal lagoon, one of many with abundant seafood. Before their first sustained contact with European pirates and traders in the 1630s, the Miskitos lived by subsistence farming, hunting, and fishing. Political organization evidently did not extend beyond the village level. Beginning in the 1640s Miskito chiefs joined with English pirates in attacks on Spanish settlements along the coast and in the interior of the country to the west. The first Africans also began to arrive on the coast—some from Jamaica, some freed from shipwrecked slave ships. Africans intermarried with the Miskitos but retained a separate identity as Creoles, whose descendants continue to dominate Bluefields and other towns on the southern Nicaraguan coast.[20]

For more than 200 years after the 1640s, the Miskitos were allies and agents of British political and commercial interests on the Atlantic Coast. Their access to firearms and British political support gave them superiority over other Indians in the region, some of whom they conquered, enslaved, or incorporated. The institution of kingship evolved from the belief among Miskito leaders that to be legitimated as chief, they had to be recognized as such by the British. In 1687 the governor of Jamaica established an English protectorate over the area and crowned a leading Miskito chief King Jeremy I. His successors governed the autonomous Mosquito Kingdom, later called Mosquitia and the Mosquito Reserve, until it was overthrown by Nicaraguan troops in 1894.

Miskito society and polity were buffeted by many external changes during the two centuries of autonomy. Spanish authorities carried out punitive expeditions in the region in the late eighteenth century but never established effective control. From 1848 to 1869 the southern part of the region was the eastern terminus of one of the major routes across Central America from New York to the California gold fields; North American cultural and commercial influence in the region was firmly established from that time onward.

In 1860, under U.S. pressure, the British government signed a treaty with the Nicaraguan government that ended its protectorate over the coast and acknowledged Nicaraguan sovereignty but that also provided for the establishment of a self-governing district in most of the area of the former kingdom. At this time the indigenous population of the coast was thought to number about 15,000, almost equally divided between Miskito Indians and Creoles. The Creoles of the coastal towns became the dominant political and economic class in the newly established Mosquito Reserve, although Miskito kings still ruled; effective authority in Miskito villages continued to be exercised by village headmen called *whita*.

The most profound change in nineteenth-century Miskito society began with the arrival of German-American Moravian missionaries from the United States at the end of the 1840s. They worked hand in hand with Miskito and Creole authorities, first to convert and educate the coastal peoples and then to inculcate in them the Protestant ethic of individual morality, moderation, and hard work. The missionaries backed Mosquitia's autonomy for both secular and religious reasons: They wanted to maintain their close working relations with local authorities, and they opposed the extension of Catholic influence to the coast. The missionaries and their native assistants came to have great administrative and political influence as well as religious authority in the villages. The Miskito pastors who gradually replaced the missionaries in the twentieth century inherited this dual secular and religious authority and have been among the strongest proponents of Miskito rights and autonomy since the 1980s.

In 1894 the Nicaraguan government decided to assert effective control over the coast in the interests of what would now be called state-building and modernization. The Nicaraguan government wanted to move troops to the region as a maneuver in its conflict with Honduras, and it sought customs duties from Mosquitia's port at Bluefields; leading merchants from the Pacific region, meanwhile, wanted to open up the coast for coffee production. Only a small contingent of troops was needed to occupy Bluefields and remove the authorities of the reserve. Creole resistance prompted intervention, at Nicaraguan request, by U.S. Marines and a few British troops. Resistance ended within a few months, and the Miskito king and 150 of his supporters were exiled to Jamaica. Miskito villagers remained mostly passive.

Nicaraguan governance of the coast, renamed the Province of Zelaya, was not repressive. Local affairs and tax revenues of Indian villages remained largely in the hands of village authorities, and after 1905, Indian villages were granted titles to their communal lands. In the late nineteenth century Mosquitia's economy changed more fundamentally than did its political status. From 1880 until the onset of the Great Depression in the 1930s, U.S. firms were heavily engaged in lumbering, running banana plantations, and mining, thus providing employment for much of the male coastal population. During World War II rubber plantations were a major source of employment; after the war, mining took on this role. The growth of a wage labor economy provided opportunities for small-scale commerce in which Miskitos and Creoles participated along with immigrant Chinese. During periodic slumps Miskito men returned to the subsistence farming that had continued to occupy their wives and children, or they worked abroad and sent their remittances home. This pattern continues to the present, with many Miskito men working on merchant ships and cruise liners.

From the Somoza Dictatorship to the Sandinista Revolution

From 1936 to 1979 Nicaragua was ruled by the Somoza family, a dictatorship whose main interests in the Atlantic Coast region were economic rather than political. Especially during the 1950s and 1960s, the Somozas promoted such projects as reforestation, commercialization of fishing, community-based cooperatives, and agrarian colonization by mestizos (people of mixed Spanish and Indian descent) from the Pacific side of the country. By 1981 the mestizos made up more than half of the population of the province, but most lived on the "agricultural frontier," near the foot of the highlands and well to the west of the areas of Miskito settlement. Some projects, like the creation of forest preserves on traditional lands, antagonized some villagers, but on balance the Miskitos benefited from government policies during this period because of employment and commercial opportunities. Many were said to admire English-speaking President Anastasio Somoza Debalye, and few Miskitos supported the Sandinista revolutionary movement that began in the Pacific region of the country in the mid-1970s.

The Miskitos began to mobilize in 1974 when Moravian pastors and young Miskito professionals founded ALPROMISU (Alliance for the Progress of Miskitos and Sumus) to promote Indian economic interests vis-à-vis the Somoza government and merchants. ALPROMISU was part of the international movement of indigenous peoples that emerged during the mid-1970s; one of its representatives became president of the Regional Council of Indigenous Peoples formed in January 1977 and served as an executive member of the World Council of Indigenous Peoples, founded two years earlier.

In 1979 the Marxist-populist Sandinistas ousted the Somoza dictatorship from power in the Nicaraguan capital of Managua and instituted the policies that drew the Miskitos into protracted and internationalized conflict. Their war is best understood as a conflict between two political movements with contradictory ideologies.[21] The Sandinista authorities had ambitious plans for revolutionary modernization of the Province of Zelaya, which made up 60 percent of the country's area. Their program of state-directed economic growth in the interests of the country's predominantly mestizo peasantry and workers was fundamentally inconsistent with the emerging political program of the Miskitos.

In November 1979, shortly after the Sandinistas came to power in Managua, a convention of 500 Indians met in Puerto Cabeza and established a successor organization to ALPROMISU called MISURASATA (Miskitos, Sumus, Ramas, and Sandinistas United). The new organization appeared at first to embrace the revolutionary program and was granted a seat on the Sandinista government's National Council of State. Within a few months, however, MISURASATA leaders were making strong claims that indigenous peoples had a fundamental right to communal land and resources and the right to promote the language and culture that set them apart from others, including the Hispanic revolutionaries. The Sandinistas agreed to policies that met some MISURASATA demands, but the officials charged with implementing revolutionary programs on the coast were Spanish-speaking mestizos. Their actions, often heavy-handed, and attitudes, often racist, undermined efforts at compromise. MISURASATA demands and tactics simultaneously became more radical and threatening to the government.

Rebellion and Reconciliation

Violent conflict began in February 1981 when Miskitos resisted Sandinista attempts to arrest MISURASATA leaders at a Moravian church in

Forum in Puerto Cabezas to protest commercial leasing of a community pier, 2001. Photo by Mark Pitsch and Robert Ritzenthaler, reproduced by permission.

Prinzapolka and four people on each side were killed. In August MIS-URASATA was banned; in December one of its leaders, Steadman Fagoth, operating from the Honduran side of the Coco River, began what the Miskitos called the Red Christmas campaign of attacks on Sandinista garrisons. The government responded in January 1982 by sending troops to forcibly remove 8,500 Miskito villagers from the south bank of the Coco River to resettlement camps fifty miles further south; about 10,000 others escaped across the river to Honduras.

Between 1982 and 1984 about four thousand armed soldiers from two Miskito groups waged guerrilla war on the Sandinistas. MISURASATA, now led by Brooklyn Rivera, operated from Costa Rica. Miskitos, Sumus, and Ramas (MISURA), led by Steadman Fagoth and armed and supplied by the U.S. Central Intelligence Agency as part of the "contra" war against the Sandinistas, operated from Honduras. Miskitos still living in Nicaragua were encouraged or coerced by contra forces to flee to Honduras.

In 1984 and 1985 the Sandinistas shifted their policies toward the coast. Zelaya province was placed under the personal control of Interior Minister Tomás Borge, and "Spanish" officials in the region were gradually replaced with local people. A National Autonomy Commission was established, and talks were begun with local and exiled Miskito leaders. Some of the talks led to limited cease-fire agreements.

In September 1987 the Nicaraguan National Assembly passed an Autonomy Statute—written with input from most coastal communities—which established two autonomous regions (north and south), each with its own representative council and administration. Substantial political, economic, and cultural rights were guaranteed. In January 1988 exiled Miskito leaders and the government began the autonomy and peace talks, referred to in the previous paragraph, that provided for the return of exiles and of 35,000 refugees from Honduras, including fighters. The September 1989 agreement mediated by Jimmy Carter guaranteed the safe return of fifty rebel leaders, including Rivera and Fagoth, so they could participate in the national elections planned for spring 1990.[22]

The unexpected outcome of the elections was the defeat of the Sandinistas. In April 1990 Miskito leaders signed an agreement with the government of newly elected President Violetta Chamorro that affirmed truce accords and plans for demobilization. The autonomous region the Miskitos call Yapti Tasba was established, and elections were held for separate forty-five-member councils for its northern and southern parts. The northern area, the Región Autónoma del Atlántico Norte, is dominated by Miskitos; the southern area, the Región del Atlántico Sur, is governed jointly by Creoles, Miskitos, and others. Each council elects a coordinator as chief executive, each area has elected representatives in the Nicaraguan National Assembly, three from the north and two from the south.

The Limits of Autonomy Arrangements

Regional autonomy has not ended conflict between the Miskitos and the central government. The councils and the Miskito political movement, Yapti Tasbaya Masrika (YATAMA, a successor to MISURASATA) have engaged for more than a decade in disputes with the Managua government over implementation of the autonomy agreement. One issue is funding: The Nicaraguan economy has never recovered from Sandinista rule and the central government is virtually bankrupt. As a consequence the coast suffers from all the ills of a poor region in a poor country. Bilingual education programs have not been funded, roads and port facilities go unmaintained, public health services are minimal, unemployment estimates range from 50 to 80 percent, and cocaine addiction has spread rapidly among adolescents.

The second issue is this: Who will control development of the natural resources of the region and its offshore waters? The Atlantic Coast region has abundant resources—inshore and offshore fisheries, tropical forests with commercially valuable mahogany and cedar, and inland mines. The Miskitos are supposed to control all fisheries inside the three-mile limit and continue to take in about 60 percent of the seafood harvested in the

Rama teacher on Rama Cay,
2001. Photo by Mark Pitsch
and Robert Ritzenthaler,
reproduced by permission.

region. But the Managua government has encouraged foreign commercial fishing by long-line boats that routinely violate the three-mile limit and overfish stocks. The central government also has attempted to give timber concessions to foreign firms without consulting the regional councils.

Miskito grievances about these issues take two political forms. Some YATAMA activists, veterans of the 1980s conflict, have continued or resumed militant political action. In the early 1990s they temporarily seized towns and ousted local officials; in 1994 ex-YATAMA members kidnapped four U.S. fisherman and held them for ransom. In the late 1990s some began to rearm and carried out a deadly attack on a military post in 1998.

Indigenous organizations also used the new institutions to promote their rights by conventional means. One indigenous group, the Awas Tingni people, used legal means to protest a thirty-year timber concession granted in the mid-1990s to a Korean firm. The case eventually was heard by the Inter-American Court of Human Rights, the concession was canceled, and the Nicaraguan government was obliged to compensate the tribe and its lawyers. Nonetheless the Managua government has persisted in efforts to "develop" the area without the consent of the regional councils—including plans announced in 2002 to build a Caribbean-to-the-Pacific rail corridor through the southern region, and to give four U.S. oil consortiums exploration rights off the Miskito coast.

Dissatisfaction with the central government's failure to respect regional rights came to a head in July 2002 when the Miskito Council of Elders announced plans to create an independent "Miskito Communal Nation." The council said that 280 communities—including those in Honduras—

had signed onto the plan, which envisions an independent state that controls all resources in the region, including those off shore islands. What will be done to implement the plan remains to be seen.[23]

CONCLUSION

Conceptual analysis and comparison of conflicts involving these two peoples are provided in Chapters 6 and 7. The history of the two groups and their fates offer useful contrasts. The Kurdish peoples' aspirations for autonomy, their cultural cohesion, and their common historical experience of subordination to other states have repeatedly motivated rebellions throughout Kurdistan. In Iraq and, to a lesser degree, Iran they have also led to frequent negotiations aimed at accommodating both government and Kurdish interests. But attempts to establish autonomous Kurdish states have failed, and they have usually been followed by repression. A decade-long experiment at establishing an autonomous Kurdish state was conducted in northern Iraq under Allied (U.S. and British) protection, but whether the main Kurdish factions will maintain their alliance and autonomy in a post-Hussein regime remains to be seen.

The Miskitos are a much smaller group than the Kurds and have been involved in fewer instances of violent struggle against outsiders and have gained significant regional autonomy without massive destruction and loss of life. One intriguing question is, Why the difference? What combination of domestic and international factors made it possible for the Miskitos to win a small victory, whereas the Kurds have suffered great and recurring losses in the largely futile pursuit of their own state? Another challenging question concerns implementation. It is increasingly evident that the quasi-democratic Nicaraguan state, now dominated by conservatives, is not prepared to respect significant aspects of the autonomy agreement. So the Miskitos' conflict has not ended, it has been transformed, and its future course is unpredictable.

The Miskitos also provide evidence for another kind of conclusion. There is a tendency in Western societies to romanticize the lives of indigenous peoples, to think of them as surviving fragments of a lost world in which people lived without conflict in simple harmony with their natural environment. It should be clear, even from our brief account, that within the semiautonomous domain of the Miskitos, their culture and ways of life have evolved by incorporating Western elements. At various points in their history, they have adapted to trade-based and wage labor economies and have converted to a strong and indigenously controlled Protestant faith. Miskito leaders did use the language and politics of the indigenous rights movement during the 1980s to justify and gain support for their opposition to the Sandinista government, and the broader war of the U.S. government against the Sandinistas did both co-opt and empower them. But the society they are protecting is not a static fragment of pre-Colombian traditional society: The Miskitos are a dynamic and outward-looking society that has used Western political means and outside support to assert a distinctive local culture and interests that can be traced only in part to indigenous origins.

DISCUSSION QUESTIONS

1. What accounts for the dispersal of the Kurds across many different countries? Does this weaken their claim to statehood?
2. What combination of international and domestic factors made it possible for the Miskitos to win regional autonomy, whereas the Kurds have suffered great and recurring losses in the largely futile pursuit of their own state?
3. Many Kurds believe they have been a distinct people since ancient times; some non-Kurdish observers think their identity was formed more recently. Does this kind of historical debate, which is echoed in debates over other ethnonational movements, have any relevance to the contemporary Kurdish struggle for independence?
4. Do changes in Miskito culture and society over the past three centuries weaken their claims to being a distinct indigenous people with special claims to the region they currently inhabit?
5. Why did some Miskitos ally first with the revolutionary Sandinista government and then switch to the U.S.-supported Contra movement that sought to overthrow the Sandinistas?

4

Protecting Group Rights in Plural Societies: The Chinese in Malaysia and Turks in Germany

The Chinese in Malaysia and the Turks in Germany are examples of two types of ethnopolitical groups identified in Chapter 2. The Chinese are communal contenders, a cohesive and culturally distinct group that is mainly concerned about using its limited political influence in a Malay-dominated society to protect Chinese economic advantages and cultural interests. They provide an illustration of the ways in which the rights of a large communal group are both protected and restricted in a rapidly developing democracy. The Turks are an ethnoclass, a classlike immigrant minority that was originally expected to work temporarily in Germany and then return to Turkey. Most of its members are now permanent residents of Germany without full citizenship, their security threatened by neo-Nazi and skinhead attacks. Their changing status has prompted intense political debate in Germany, leading to reconsideration and legal redefinition of what it means to be "German." Their situation parallels that of the growing numbers of visible minorities in other advanced industrial democracies.

THE CHINESE IN MALAYSIA

During what became known as "the Emergency" in the British protectorate of Malaya (1948–1960), 6,710 Chinese insurgents and 2,473 civilians were killed (and 510 civilians were missing), whereas 1,865 members of the government forces died. The government forces consisted mainly of British Europeans and Malays; all of their opponents were Chinese, who were concentrated on the country's west coast, as shown in Map 4.1. The Emergency was one of the numerous insurrections that swept Southeast Asia following World War II. Founded in 1930, the Chinese Communist Party became the principal resistance force during the Japanese occupation. Although it collaborated loosely with Allied forces during World

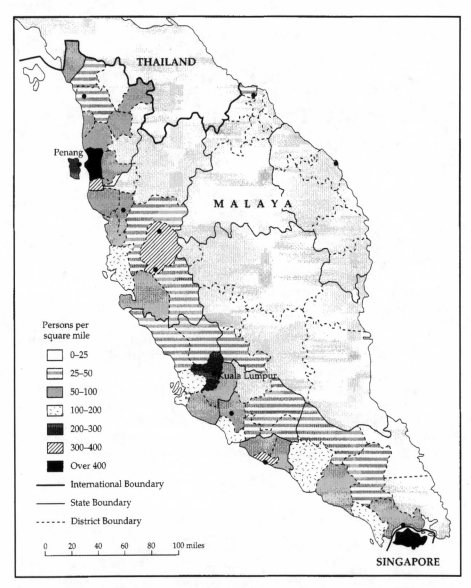

MAP 4.1 Distribution of Chinese population in Malaya, 1957. *Source:* Ooi Jin-Bee, *Land, People, and Economy in Malaya* (New York: Longman, 1963).

War II, its main goal was to drive the British out of Malaya. Its youthful leader, Chin Peng, received his ideological direction from Moscow by way of the Comintern (International Communist Movement) and his revolutionary modus operandi from the Communists in China.

During the 1930s the Malay Communist Party followed a rather unorthodox path by abandoning class struggle in favor of winning over labor unions and emphasizing the democratic and nationalistic character of the movement. This changed in 1948 when Peng's party was declared an illegal organization and, thus, was forced underground. Harsh British policies coupled with Malay reprisals led to the deaths described in the previous paragraph.[1]

The Status of the Chinese in Malaysian Society

Despite hardship, because of Japanese occupation and also as a result of the suppression of Chinese guerrilla activity, the Chinese have become prosperous in their adopted land. Although the Malay-dominated government has actively pursued Malay advancement through ethnic hiring quotas for the professions, commercial ventures, and the civil service, all citizens are guaranteed equal protection under the law. The government has justified preferential policies by arguing that if Malays continue to be less prosperous than their Chinese counterparts, ethnic tension will increase.

Since independence, Malaysia has been committed to a multiparty parliamentary form of government, a working democracy in which Chinese and other minorities are represented. Nonetheless, the underlying competition and conflict between Chinese and Malays has dominated all political discourse.

In the eyes of many Malays, the Chinese are immigrants who have no particular loyalties to the overwhelmingly Malay political establishment. Distrust has also existed in Chinese circles, as has been evident in the platform of opposition parties challenging policies favoring Malays (one example is the Democratic Action Party, founded in 1965). With the increase in Islamic orthodoxy worldwide, some Malay Muslims now call for an Islamic polity that, if instituted, would further circumscribe Chinese political participation.[2]

Despite ethnic rivalries, with the exception of communal riots in 1969 that led to a brief period in which democracy was suspended and a state of emergency declared, Malaysia's political elite has managed to maintain relative ethnic harmony. However, with the flare-up of ethnic violence worldwide and the increase in Islamic militancy, Malay-Chinese relations are vulnerable. The government has taken precautionary steps to counteract extremist propaganda by legally limiting civil liberties, especially in the area of freedom of communication. Thus, all opposition voices have been muted and public discussion of sensitive issues curtailed through the Internal Security Act of 1960 and later legislation. Unfortunately, by suppressing expressions of discontent, a sense of how deeply grievances are rooted is also lost. It is an open question whether Chinese-Malay relations will deteriorate in the present global climate of worldwide ethnic and religious assertiveness

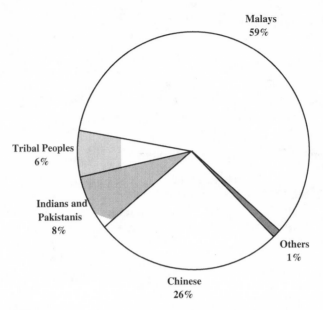

FIGURE 4.1   The population of Malaysia, 2000

or whether both peoples will find the common ground needed to build a successful multiethnic polity.

Ethnic Divisions in Malaysia

Approximately 26 percent of Malaysia's multiethnic population of 21.9 million people (2000 census) is of Chinese background, 59 percent is Malay, 8 percent is Indian, and 6 percent is of tribal and other origin, as shown in Figure 4.1. Most of the latter are tribal people of Sabah and Sarawak (see Map 4.2), such as the Iban Dayak and the Kadazan-Dusun, who are close cultural kindred of the Malays. The population also includes about 100,000 indigenous peoples, descendants of the aboriginal peoples of the Southeast Asian peninsula and Borneo. They are known collectively as Asal, a name assigned by the governing authorities.

Malays have populated the states of modern-day Malaysia for millennia, whereas most Chinese and Indians arrived during the late nineteenth century. Malay origin is uncertain: Myth and oral history claim they are descendants of a Caucasian tribe originating in China that migrated to the Malay peninsula seven thousand to four thousand years ago. Most Chinese immigrants arrived from South China after 1860, lured by British promises of a better life. Some trace their ancestry back to migrants in earlier centuries called Straits Chinese, who settled in the islands of Penang and Singapore and in Malacca. Indians are largely Tamils from southern

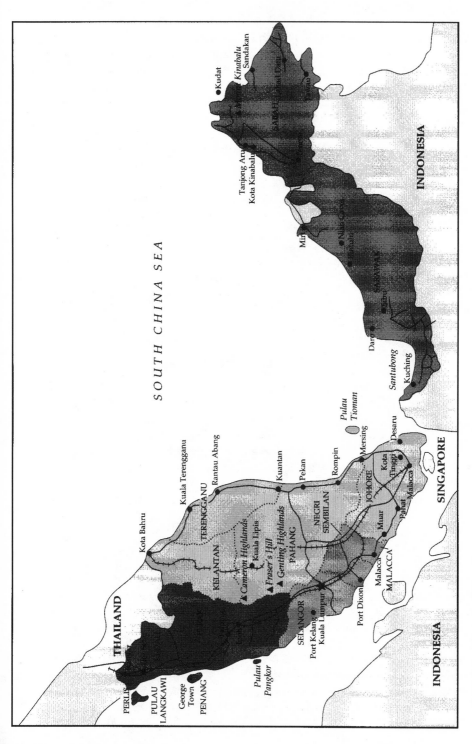

MAP 4.2   Modern Malaysia

India brought by the British colonizers to work the rubber plantations. Sabah and Sarawak Chinese have a somewhat different history. Sabah was ceded to a private company, the British North Borneo Company (1881), which actively recruited Chinese laborers, at times primarily Christian Chinese from Hong Kong. Today Chinese account for 12 percent of the Sabah population. Sarawak was run by "white Rajahs," the Brooke family, who actively recruited Chinese from the mainland. Chinese gold miners from Indonesia were followed by the Fuzhou Chinese, who included large numbers of Methodists. The Chinese account for 29 percent of the local population of about 2.1 million.

Malays are Sunni Muslims, Indians are largely Hindus, and the Chinese are predominantly Buddhists, with some Confucianists, Taoists, and a few Christians. The indigenous peoples are mainly Animists, and the few Eurasians and Europeans are Christians. Before World War II, Malays were overwhelmingly agriculturalists; they were also heavily represented on the police force, and some were civil servants. The Chinese provided most of the labor for building roads and plantations and for working the tin mines; later they dominated the commercial sector. Most Indians worked in the mines and on the rubber plantations; some moved to the cities and opened small businesses. The tribal peoples are largely hunters and fishers, and they occasionally farm.

Before independence in 1957, Malaya's ethnic communities were not only separated by language, religion, custom, and geography but were divided among themselves. Ethnic consciousness and divisiveness were probably enhanced by the colonial experience. For example, Chinese elite consciousness was fostered and encouraged by the British, who from the early nineteenth century onward used the Straits Chinese as clerks in their firms. These Chinese often spoke English as their first language and had only a rudimentary understanding of Mandarin, Cantonese, or other Chinese dialects (Hokkien, Hakka, and Cantonese dialects are fairly different from one another and are not readily understood). Most of these people were descendants of longtime residents of Malaya, and they saw themselves as "Malay" citizens (a term used to describe people living in colonial Malaya) of the empire. Some of the more recent immigrants from China also came to see Malaya as their home, especially those who fled the civil war in China in the 1930s and 1940s. Others wavered in their sympathies between China and Malaya, and they envisioned Malaya as a temporary residence away from the Chinese motherland. Businesspeople, whose political sympathies were with the anti-Communist Kuomintang forces in China (before their defeat in 1949), were basically loyal as long as their business interests were protected by the local and colonial elites.

Malays were mostly rural people who lived in areas belonging to one of the nine sultanates that eventually became part of modern Malaysia. Malays seemed content to live under the patronage of their respective sultans, whose feudal systems remained largely intact until World War II. Dependence on the benevolence of individual autocratic rulers was firmly imbedded in Malay political culture prior to independence. Although sultans had an open-door policy under which citizens could ask for personal favors, voice their grievances, and utter complaints, once they reached a decision individuals had few avenues for redress.

Most Malays were illiterate, partly because the sultans discouraged Western-style education. In most instances people had to rely on their local qadis (Muslim judges) and religious leaders for education and dispute settlement. Literacy was further impeded because some of the classical texts of Malay literature were written in Arabic, reflecting the Islamic impact on civic culture. Cultural exchanges with Europeans, Chinese, and Indians were discouraged by local leaders for fear of having their authority undermined.

Wealthier Chinese established their own elementary and secondary schools prior to independence, but most attended the secular institutions established by the British. Secret societies and special bureaus (established by the British) that dealt specifically with Chinese civil affairs served as the equivalent of a modern-day patronage system in preindependence Malaya. Under the colonial system the Chinese were restricted in their access to ownership of land, to which they responded by becoming traders; from there they moved on to become bankers and manufacturers.

Indians who worked on rubber plantations had their own security system and social services; the plantations were largely self-contained units. Indians typically divided their loyalties among the Crown, their home provinces in India, and Malaya. Most were either subjects of the Crown or Indian citizens; thus, they were doubly dependent on the British.[3]

The Emergence of Democratic Malaysia

Britain's role in Malaya was largely that of a protector rather than a colonizer, with the notable exception of the Crown colonies of Singapore, Malacca, and Penang. Penang effectively became a dominion of the British East India Company (the commercial predecessor of Imperial Britain) in 1785, when the sultan of Kedah ceded the island in return for military support and an annual salary. Singapore was similarly taken over by 1824, and Sarawak and Sabah on the island of Borneo became Crown colonies in the late nineteenth century. Malacca was first held by the Dutch, who gave it to the British in 1796. The interior of Malaya was never effectively colonized. By playing one sultan against the other and offering military assistance, the British were able to establish dominion over the sultanates of Negri Sembilan, Selangor, Perak, and Pahang by 1875. These states merged into a federation known as the Federated States of Malaya. The sultanates of Kedah, Perlis, Kelantan, and Trengganu, all either previously allied with Thailand or vassals of the same, were freed of Thai domination by 1909 but at first declined to join the British-sponsored Malay Federation. Johore, the last independent sultanate, formally accepted British supervision in 1923.

Britain's rule was relatively benign, although colonial officials interfered in dynastic conflicts among the pretenders to the sultan's throne and similarly intervened when hostilities broke out among the Chinese secret societies.

At the beginning of the twentieth century, political power was divided among the British governor and high commissioner, the Conference of Rulers, the prime minister of each state, and members of the Legislative Council. The council included representatives of the trade unions and chambers of commerce (including Chinese), who were chosen by their respective organizations and appointed by the high commissioner.

World War II and the Japanese invasion of the peninsula exposed the tenuousness of British rule in Malaya. The Chinese especially were the targets of ruthless treatment by the invading Japanese. When the Japanese invaded China in 1937, all Chinese in Asia were treated as enemies. Deprived of work, they became impoverished squatters on the fringes of the Malayan jungle.

After World War II the British were slow to reestablish colonial rule in interior Malaya. Visible only in Penang and Singapore, their tentative plans to extend central rule triggered widespread Malay protests. Compromises between the British and communal leaders in the late 1940s and early 1950s led to a formal alliance of three important communally based parties. What emerged in 1957 as the independent country of Malaya consisted of eleven states; in 1963 Sabah and Sarawak (on the island of Borneo) and Singapore (for a period of two years) joined the federation and formed the country of Malaysia.

During decolonization and the early stages of independence, executive and legislative powers were somewhat decentralized, as each state retained the power to run its own internal affairs. This situation changed when Malaysia entered a new era that included what became known as "the Emergency."[4]

The Emergency

Subsidized by the British during World War II as a local resistance force against the Japanese occupiers, the Malayan Communists (members included few if any ethnic Malays) gained a degree of respectability among ethnically divided Malayans. The Chinese and the Communists were the prime targets of ruthless Japanese elimination campaigns. Communist sympathizers were often killed on mere suspicion. Upon the Japanese surrender, the British sought to disarm the guerrillas, of which there were

Chinese Malaysians' voter registrations are checked on election day in Kuala Lumpur, November 29, 1999. © AP WorldWide Photos.

about 6,000 in 1945. Alarmed by what the Chinese perceived as the British catering to Malay dominance, the guerrillas refused to disarm. The sultans' refusal to join a more centrally organized federation that would give representation and full citizenship to minorities added to the mistrust. Chinese Communists were convinced that only full independence, preferably under their leadership, would lead to full emancipation of all ethnic groups in postcolonial Malaya.

Authorities' treatment of the Chinese was often harsh and discriminatory. Until 1948, for example, Chinese accused of the tiniest infractions were regularly sent back to China. In 1948, emboldened and inspired by the impending Communist victory in China, the Communist Party of Malaya embraced armed struggle. The British responded with a scheme whereby thousands of squatters were resettled into camps hermetically closed off from their surroundings. The Chinese were given land and were allowed to farm but were simultaneously deprived of free movement. Villagers became pawns of the Communists and the British. Totally dependent at first on British support and often forced to collaborate with Communist infiltrators, they were targeted by both sides. Informants were typically killed by the Communists; upon suspicion of Communist support, government forces responded with food rationing, deportations, prison sentences, and other forms of collective punishment. Eventually, the hamlet policy, as it was known, of closing off the villages from the outside world robbed the guerrillas of the much-needed political and physical support of the Chinese squatters and, thus, gradually led to the dissipation of the movement.

The Emergency disclosed the weakness of a decentralized political system and forced a reevaluation of existing arrangements. With the realization that the insurgents were a force to be reckoned with, state-level executive committees cooperated with federal authorities, local police chiefs, and army commanders to fight the insurgents. At first, lacking military and police forces to fight the rebels, the British passed emergency regulations that gave the police extraordinary powers. They created special forces trained in jungle warfare, gave arms to community guards, and, later, encouraged non-Malays to join the struggle against the Communists. By the early 1950s the insurgency had faded, and Malays and Chinese, under the able leadership of Tunku Abdul Rahman, joined to form an alliance that became the basis for cooperation among the three ethnic groups.

The son of the sultan of Kedah and a Thai princess, Tunku Abdul Rahman was one of the bright nationalists who organized the Alliance Party in 1952 (the forerunner of UMNO—the United Malay National Organization), which convinced the British that Malaya was ready for independence. The party consisted of the Malay Nationalist Organization, the Malayan Chinese Association, and the Malayan Indian Congress. Until 1969 it provided the type of political formula that led to relative ethnic stability. The formula consisted of a series of compromises that favored the Malays: The Malays were to dominate politics, the official religion was to be Islam, the official language would be Malay, and the head of state was to be a sultan elected from among the nine hereditary rulers.

Malaysia Since 1969

The preindependence social contract that favored Malay status and protected non-Malay cultures, which allowed for relative ethnic harmony, collapsed in the riots that followed the elections of 1969. In retrospect that came as no surprise. The Malaysian Constitution differentiates between the indigenous status of citizens and that of "immigrants." This distinction is inherent in the designation of bumiputera (literally son of the soil). All Malays and indigenous groups of the peninsula and Sabah and Sarawak are bumiputera, all other are not, which includes Indians, Chinese, Pakistanis, and others. This so-called social contract was negotiated among the elites, with little or no input from the general population. In 1969, by running on a platform of equal rights for all citizens regardless of

Chinese Malaysian children sit below posters of the Democratic Action Party criticizing Prime Minister Mahathir Mohamad for declaring Malaysia is "in effect" an Islamic state, June 2002. Copyright © AP WorldWide Photos.

race, the urban-based, largely Chinese Democratic Action Party had wrested votes from the Malaysian Chinese Association. This position directly opposed the aims of the Alliance Party, which promoted racial harmony by acquiescing to Malay political hegemony. The electoral gain of the Democratic Action Party was interpreted by impoverished Malays as a direct threat to the continuance of their political dominance. In the ensuing riots 143 Chinese, 25 Malays, 13 Indians, and 15 others were killed.

These riots led to the emergence of a new generation of leaders committed to protecting communal rights, but as it turns out at the expense of the Chinese. New policies were enacted to eliminate poverty especially among all communal groups. This included long-term objectives such as eliminating or at least narrowing the gap between rural poverty and urban wealth and to eliminate economic inequalities between the Chinese and the Malays. Estimates showed that in 1969, nearly 65 percent of all Malays lived below the official poverty line, compared with 26 percent of the Chinese and 39 percent of the Indian households.

Broader initiatives included funding for research and development, especially in technical fields, providing additional funds for regional development schemes, stressing the value of education, and encouraging peasants to take wage-earning jobs. Furthermore, the government hoped to reduce foreign investment by replacing foreign corporations with Malaysian owned and managed ones. In 1969, an estimated 62 percent of all corporate assets were foreign owned, whereas Chinese Malays owned more than 30 percent and Malays less than 2 percent. Government policy aimed to change this within twenty years to 30 percent foreign, 40 percent non-Malay, and 30 percent Malay. Although the Malay-owned percentage had increased significantly by the year 2000, it still fell short of these targets.

In reality, the New Economic Policy (NEP), as it was called, favored the Malays through special subsidies. Newly established government-financed agencies served as clearinghouses in commercial ventures, job quotas were introduced, Chinese quotas were introduced at universities, and various other programs were instituted that were designed to help Malays gain economic parity with the Chinese.

To many Chinese these policies amounted to a Malay takeover and an attempt to convert potential Chinese economic losses into Malay gains. For the Malays the change of direction was long overdue. Although many earlier policies had favored Malays by requiring quotas in occupations, they had done little to alleviate rural Malay poverty. Thus, the new policies were directed primarily toward trying to narrow the gap between rural poverty and urban wealth and eliminating economic inequalities between the Chinese and the Malays. The official goal was to "eliminate the identification of race with economic function."[5]

Since the implementation of the New Economic Policy, Malays have enrolled in universities in unprecedented numbers, whereas because of quotas, many Malaysian Chinese study abroad. Malays are still underrepresented in the professions and in technical jobs. All ethnic groups have gained in relative income, but the distribution among ethnic groups has changed only slightly in favor of Malays, and income disparities remain. Malaysia's export-oriented economy is not easily manipulated through government-sponsored programs. Economic growth may promote more overall wealth but without changing existing income inequalities, despite governmental intervention, because of the independent nature of a globally oriented market economy. The very real Malay gains in education may eventually challenge Chinese domination in the professional and technical fields and, thus, in the long run improve overall Malay economic standing.

Malaysia in the 1990s

Despite regular elections, an orderly leadership succession, a federal bicameral legislature, and a sharing of legislative powers with thirteen states, democracy in Malaysia is still limited. After the 1969 riots the democratic system was suspended for eighteen months and replaced with a National Operations Council with full emergency powers. Also, emergency legislation was enacted that continues in force. Under the provisions of the Internal Security Act, party activists, Christian evangelists, and other activists from various community organizations have been arrested. The act is supposed to allow people to criticize the government as long as the criticism has no racial or ethnic connotations. The curtailment of freedom of expression to such a degree, coupled with the occasional use of preventive detention, is incompatible with democratic values.

The political situation has not improved in the early 2000s. The Chinese continue to face discrimination in employment in the public sector and educational advancement; in addition, many small Chinese-owned businesses are floundering. Discrimination in education is especially glaring. Bahasa Malay is the official language of instruction in all government-funded institutions, including primary and secondary schools. Certificates from private Chinese schools are not recognized and the schools receive no government funding. A strict quota system is in place in universities, officially 55 percent bumiputera and 45 percent all others whereas in reality 70 percent of the student body is bumiputera. Most government funds for overseas education (about 95 percent) go to ethnic Malays. It is of course widely known that Chinese students often outperform their Malay counterparts, but that is of little consequence to their overall chances for admission to a public university. During the mid-1990s the government allowed foreign universities to set up branches in Malaysia, a practice that has benefitted the Chinese because foreign-based universities readily accept certificates from private Chinese schools.

Ethnic Chinese have little or no chance of serving in the public sector. The official bumiputera-first policy has resulted in an overall ratio of ten ethnic Malays for every non-bumiputera in the civil service.

In the business sector ethnic Malays are given preferential treatment in regard to government contracts, licensing, and loans. This has resulted in some dubious practices. Chinese firms use nominal Malay ownership to conduct business and ethnic Malays in return have prospered but have shown little inclination to become genuine entrepreneurs. Most firms are required to hire up to 30 percent bumiputeras, but some Malay-owned corporations do not hire any non-bumiputeras. By 2002 the Chinese share of the economy had declined by at least 10 percent since the early 1990s.

Discrimination is also prevalent in the cultural domain. The government has actively pursued a pro-Islam course. Proselytizing of Muslims is forbidden; mosques, Islamic-based schools, and a university have been funded by the government, whereas few new temples or churches can be built. All government-funded schools are required to offer a course on

Islamic culture and religion and taking such courses is mandatory for all students irrespective of religious affiliation.

On the other hand, there is some continuity in the democratic process, and relatively few question politicians' commitment to parliamentary democracy. Whether fear or lack of opportunity is the motive one cannot tell, but it is a given that ethnic questions cannot be brought into parliamentary debate. On the positive side, the Constitution guarantees religious freedom. Malaysians have somewhat prospered and enjoy relative freedoms in a quasi-democracy, rare accomplishments among multiethnic Second and Third World countries.

It is important to reiterate that obstacles to complete ethnic harmony in Malaysia still remain, obstacles that would present a tremendous challenge to any polity. Malays have yet to achieve economic parity in their native land. **Islamic fundamentalists** who are found in universities and in politics stress the Islamic character of the polity. Kinship ties remain a strong force in Malay life—Chinese can only enter the circle if they convert to Islam, as a few have done. A conversion to Islam cannot be reversed, and typically Chinese converts change names and cultural identity, but to become what? The generally accepted view is that, once converted, Chinese also change ethnic identity. In contrast, some Chinese have converted to Christianity, which is an affront to pious Muslims, who see proselytization as an attempt to diminish their faith.

Quotas preventing Chinese from entering universities have led to emigration and to a brain drain of needed professionals. State legislatures have frequently challenged the central government, especially those legislatures controlled by opposition parties. In response, the federal government has sometimes invoked emergency powers to remove opposition leaders. Divisions exist not only between Chinese and Malays but also between the educated elite and their rural counterparts. Communal tensions are exacerbated by the various demands of indigenous groups in Sarawak and Sabah, who, although they are ethnically related to Malays, have interests similar to those of indigenous peoples elsewhere. Aborigines in peninsular Malaysia form yet another group within the communal pie. Indians, the third-largest ethnic group in Malaysia, are largely ignored in the ongoing struggle involving Malay political dominance and Chinese economic preponderance.

Malaysia enjoyed healthy economic growth during the 1980s, until the retrenchment of the global economy in the early 1990s, and the currency crisis of 1997 (when the ringgit was devalued by 50 percent). Until then it was considered one of the fastest-growing economies in Asia. After the crisis many foreign laborers were sent home (about 20 percent of the workforce consisted of foreigners). Although international demand for natural rubber and tin has slowed, Malaysia has other valuable resources and is open to foreign investment. Its ambitious development plans provide for the creation of free zones where export-oriented businesses are allowed duty-free imports of raw materials. Its growth targets include biotechnology, microelectronics, and information technology. By 2000 Malaysia was recovering from a serious recession. However the future stability of Malaysia depends in part on international economic factors beyond the control of its multiethnic government.

Recent events have not helped the Malaysian polity. Malaysia is seen by some in the West as a country steering an ever more conservative Islamic course. Post-9/11 that does not inspire creditor or investor confidence. Al-Qaeda ideologues have some support among a fraction of the population, albeit concrete evidence of their activities is largely lacking. The ethnic connection with Indonesia further undermines Western trust in Malaysia. In nearby Indonesia the Chinese, other ethnic minorities, and Christians are targets not just of discrimination but of episodes of torture, assassination, and mass violence. In addition, Islamic extremists have found a refuge in the largest Muslim nation on earth and Indonesia has yet to recover from years of autocratic rule, corruption, the devastation of the economy, and a multitude of other societal ills. One can only speculate how this may affect Malysia. Mahathir, the world's longest-serving elected prime minister, has become ever more autocratic—literally hand-picking his successor.

What we can expect? Malaysia's neighbor to the south, Singapore, has voiced its concern about the treatment of their ethnic brethren; Singapore's population is overwhelmingly Chinese, with Malay and Indian minorities, who are given equal rights. Given the increasing economic and military status allotted to Singapore by the Western alliances, their voice matters. Malaysia's primary economic partners, the United States, Singapore, and Japan, may also have some legitimate concerns about Malaysia's political direction. In our view Malaysia's treatment of its ethnic minorities is unfortunate, counterproductive, and a likely source of future instability.[6]

TURKISH IMMIGRANTS IN GERMANY

On November 23, 1992, a fifty-one-year-old Turkish woman and two Turkish girls, ages fourteen and ten, were killed and eight other Turks injured by the firebombings of two apartment buildings in the western German town of Moelln, near Hamburg. Ten days later two neo-Nazis, ages nineteen and twenty-five, confessed to having thrown the gasoline bombs. This was one of the most deadly episodes in a yearlong wave of more than 4,500 attacks on foreigners and citizens who were thought to be foreign in recently reunited Germany. The arrested killers were typical

Turks and others pray in front of a burned-out house in Solingen, Germany, on May 30, 1993. Five Turks died and three were injured when the house was destroyed by neo-Nazis in an arson attack. Photo courtesy of Reuters/Bettmann.

of the young skinheads who were responsible for virtually all of the attacks. The victims, however, were atypical, because most targets of antiforeign attacks in 1992 were recent refugees such as Vietnamese, Angolans, and Romanian gypsies, who were protected by German law, which at that time guaranteed temporary asylum—including shelter and support—to people fleeing from repression. In 1993, attacks on Turks escalated; the worst episode occurred in Solingen on May 29, when three Turkish women and two girls were killed in another firebombing.

The immediate political questions raised by these incidents are why there is a Turkish minority in Germany, and why they and other foreigners should be targets of sometimes-deadly hostility. The larger questions are whether an analysis of the German situation helps explain the rise in antiforeign sentiment in other European democracies, and what kinds of public policies are being devised to cope with such problems.

Origins and Status of Turks in Germany

At the beginning of 2001 Germany had 7.3 million registered foreigners, about 9 percent of its population. The largest proportion of foreigners were Turks, numbering 2 million. Another 320,000 people of Turkish descent held German citizenship. Most noncitizen Turks are longtime residents who make a major contribution to the German economy. Many, like the two girls who died in Moelln, were born in Germany, went to local elementary and secondary schools, and are bilingual and bicultural. Their situation within German society is deeply ambiguous, however. The great majority want and expect to stay in Germany, but until very recently official policy was that Germany is not a "society of immigration," a policy that justified raising high barriers for Turks and other foreign residents who sought citizenship. Turks are entitled to full social benefits, but those who are not citizens cannot vote or run for political office. Their lack of citizenship symbolizes foreigners' exclusion from the community of Germans and provides a kind of implicit license allowing subtle, yet persistent and widespread, discrimination.

The presence of Turks in Germany is a consequence of policies of the former West German and the Turkish governments. Germany's rapid economic growth in the 1950s and 1960s created a demand for labor that could only be satisfied by encouraging immigration of workers from poorer countries. At first they were recruited mainly from Italy, Greece, and Yugoslavia, but in 1961 the governments of West Germany and Turkey signed a bilateral agreement that regulated the recruitment, employment, and wages of Turkish workers. During the next fifteen years 650,000 Turks migrated to Germany—two-thirds of them recruited by the Turkish Employment Service, one-third nominated by German employers. Contrary to the popular German image of migrants as unskilled Anatolian villagers, more than half came from urban areas, one-third were skilled workers, and one-fifth were women. Many were members of Turkey's Kurdish minority, some of whom were recruited into Kurdish nationalist organizations that soon established branches in Germany. News accounts from the late 1990s estimated that Kurds in Germany numbered about 400,000, or one-fifth of the registered Turkish population.

Both governments expected that the workers' stay was temporary and that they would return to their homeland. One-third of Turkey's skilled workers emigrated during the 1960s and early 1970s, mainly to West Germany, and the Turkish government was eager for their return.[7] In the early 1970s all West European economies were hit by recession and rising unemployment, and the federal German government promptly moved to halt emigration, beginning with the *Anwerbestop* (recruitment stoppage) legislation of 1973. The influx of new workers slowed to a trickle, but most Turks already had long-term residence permits and were reluctant to leave. During the next decade new restrictions were imposed, and new incentives to return to Turkey were established. To discourage family reunions, for example, work permits were denied to dependents who emigrated after December 1, 1974, until authorities realized that the policy was creating a subclass of unemployed, potentially delinquent youths. In the early 1980s tougher restrictions were placed on family reunions, Turks were offered substantial premiums and early payouts of social security benefits if they left the country, and additional grounds for deportation were specified. Although some Turks left voluntarily, the restrictions increased the determination of most Turks to bring in their spouses and children from Turkey and to maintain permanent residence.[8]

By 2001 almost all of the 2 million registered noncitizen Turks in Germany were permanent residents, most of whom lived with their families in old inner-city neighborhoods like Berlin's Kreuzberg district, where 150,000 Turks make up a third of the population. In the industrial city of Duisberg the population of 550,000 includes 60,000 Turks. In the late 1980s more than 400,000 Turkish youths were enrolled in primary, secondary, and technical schools—nearly 20,000 of them in Gymnasiums, the academic secondary schools that are the gateway to universities and professional training. Polls show that more than 80 percent of Turks want to remain in Germany, including virtually all of those born in the country. Many Turks, like other immigrants to Germany, still work at menial, entry-level jobs but some have been modestly successful: in the early 1990s there were 33,000 Turkish-owned businesses, mostly small retail and service enterprises. Turkish unemployment rates reportedly are lower than those of German workers, and Turks are enthusiastic consumers—for example, only one German in thirteen drives a Mercedes, but one Turk in five does so. As one authority remarked, German-born Turks are "not foreigners with German residence permits, but Germans with foreign passports."[9]

THE END OF THE COLD WAR AND
IMMIGRATION PRESSURES IN GERMANY

Events following the dissolution of the Soviet bloc in 1990 and 1991 and the unification of Germany in mid-1991 added greatly to antiforeign sentiment. First, other flows of immigration to Germany increased greatly. Germany's liberal political asylum law attracted more than 2 million asylum seekers to Germany in the early 1990s, more than half of whom arrived in 1992. They are given housing and support while their cases are being reviewed, which is a source of German resentment. Until late 1993 there were long delays in reviewing applications for asylum. Most of the right-wing attacks mentioned previously have been targeted at these immigrants and the temporary quarters in which they live.

Second, after 1988 more than 2.5 million *Aussiedler* arrived in Germany from Poland, the former Soviet Union, and Romania. They are descendants of Germans who settled in eastern lands sometimes as much as five centuries ago. German law, in effect since 1913, grants citizenship to any immigrant who can demonstrate that he or she is of German descent. Public policy guarantees these immigrants housing and support as well as citizenship. Third, economic crisis in the former East Germany pushed many people, an estimated 200,000 in 1991 alone, to emigrate to the former West Germany.[10]

Thus, German society in the early 1990s was under great pressures from outsiders. By the end of the decade the pressures had eased somewhat: in 1998–1999 the annual numbers of new immigrants were 104,000 ethnic Germans, 97,000 asylum seekers, and a net gain of 75,000 workers from outside the European Union. The costs of accommodating these people remain high, and they are especially resented because of the economic problems, including high levels of unemployment, especially in the former East Germany. It is not surprising, then, that foreigners are attacked mainly by unskilled and semiskilled youths, many of whom are unemployed. Nor is it surprising that antiforeign sentiment spills over onto Turks and anyone else of visibly foreign origin.

Social Discrimination

A special liability faced by Turks is widespread prejudice and social discrimination, based on the pervasive perception that Turks are a culturally alien group who cannot be assimilated into European society. Opinion polls in the 1980s showed widespread resentment against Turks; two-thirds of Germans thought that guest workers *(Gastarbeiter)* should return to their homelands, regardless of their own wishes. Antiforeign attitudes are especially common among young people. A survey in 2000 showed that 46 percent of people in the 14–25 age bracket in the former East Germany thought there were too many foreigners in Germany, compared with 40 percent in the former West Germany.

These antiforeign attitudes are directed at least as much at recent refugees from the Balkans, the Middle East, and Africa. The sources of resentment include the belief that foreigners compete with Germans for jobs, that they take undue advantage of social programs, that they are potential supporters of militant Islam or extreme Kurdish nationalism, and that they are dirty and disorderly. Antidiscrimination laws are on the books, but enforcement efforts appear limited. These attitudes and practices translate into day-to-day acts of discrimination and hostility that limit Turks' personal security, cultural expression, and access to housing and private facilities. Two examples from 1997 serve to illustrate. In Duisburg leaders of two mosques applied to the city to broadcast their muezzins' call to prayer once a week, as in other cities in the region. The application, though approved, prompted hundreds of protest letters and newspaper advertisements decrying "Islamic sovereign territory Duisburg." On New Year's Eve, in a village near Berlin, ten skinheads attacked the Turkish proprietor of a fast-food stand. He defended himself with a meat cleaver. When police arrived, they let the skinheads go but arrested the proprietor and held him for two days.

The most serious manifestations of antiforeigner discrimination have taken the form of deadly arson attacks on foreigners' residences and assaults, some of them fatal, on foreigners in public places. The attacks began in the context of widespread insecurity in Germany due to the economic impact of reunification in 1991, discussed above. They were perpetrated mainly by skinheads and neo-Nazis, whom authorities estimated in 1997 to number about 48,000. The attacks were directed more or less indiscriminately against all visible minorities, not just Turks, and were gradually brought under control by state authorities. Right-wing attacks against all targets declined from 1992 to 1994 by nearly two-thirds, from 2,277 to 860. In 1997 the German agency that monitors such attacks reported 669 episodes, more than half aimed at foreigners. But by 2000 there was evidence of a resurgence in xenophobic crimes and also in anti-Semitic offenses such as defacing Jewish cemeteries. The attacks and lesser acts of harassment continue to occur disproportionately in the towns and villages of former East Germany, where foreigners make up a much smaller proportion of the population than in the former West, but where unemployed youths are numerous and neo-Nazi sentiments are widely held.[11]

The Changing Political Situation of Turks

Xenophobic attitudes have prompted right-wing political parties to campaign against the foreign presence in Germany. From the 1960s to the 1980s the National Democratic Party advocated compulsory repatriation and other restrictive measures, although it never won seats in the federal German legislature, the Bundestag. In 1989 a new right-wing party, the Republicans (founded in 1983), capitalized on antiforeign sentiment and won seats in Berlin and later in several other German localities. In the industrial city of Essen, for example, the Republicans increased their share of the votes from less than 1 percent in 1989 to 8.3 percent in 1993, but never gained a foothold in national politics.[12]

Although political threats to the Turkish community come from a small right-wing minority, of greater import is government policy, the effect of

Cem Oezdemir, Turkish-German member of the Bundestag from 1994 to 2002 and influential advocate of integration. Copyright © AP WorldWide Photos.

"Day of the Turks" parade in Berlin, May 25, 2002, promoting friendship between Germans and the Turkish community. Copyright © AP WorldWide Photos.

which has been to restrict the citizenship rights of Turks. The basic assumption of (West) German public policy, until recently, was that the Turks were temporary residents, which justified raising barriers to their citizenship and, hence, to their political participation. All immigrant workers also face legal liabilities. The *Auslaendergesetz* of 1965 gave the government the right to restrict their freedom of assembly, association, movement, and choice of occupation. Unless they acquire citizenship, they cannot vote in national or most local elections, although they can and do participate in unions and civic organizations. The elected head of one of Germany's largest trade unions in 1999 was of Turkish origin. Ironically, despite the economic power he wielded, as a noncitizen he could not vote in national elections. Employed workers from countries of the European Community (since 1993 the European Union) have long had automatically renewable residence permits, whereas, until recently, Turks could qualify as permanent resident aliens only after eight consecutive years of work and residence.

Restrictions on citizenship have been a major source of grievance for longtime Turkish residents and their children. Under German law citizenship is generally limited to those of German descent, and the law excludes from citizenship children born and raised in Germany by foreign nationals. The law in effect in 1998 allowed foreigners who had lived in Germany for fifteen years—or for eight years if they were under the age of twenty-three—to apply for citizenship. Doing so meant giving up foreign citizenship, which many migrants have been reluctant to do because it precludes a future return to Turkey or inheritance of property in Turkey. Further, substantial fees were required, and many applicants reportedly were rejected by police investigators on technicalities. As a consequence only 13,000 Turks were able to gain citizenship between 1977 and 1990. In the 1990s the process was eased so that in 1996 citizenship was granted to 46,300 Turks and in 1998 to 60,000. But only 160,000 Turks were eligible to vote in the 1998 federal elections, less than 0.5 percent of the electorate, and only one of 672 members of parliament, a representative of the Green Party, was of Turkish origin.

In late 1998 the new government in Bonn, a coalition of Social Democrats and Greens, proposed legislation to reduce the residency requirement for all foreigners to eight years and to allow dual citizenship. The proposal was fiercely opposed by the Christian Democratic opposition, not least because virtually all Turkish-German citizens voted for the Social Democrats in 1998. Public resistance to the proposal also contributed to the Social Democrats' electoral defeat in subsequent elections in the State of Hesse, a long-time party stronghold. The new Nationality Code that went into effect on January 1, 2000, provides that children with foreign-national parents who have lived eight years or more in Germany have dual citizenship until the age of twenty-three, when they must choose between German citizenship or that of their parents. One consequence of liberalization of the citizenship law became clear in the September 2002 elections, in which the Social Democrats and their coalition partner, the Greens, won a very narrow victory. A survey showed that 70 percent of the 400,000 Germans of Turkish origin who were eligible to vote had done so and gave 80 percent of their votes to the coalition partners. Turkish

Germans therefore have become a key political player in electoral politics and can be expected to press for greater political representation and more favorable public policies.

There is much evidence that mainstream German society deplores antiforeign violence and discrimination. Attacks against foreigners in the 1990s prompted public reactions throughout Germany: Thousands of people acted as human barricades between neo-Nazis and immigrant hostels, and hundreds of thousands marched in protests against right-wing violence. The federal government has cracked down on the right-wing organizations most directly responsible for the attacks. Domestic pressures on German politicians to take further action has led to two kinds of responses. One, discussed previously, involved liberalizing citizenship laws for most long-term foreign residents, especially the Turks. The other was to restrict the rights of asylum seekers to cross the German border; this was the aim of a new law that went into effect in 1993. Moreover, Germans are keenly aware of international concern and criticism, which provides added incentives to put their house in order.

Group Identity and Political Action

Given our concern with analyzing ethnic protest and rebellion, we can ask why Turks have not organized sustained political action to improve their status. In fact, some of them have done so. In the 1970s, encouraged by grassroots political organizations, some Turks participated in major strikes, demonstrations, and building takeovers to protest poor housing conditions. A Federation of Turkish Workers was established in 1977. Many Turkish workers joined trade unions, and some have joined political parties—despite the fact that they cannot vote—and have participated in special advisory councils set up in some localities to represent foreign workers. A number of ad hoc groups composed of German citizens and immigrants have been formed locally and regionally to pursue common interests.[13] In the 1990s Turks often joined German citizens in demonstrations and vigils to protest antiforeign arson and murder.

But in spite of political and social discrimination, Turks have rarely joined in collective action against German authorities. On the other hand many have organized and acted in behalf of Islamic and Kurdish causes, prompting public and official concern. The German domestic intelligence service reported in 1997 that some 28,000 Turks belonged to militant Islamic organizations such as the Islamic Community Milli Görues, which wants to replace the Turkish secular state with an Islamic republic. Kurds in Germany have repeatedly reacted to policies of the Turkish government, including large demonstrations in 1999 to protest the Turkish government's arrest of the leader of the revolutionary Kurdish Workers Party

(PKK), Abdullah Öcalan. In another of many examples, on March 23, 2002, the Kurdish New Year, more than 30,000 Kurds marched in Düsseldorf to demand more rights for Kurds in Turkey, Iraq, and Iran. The PKK and other militant Turkish organizions were banned in Germany in the early 1990s and their activists have been regularly expelled by Germany authorities. But protest marches are legal and participants are not subject to harrassment.

Political action by Turks (and Kurds) in Germany thus poses a puzzle. Their lack of protest against discrimination suggests a degree of complacency about a status that German and other observers think is insecure and inequitable, especially given the proactive efforts to incorporate immigrants by some of Germany's neighbors.[14] On the other hand, Turks and Kurds are quick to engage in political action in behalf of contentious issues in the Middle East, which suggests continued identification with groups and issues in their homeland. The answer to the puzzle is this: As many studies have shown, Turks in Germany are not a cohesive group, except perhaps in the perceptions of many Germans. Second- and third-generation Turkish Germans probably have enough of a stake and enough security in Germany that they identify more with German than Turkish society. More recent immigrants, though, are still outsiders—a status reinforced by government policy and social discrimination—and therefore are more likely to value their old communal ties. Many came as political refugees in the 1980s and are responsive to the appeals of political entrepreneurs to take sides in homeland politics.[15]

MINORITIES IN OTHER WESTERN EUROPEAN SOCIETIES

The problems posed by immigrant minorities in Germany are greater in magnitude but otherwise similar to those in other Western European democracies. In 2000 the legally resident foreign population of thirteen countries in northern and western Europe totaled nearly 20 million, as shown in Figure 4.2. During the 1990s France, with 3.3 million foreigners, and the United Kingdom, with about 2.4 million, both experienced an upsurge in antiforeign violence and demands from right-wing political organizations to stop future immigration and to force those already there to return to their countries of origin. In both these countries the numbers and proportion of foreign residents were significantly less than in Germany. These demands did not check legal and illegal migration. In 1999 over 700,000 legal immigrants—including refugees and asylum seekers—arrived in the European Union countries along with an estimated 500,000 illegal immigrants.[16]

The main targets of these antiimmigrant pressures in France are the Maghrebins, Muslims from North African countries. The openly racist

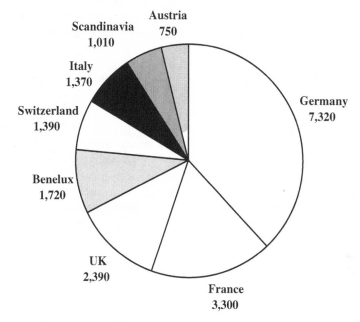

FIGURE 4.2 Foreign populations of thirteen European
countries, 2000 (in thousands)

National Front Party advocates their repatriation; the party's leader, Jean-
Marie Le Pen, received 17 percent of the votes in the second round of the
presidential elections held in 2002. In the United Kingdom the targets include Afro-Caribbeans from Jamaica, Trinidad, and other West Indian islands, and Asian immigrants from India, Pakistan, and Bangladesh.
British officials report that there were 7,700 racial attacks against members of these groups in 1992 and that about a dozen people died from
such attacks in 1992 and 1993.[17]

The attacks on visible minorities in these societies raise serious questions about the ability and the will of Western democracies to protect the
basic rights of all of their residents. Citizenship is the key symbolic issue
for German Turks. The underlying issue is that of popular resentment
against visible minorities, whatever their legal status. Many French Muslims and most Afro-Caribbeans and Asians in Britain have citizenship,
but it does not protect them from individual attacks or demands to send
them back to their countries of origin. Resentment of visible minorities
has increased virtually everywhere in Europe for a combination of reasons. The first is slow economic growth and high unemployment in most
West European countries, which increases hostility against "outsiders"
who are thought to take jobs away from "real" citizens. The second is the

continuing influx of refugees, asylum seekers, and economic migrants. The third is the susceptibility of democratically elected politicians to public pressures, which means it can be very risky for a governing party's leaders to ignore demands for restrictions on foreigners.

In response to this situation, a two-track policy is being charted by virtually all West European governments. One is to devise increasingly tighter restrictions on new immigrants and refugees. In Britain such policies date back to the 1960s; in Germany they are more recent, but they share a common objective: to restrict the influx. The parallel policy is to speed up the incorporation of people of foreign origin who have already established residence. This has also been a long-standing policy in some countries, but it is being accelerated, especially in Germany and France. There are and will be significant differences among European governments in the details, timing, and emphasis of these two policies. Their larger objectives are clear: to close the gates to outsiders, and to incorporate or assimilate immigrants already inside the gates into the dominant culture.

CONCLUSION

The internal dynamics of the conflicts in which the Malaysian Chinese and the German Turks have been involved are analyzed in Chapter 6; their international dimensions are assessed in Chapter 7. Here we can point out that both cases provide correctives to some simplistic assumptions about the nature and outcomes of communal conflict at the beginning of the twenty-first century.

First, at a time when serious ethnopolitical conflicts afflict much of Africa and Asia, Malaysia offers a modest success story. It shows that restraint and accommodation can be more effective than policies of cooptation and repression. Despite often mutually exclusive communal demands, Malaysian authorities have not succumbed to temptations to replace democratic rule with autocracy, although present policies favor Malays and restrict the expression of potentially divisive communal demands. Malaysia's remarkable economic growth, though interrupted by the Asian economic crisis, results in no small part from a political system that balances contending communal interests, and the country's return to growth in turn reinforces all groups' acceptance of its political arrangements.

Second, the German case highlights some of the dilemmas facing prosperous Western democracies. Many people in Western societies are smugly confident that their systems have an almost infinite capacity to respond to internal crises. Germany in the 1990s came up against the limits:

It simultaneously sought to incorporate the crippled economy of former East Germany, rebuild that region's civil administration and infrastructure, *and* accommodate a flood of immigrants and refugees that, in proportional terms, was probably unparalleled in the history of Western societies. German democracy and its economy survived the process, and it now seems likely that long-term immigrants will gradually be incorporated. But Germany also illustrates a dilemma common to all democracies that face the challenge of incorporating visible minorities. Germans who oppose further immigration or citizenship for people of Third World origin have the right to work for those objectives within the political system. And if their views are widely shared, they will almost inevitably shape future public policy in ways that will restrict the influx and rights of noncitizens. Political leaders in all democracies, including the United States, are obliged by the basic rules of their political systems to create compromises among the rights, interests, and demands of both majorities and minorities.

DISCUSSION QUESTIONS

1. Why did the Malay Communists rebel in 1948? Did the rebellion have any lasting effect on the status of the Chinese in Malaysia?
2. Most former European colonies shifted toward socialist or autocratic governments following independence. Why do you think the Malaysian state retained its essentially democratic character?
3. Are the restrictions on the Chinese in Malaysia consistent with Western democratic principles and practices? To what extent do you think the restrictions are justified?
4. What kinds of groups, excepting foreign workers like the Turks, have moved to Germany in recent years? How has their arrival affected the situation of the Turks?
5. List all of the factors that seem to contribute to the 1990s wave of antiforeigner attacks in Germany. Can you rank them in order of importance? Do you think they are caused in part by Germany's historical legacy of Nazism?

5

A Framework for
Analysis of Ethnopolitical
Mobilization and Conflict

In Chapters 3 and 4, we recounted the distinctive historical, political, economic, and social experiences that shaped the identities, status, and grievances of four different ethnopolitical groups. We also showed when and how each group became involved in political conflict with the states in which it lives and pointed out the ways in which members of each group have been restricted and sometimes victimized by governments.

Most social scientists are committed to going beyond describing single cases to provide more general explanations. How do we explain the reasons for, and the causes of, ethnic conflicts in general? In this chapter we begin with a brief review of some social science approaches (or theories) for explaining why ethnic groups mobilize and become involved in conflict. We then introduce a variety of concepts and **propositions** that together form a preliminary theory of mobilization for ethnopolitical conflict. By identifying general determinants of ethnic groups' political actions, our aim is to provide the common ground that will enable students to critically analyze accepted wisdom about what causes ethnic conflict. In subsequent chapters we use information from the four cases in the previous chapters to illustrate our propositions and try to strike a balance between providing a theory to explain all cases of ethnopolitical conflict and offering historical interpretations of single cases.

APPROACHES TO EXPLAINING ETHNOPOLITICAL CONFLICT

Many theories have been proposed to explain political conflict and violence, either in general or in specific forms such as revolution.[1] But there is no comprehensive and widely accepted empirical theory of the causes and consequences of ethnopolitical conflict. Rather, there are approaches and **hypotheses** that seek to explain particular aspects of ethnic conflict. Some of these are concerned with how ethnic identities form and change

95

over time.[2] Others examine the sources of competition and conflict between ethnic groups.[3] The first and second authors have developed testable models of genocide and political mass murder and of ethnopolitical conflict, respectively. The model presented here is an amalgam of our different yet complimentary foci. We are most interested in explanations of why and how ethnic groups **mobilize** (organize for political action) and enter into open—often violent—conflict with the governments that claim to rule them. Although not part of explicit theory, we are also interested in what determines government responses—why some repress and others accommodate.

New theories usually begin as efforts to explain puzzles—that is, new political phenomena that are not explained by older theories. This is clearly the case with ethnopolitical conflict. In the 1950s and 1960s many social scientists thought economic development, the migration of rural peoples to cities, and growing literacy would lead to the creation of complex and integrated societies throughout the world. **Modernization** theory, as this argument was called, made a specific prediction about ethnic identities: that greater political and economic interaction among people and widespread communication networks would break down people's "parochial" identities with ethnic groups and replace them with loyalties to larger communities such as Canada, the European Community, or an emerging pan-Africa. The political facts of the 1970s and 1980s contradicted this prediction: Rather than declining, conflicts based on the assertion of ethnic identities and interests increased sharply. Moreover, ethnopolitical conflicts increased not only in modernizing societies but also in developed Western societies, which experienced an upsurge in regional **separatist** movements and ethnoclass protests in the 1960s.[4]

Several alternative approaches have been used to explain the persistence of ethnic conflict in a modernizing world. One approach argues that people's ethnic and religious identities have deep social, historical, and genetic foundations. From this perspective, sometimes called **primordialism,** modernization is a threat to ethnic solidarities that prompts minorities to mobilize in defense of their culture and way of life.[5] A second alternative emphasizes the **instrumental** nature of ethnic mobilization. The main goals of a group are assumed to be material and political gains; cultural identity is invoked mainly as a means to attain those goals. In this perspective the most important effect of modernization is to increase economic differences, or awareness and resentment of differences, between dominant groups and minorities. "Political entrepreneurs" capitalize on these differences to establish ethnically based political movements aimed at increasing the economic and political well-being of their group or region. A version of this argument, called *internal colonialism,* was proposed to explain one source of growing ethnic conflict in developed European societies—the regional separatist movements like those of the Welsh and Scots in Britain, the Bretons and Corsicans in France, and the Basques in Spain.[6]

A third approach is the **constructivist** interpretation, which emphasizes the ways in which group identities emerge and change over time. An identity such as "the Kurdish nation" or "African-American" is a social construction that may have been imposed by outsiders, shaped by intellectuals, and reinforced by conflict with other groups. However identities originate, they are passed on by families and teachers, reinforced and reshaped by leaders, and used by political movements. This does not mean that ethnic identities are totally malleable. On the contrary, they are enduring social constructions that are based on many collective memories and experiences.[7]

The three approaches emphasize different but complementary aspects of ethnic mobilization and conflict. The primordial approach helps explain the intensity and persistence of ethnic political action. The instrumental approach stresses the importance of group material and political interests. The constructivist approach ties them together by showing how ethnic interests are defined and how the salience (importance) of ethnic identities change over time. We think ethnic groups are most likely to mobilize when all conditions—a strong sense of ethnic identity, based on "primordial" attachments, in combination with imposed disadvantages—are present. Recent theories of specific kinds of ethnic conflict incorporate all conditions. We think, for example, that secessionist movements like those of the Kurds and the Miskitos result from three general conditions: (1) the existence of a separate ethnic community or society with a territorial base, (2) a symbolic conception of the group as a nation or people, and (3) actual or perceived disadvantages in comparison with the dominant society. If we borrow from international legal arguments, an ethnonational group's territorial base shapes its decision to pursue its interests by fighting wars of secession.[8] We also find primordial, instrumental, and constructivist elements in theories designed to explain how conflict arises in multiethnic societies like Malaysia and modern Germany, where peoples of different ethnic origins compete with one another in the pursuit of jobs, political influence, and status. A common argument is that when peoples of different ethnic groups compete *directly* for the same scarce resources and positions, their ethnic identities become more important to them and group boundaries are more sharply defined. And if some groups are more successful than others, inequalities increase, which provides the third general condition for ethnic mobilization and conflict.[9]

The mobilization of ethnic groups is the immediate precursor of the political actions used to make demands on governments. The extent and intensity of the resulting conflict depend upon the strategies followed by ethnic groups' leaders *and* those followed by governments. Few theorists have tried to explain what strategies governments have used in response to challenging groups in general or to ethnic groups in particular. The first author's empirical work on the etiology of genocide and political mass murder is directly relevant to our subject: We show how competition between subordinate ethnic groups and dominant groups can lead to discrimination and repression of subordinate groups. In response to privation and repression, some ethnic groups mobilize for political action, which is then used by threatened elites to justify their destruction. Others, like the victims of the Holocaust and the Muslim Chams in Cambodia under the Khmer Rouge, are targeted because they are defined in the dominant group's ideology as a threatening group.[10]

A brief sketch of the model follows: seven factors are identified that, in combination, make genocides and politicides likely: (1) elites have a history of relying on repression to maintain power, including prior genocidal violence; (2) the country is ruled by an autocracy; (3) elites use their power to reward groups differentially for their loyalty; (4) the society has recently experienced a political upheaval, for example, a revolution or a defeat in war; (5) exclusionary ideologies arise that define target groups as expendable; (6) political elites typically are members of an ethnic minority; and (7) the country has weak economic and political ties with other states, therefore elites face few limits on how they deal with target groups.[11]

When all of these factors are present, ethnopolitical conflict is likely to have genocidal consequences and in fact most genocides were preceded by or happened during periods of ethnic and revolutionary conflict. Thus, it is neither desirable nor particularly useful to draw sharp distinctions between arguments about the causes of ethnic mobilization, conflict, and genocide. Most scholars build on others' work and thus we are indebted to many scholars, not all of whom are mentioned here.

USING SOCIAL SCIENCE THEORIES TO EXPLAIN ETHNOPOLITICAL CONFLICT

Some people think the terms *theory* and *model* are too removed from political realities. Theories use abstract concepts, which some regard as irrelevant to their perceptions of events in the real world. We recognize that there are different ways of looking at the world of ethnopolitical groups, one of which is to rely on direct observation, so that one gains an almost intuitive understanding of group members' perceptions and intentions.

Our view is that systematic comparison of different cases is needed to reach more general conclusions about how and why ethnic groups become involved in conflict and with what consequences. Therefore, we provide here a rationale and guidelines for students who seek more general, empirically grounded knowledge about ethnic conflict. Use of the theories and language of social science can generate the kind of satisfaction that comes with an increased understanding and appreciation of the complexity of political life. The reasons are not just "scientific"; we think general knowledge is essential if scholars and policymakers are to understand, anticipate, and respond to ethnic conflicts in ways that can reduce human suffering and improve the chances for accommodation.

Scientific analysis requires precise communication, a key to which is the development of a common vocabulary. The technical language of the social sciences is supposed to convey the same meanings to anyone who reads or reanalyzes a researcher's findings. Scientific analysis also requires the use of standardized concepts, categories, and indicators so as to eliminate as much as possible the observer's own subjective interpretations. Objectivity and logic, after all, are the tools of the scientist.

But scientific analysis has its critics. We briefly identify some of the key arguments.

1. The *"verstehen"* (German for understanding) argument is that, to truly understand human behavior and social interaction, one must immerse oneself in the minds of peoples and cultures. The best way to do so is through first-hand observation and case studies.
2. Empirical social science analyses has yielded few earthshaking revelations, despite the expenditure of enormous intellectual energy and financial support.
3. Empirical theory is not value-free because it is shaped by scholars' own ideological or normative preferences.
4. Empirical analyses are theory poor, the availability of data drives analyses or, worse yet, one crunches numbers in hope of finding a theory.

Although these critical observations apply to some studies, if they are targeted at all empirically driven analyses, the critics miss the point. First, what are the alternatives? Should social scientists no longer be considered scientists? Should we be rather historians (though historians use systematic analyses) or journalists? Or should we acknowledge that some empirical analyses have yielded significant results, far beyond what we knew just twenty years ago? The most important issue is that one cannot generate or test general explanations by doing a few case studies. Many empiricists have also done case studies, some are area specialists and think it desirable to immerse themselves in particular cultures, but are not satisfied with case-specific answers. Both authors belong to the latter category—

we have done extensive case studies, have area expertise, and were dissatisfied with our local knowledge, which yielded little to our understanding of why ethnic conflict and genocide are worldwide phenomena, and why they increased and then decreased over time. Thus, our emphasis on scientific analysis. We also reiterate that the following model has a solid theoretical base, it is anchored in the literature.

Let us do a brief mental exercise. Assume one wants to argue that the UN-sponsored **sanctions** against Iraq before the 1991 Gulf War increased the conflict potential of the region. The argument can be extended to the year 2002, when sanctions were still in place, but prior to the U.S.-led invasion of Iraq in 2003. The concepts—here, sanctions and conflict—ought to have the same meaning to all and should be measured by commonly accepted indicators. In order to describe something, we need to be able to observe something. We know that UN-sponsored resolutions were in place (the actual texts are readily available) and we can do a before-and-after analysis by looking at quality-of-life indicators (such as decline in economic well-being, etc.). But, in order to be persuasive, we need to demonstrate that the conflict potential increased when sanctions were applied, that is, establish that there is a direct connection.

Now let us assume the following hypothetical scenario. The United States unilaterally cuts off trade relations with all Middle Eastern states that are either neutral in their policy toward Iraq or that subvert UN-sponsored sanctions against Iraq. This scenario is very relevant in the post 9/11 fight against international terrorism—see President Bush's declaration that either "you are with us or against us." The U.S. action is designed to enforce compliance with the sanctions and to help us find and neutralize terrorists. The targeted states respond by accommodating the United States: They abandon their hostile rhetoric and stop letting Iraq use their territory to smuggle in military supplies. Saddam Hussein reacts with open defiance by attacking Kurdish villagers and imprisoning some foreign nationals. The Kurds in turn attack Iraqi positions. Turkey, fearing unrest among its own Kurds, attacks Kurdish areas inside Iraq. It seems that the U.S. trade embargo has had the desired impact by forcing a change in the behavior of the target states. Yet it led simultaneously to the Iraqi attack against Kurdish areas and to Turkey's intervention. At this stage of analysis, we cannot assume that the changes in political behavior resulted from U.S. pressure, however likely this may seem. Perhaps Saddam Hussein had long planned an attack to reestablish government control over Kurdish rebels, and Turkey had used the circumstances to resurrect a long-standing policy of intimidating Kurds by force. Thus, we need to further test our argument.

An untested argument or idea about a specific kind of relationship is called a proposition. How do we test our proposition that sanctions against Iraq increased the conflict potential within the region? The standard procedure used by social scientists is to put the proposition into testable form: A testable proposition is a hypothesis. If we expand our ideas to include more than one hypothesis about the conflict potential within the region, we can call this a theory. In other words, logically related testable ideas (hypotheses) that specify relationships between concepts are commonly called a theory.

The term *theory* is often used more loosely, that is, any general idea about what factors contribute to particular outcomes is called a theory by some scholars. Here we use the term more narrowly—we think of theory as a number of hypotheses (testable propositions) that are interconnected to explain a previously defined phenomena, e.g., ethnic conflict.

Our previous argument that sanctions against Iraq increase the conflict potential in the region is simply an untested idea (proposition) unless we change propositions into testable hypotheses. Let us briefly conclude our theoretical excursion by transforming our proposition into a hypothesis and **operationalizing** its concepts.

The hypothesis states that the degree of compliance in countries' political behavior increases relative to the strength of sanctions imposed by external actors. Sanctions imposed on states engaged in open conflict increase their degree of hostility toward internal and external opponents.

By specifying the type of pressure applied by the United States and relating it to a specific type of performance (stop supporting Iraq), we can determine with much greater confidence whether and under what conditions the United States is able to influence a specific type of political behavior. Of course, we cannot assume that all of the countries in question would act similarly if the United States were to ask them to disarm, for example. In the second part of the hypothesis we argue that once a country is involved in open conflict, sanctions may have the opposite effect—they may increase conflict behavior. Thus, we have qualified our statement because we recognize that political behavior and conflict are multifaceted phenomena, that they occur in different domains (domestic policies versus foreign policy behavior), and that they are applied with different degrees of strength (sanctions that force total versus partial compliance).

Another important step in social science analysis is to introduce criteria that enable us to disprove a hypothesis. If we were to identify only those instances in which the targeted countries complied with U.S. demands and ignored instances in which they did not, our task would be easy and our conclusions wrong. By selecting information to suit our particular argument, we overlook other information and may reach false conclusions.

What have we learned about states' behavior in our example? If we have observed the region's relations with the United States for some time, we probably recognize that many states were already in the process of changing their behavior vis-à-vis Iraq and only reacted more quickly than they would otherwise have done because the United States exerted pressure. This implies that the United States truly influenced some states' behavior, but possibly not to the extent we had thought. And we do not know with any certainty whether either Turkey or Iraq responded with increased hostility toward Kurds because of the U.S. sanctions or because they had long-standing designs to do so anyway. How much influence did the United States truly exert compared with states' own desire for change? Answering this question is far more complicated. Only if we were able to observe the same sequence of events at another time or in another area and find similar outcomes could we say with increased certainty that in some instances U.S. policy leads to changes in political behavior and under particular circumstances increases the conflict potential of a particular area.

Because of these difficulties we more often propose *likely* explanations rather than definitive ones, our statements are more often tentative than conclusive, and our tested statements (hypotheses) are **probability statements** rather than truths. Students should consider these obstacles as challenges, not barriers. The best we can do in most instances is to be as specific as possible, to be modest in our goals and objectives, to scrutinize as much information as we can obtain, and to follow procedures that can easily be duplicated by others.

Is the scientific approach we have just described worth using? Consider the alternatives. In the early stages of social science, scholars offered little more than learned opinions. The social sciences had little or no basis for claiming that their explanations had any general validity. Political science was mostly a combination of descriptive historical interpretation and philosophical discourse on human destiny. We have advanced at least to the stage of weather forecasting—that is, we can assert with some plausibility that certain conditions and actions lead to likely outcomes.

What, then, is our goal in this chapter? Our propositions about ethnic mobilization and conflict are essentially statements describing likely relationships. We invite students to develop hypotheses based on the propositions and to test them against the reality of ethnic groups in various situations. Our model introduces a set of testable hypotheses (theory) and operationalizes some of the concepts (the building blocks of propositions and hypotheses). Operationalization involves the process of defining the concepts so they can be measured in real quantities. Thus, for example, if conflict is the concept, its **variable** properties can include the amount of conflict—such as numbers of armed attacks involving two countries, the extent of participation in street protests, or a number of other properties. In other words, variable properties differ depending on the context in which they are observed.

EXPLAINING ETHNOPOLITICAL
MOBILIZATION AND CONFLICT

What contributes to ethnic mobilization? One can call our model a mobilization model, based on the assumption that mobilization may lead to either conflict or accommodation. The following describes the evolution of the model.

Before we elaborate on the model, a word of advice to students. If additional variables seem to matter for a particular case, add them. If reliable data on the indicators listed for the model are not available, consider coding them from narrative information, or look for substitute indicators. The first author's students have found the model useful in estimating the mobilization potential of Islamic groups (such as Islamic Jihad, Hammas, or al-Qaeda). They changed the identity variable to include other factors such as length of group existence, existence of an utopian or revolutionary component in religious doctrine, and insistence on Shari'ah (Islamic law) as the basis of governance.

Model concepts: (concept 1) discrimination and (concept 2) ethnic group identity. By discrimination we mean the extent of socially derived inequalities in group members' material well-being or political access in comparison with other social groups. An ethnic group consists of people whose identity is based on shared traits such as religion, culture, common history, place of residence, and race.

On the most basic level, people resent and react against discriminatory treatment. They may use their anger constructively or destructively, or they may be apathetic. In the former case they may opt for peaceful activism, channel anger into greater personal efforts to succeed, or emigrate to escape discrimination. Others are willing to openly challenge their opponents and attack the principal sources of their discontent. The extent of their grievances usually varies with the extent of their actions, and vice versa. Let us examine these arguments more closely.

We propose that when people with a shared ethnic identity are discriminated against, they are likely to be resentful and angry. Anger is expressed in a number of ways: Some people opt for accommodation; others vent their frustrations openly (proposition 1). For people who are motivated to action, the greater the discrimination they experience, the more likely they are to organize for action against the sources of discrimination (hypothesis 1).

Rare is the individual who single-handedly challenges institutions or society at large. Finding like-minded individuals with similar grievances intensifies discontent and increases willingness to take action (proposition 2). The more strongly a person identifies with an ethnic group that is subject to discrimination, the more likely he or she is to be motivated into action (hypothesis 2a). Factors other than shared grievances, including a shared religion, language, history and culture, and place of residence, strengthen group identity. The greater the number of traits common to a group, the stronger the group identity (hypothesis 2b).

What triggers political action and turns action into open conflict with the government and other groups? And what kinds of action or types of violence are most likely to occur? Collective actions are shaped by the political context in which an ethnic group is situated. The type and extent of political conflict are determined by such factors as the **cohesion of the group (concept 3)**, the strategies and tactics of its leaders, the nature of the political system that governs it, and outside encouragement. Here we examine group cohesion and ethnopolitical leadership, the political environment, the severity of force used by governments, and outside encouragement. We examine each of these in turn.

A major determinant of the occurrence of ethnopolitical conflict is the cohesion of the challenging ethnic group and the strength and unity of its leadership (proposition 3). Cohesive groups are those that have dense networks of communication and interaction that link leaders with followers. Strong ethnopolitical leaders generate the type of climate in which peoples willingly subordinate personal preferences to group preferences. Cohesive groups with autocratic leaders are not likely to face internal constraints on decisions to use violent forms of political action, whereas democratically organized challengers are typically less cohesive and have more diverse views about the preferred form of action.

Group cohesion increases to the extent that groups are regionally concentrated, accept the social order within the group, and have widely accepted autocratic leadership (hypothesis 3). Thus, if and when leaders decide to use violent forms of political action to protest grievances, they are more likely to do so in cohesive groups that share a history of discrimination and that accept strong, autocratic leadership.

The concept of **political environment (concept 4)** refers to the type of regime governing a state. We distinguish four types: institutionalized democracies and **autocracies,** and **socialist** and **populist states.** Democracies typically tolerate a wide range of political participation that at various times includes protests, riots, and open rebellion (proposition 4). However, we must keep in mind that fully functional democracies protect core values, such as equality before the law and full political and civil rights; therefore, discrimination is less likely, and violent protest and rebellion are less common. Thus, the more democratic the political environment, the more likely ethnopolitical groups will be to voice opposition nonviolently (hypothesis 4).

In political environments other than democracies, violence is more likely to be used to quell protest and riots (proposition 5a). The more violence is used by political authorities, the greater the likelihood that challengers will respond with open rebellion (hypothesis 5a). However, state authorities that have used **extreme force (concept 5, use of violence by governments)** such as massacres, torture, and genocide, to subdue challengers are also less likely to be openly challenged (proposition 5b), either because groups cannot organize open resistance or they fear the consequences of doing so. Thus, the more *extreme* force is used, the less likely the chances for open rebellion (hypothesis 5b). A curvilinear relationship thus exists between state violence and the extent and level of violence of political action taken by the challengers. Clandestine movements that use terrorism and guerrilla warfare are typically responses to situations in which government authorities have used deadly force in dealing with challengers.

What external factors contribute to ethnic conflict? Here we develop two concepts that relate to the international environment in which ethnopolitical groups act: **external support** and **economic status (concepts 6 and 7).**

As shown previously, the domestic political environment substantially determines the kinds of actions chosen by ethnopolitical groups. In addition, many groups depend on external support (proposition 6), which includes verbal encouragement, financial support, weaponry, military personnel, and other forms of active or passive support the ethnic group receives from outside the state. This may include verbal support or other forms of encouragement from ethnic brethren in neighboring states. The greater their external support, the greater the chances groups will use violent means to challenge authorities (hypothesis 6). Of course, we need to point out that minor grievances do not ordinarily provoke violent political action. Thus, the kind of action taken depends on the combination or interaction of the political environment (type of regime, external support) with the severity of discrimination.

A second external factor is the status attributed by the international community to the government that is facing ethnopolitical challenges. International status is attributed to groups and states according to the number and value of economic resources they command. States blessed with an abundance of resources are more likely to enjoy the support of the international community, which is dependent on such resources (proposition 7). They are also more likely to be free from unwanted interference than are those with fewer resources. Domestic stability, by whatever means it is achieved, guarantees the free flow of goods, currency, and primary resources. Therefore, the greater international status accorded to a state, the less it is likely that its challengers are externally supported (hypothesis 7). In addition, the extent of a state's economic interaction—via trade and investment—with foreign partners suggests some degree of openness and flexibility in dealing with international demands, which may include easing internal tension by accommodating challengers.

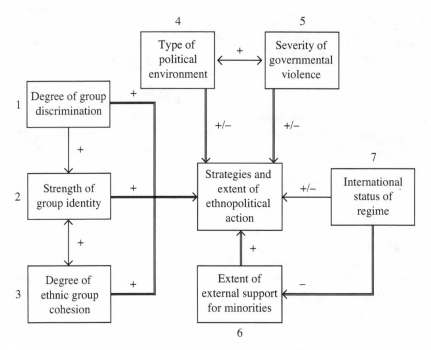

Numbers refer to the propositions and hypotheses that develop these concepts.

———— relations for which hypotheses are developed in the text

———— relations for which hypotheses are not developed in the text

FIGURE 5.1 Framework for explaining ethnopolitical violence.

During the Cold War two factors combined to favor ethnic and other challengers to Communist rule. First, the centrally planned, or "command," economies of Communist states rarely interacted in the global economy to the same degree as their capitalist counterparts. Second, internal challengers opposed to Communist rule were more likely to find outside support from states that opposed communism than they were to find challengers among states closely tied to the global economy. Post–Cold War ethnic challengers had to find other avenues of support and often could not. As the second author has documented, ethnic challenges increased immediately after the Cold War. However since 1994 many conflicts have been peacefully settled and new ethnic conflicts declined due in part to lack of external support. But some protracted conflicts continued because it would take major sacrifices on both sides to settle (for example, the Israeli/Palestinian conflict).

The propositions and hypotheses spelled out in this section describe interactive relationships among concepts. Together they constitute a model that is shown schematically in Figure 5.1. The relationships are represented in the figure by bold arrows that connect the variables. No attempt is made to express the model in more formal ways, such as by using mathematical expressions. Positive relations (an increase in x leads to an increase in y) are represented by plus signs. Combined plus and minus signs represent complex relationships—for example, the argument, in hypotheses 4, 5a, and 5b, that ethnic mobilization and conflict are likely to be greater in authoritarian political environments than in democratic ones. In Figure 5.1 we use thin arrows to depict potentially important connections among the variables that are not discussed in the text. For example, the double-headed arrow between strength of group identity and degree of group cohesion summarizes two kinds of probable relationships: First, groups with strong identity are likely to be more readily organized into cohesive groups, and second, once cohesive leader-follower networks are established, group identity tends to become even stronger. This kind of mutually reinforcing connection is sometimes called a feedback relationship. Students are encouraged to identify and analyze other significant relations that are not developed in this chapter.

Next, we briefly review the concepts and variables introduced in this section and then suggest indicators for the variables. However crude some indicators may appear, they should guide students' efforts to collect and evaluate information more systematically.

CONCEPTS, VARIABLES, AND INDICATORS

In general, social scientists seek to minimize error in the interpretation of theoretical ideas by describing concepts like group identity and external support in clear and unambiguous ways. Concepts derive their meaning from careful observation of real-life situations. The challenge for researchers is to define variables and construct standardized indicators of those variables that can be used to make reliable observations of a number of groups and situations. Observations, or measurements, are said to be reliable if similar measurements are obtained by anyone who collects information. We group indicators into three categories based on their likely significance or importance—high, medium, and low.

A simple example involves the concept of the size of ethnic groups. The variable property is the number of people who belong to each group. But alternative indicators might be used for "belonging." One such alternative is to estimate the number of people who share the group's culture (which is difficult to observe in most cases). Another is to count the number who live in the group's homeland (but some will have emigrated, and outsiders may have moved in). A third is to rely on censuses that use standardized procedures for determining people's ethnic identification. Census data are usually the most reliable indicators for measuring and comparing the sizes of different groups, but not all governments conduct censuses or ask people's ethnic identity. If census data are not available, less precise indicators of group size must be found.

Now we turn to concepts identified in the hypotheses of the theoretical model.

Concept 1: Discrimination

Variable property: degree of discrimination. The concept of discrimination was defined in the previous section as the extent of socially derived inequalities in ethnic group members' material well-being or political access in comparison with other social groups. The greater the differences in status by comparison to other groups, the greater the degree of discrimination.

Indicators of discrimination. Government policies that treat ethnic groups unequally are the least ambiguous indicators of discrimination. Inequalities between ethnic groups may also result from historical discrimination or from economic and cultural differences that give some groups persistent advantages over others.

Indicators of economic discrimination

- Public policies that restrict the economic activities or roles of group members (high)
- Limited group access to education, especially higher education (high)
- Low income, poor housing, and high infant mortality rates compared with other groups in the society (medium)
- Proportionally few group members in commercial, managerial, or professional positions (medium)

Indicators of political discrimination

- Public policies that limit the group's participation in politics and access to political office (high)
- Low participation in politics compared with other groups in the society (medium)
- Proportionally few group members in elective offices, civil service, or higher-ranking police and military positions (medium)

Concept 2: Group Identity

Variable property: strength of group identity. We proposed in the previous section that the strength of ethnic group identity depends upon the number of traits shared by group members. The greater the number of shared traits, such as religion, culture, common history, place of residence, and race, the greater the strength of identity.

Indicators of strength of group identity. The more of the following traits members of an ethnic group have in common, the greater the strength of group identity.

- The extent to which they share and use a common language (high)
- The proportion of people who share a common religious belief (high—if used for religious groups the indicators need to be expanded—see the discussion above re Islamic groups; otherwise medium)
- Visible racial characteristics (high)
- A shared history over at least a 100-year period (medium)
- A common culture—identifiable social and legal customs developed and practiced within close proximity (low)

Concept 3: Ethnopolitical Leadership and Group Cohesion

Variable property: degree of cohesion among leaders and followers. Cohesive groups are those that have a unifying belief system or ideology and dense networks of communication and interaction linking leaders with followers. The more ideological disputes and factions that exist within the group, the less cohesive it is. We proposed in the previous section that the type of leadership also influences cohesion within the group. Strong leaders generate a climate in which people willingly subordinate personal preferences to group preferences. Autocratic leaders are more likely to be able to mobilize people than their democratic counterparts, because democratic practices emphasize individual rights rather than the rights of the collective body over and above the individual.

Indicators of ethnopolitical leadership and group cohesion. Cohesion within ethnic groups increases with increased communication and interaction. In contrast, the greater the number of factions or self-proclaimed leaders, the less cohesive the group. Factors indicative of cohesion include

- Degree of acceptance of established social order within the group (high)
- Extent of acceptance of a common belief within the group (high)
- Number of factions within the group (high)
- Extent of open conflict within the group (high)
- Number of identifiable leaders within the group (medium)
- Degree of acceptance of traditional roles of leaders (medium)
- Number of newspapers and radio stations used by the group (medium)

Concept 4: Political Environment

Variable property: type of political environment. The political environment sets the stage for political action. Here we propose guidelines for identifying the four types of regimes with which ethnopolitical groups may come in conflict: institutionalized democracies, autocracies, and socialist and populist states. Note that most contemporary states have one of these four types of political regimes; a few combine elements of several.

Indicators of institutionalized democracies

- Guarantee of political and civil rights for all citizens (high)
- Effective constitutional limitations on the power of the executive (high)
- Multiple political parties that compete for office and transfer power by constitutionally prescribed means (medium)

Indicators of institutionalized autocracies

- Concentrate most or all political power in the executive (high)
- Limit or ban political parties and sharply restrict civil rights and political participation (high)
- Political power usually transferred and distributed among members of a tiny political elite (medium)

Indicators of socialist states

- Concentrate power in a single party used by the elite to mobilize mass support for the regime (high)
- Encourage participation only within the party and restrict other political and civil rights (high)
- Transfer political power through competition within the party (medium)

Indicators of populist states

- Weakly institutionalized political systems in a transitional state to either democracy or increased autocracy (high)
- Transfer political power through military coups or popular uprisings, short of revolution (high)
- Frequent leadership changes, with no predictive sequence (medium)
- Wide, often disruptive political participation through functional groups, and many transient political parties and movements (low)

Concept 5: Use of Violence by Governments

Variable property: the severity of force used by governments against ethnic groups. The systematic annihilation of an ethnic people is the rarest and most severe form of violence used by governments and is called genocide. Less severe kinds of force include massacre, torture, execution, detention without due process, forcible relocation of a people, and many others.

Indicators for use of force by governments against ethnic groups. Governmental violence directed against ethnic groups varies with the type of government. Autocracies and socialist states use violence against political challengers more often than do their democratic counterparts. Populist states often alternate erratically between severe repression and accommodation. Means used to oppress ethnic challengers, in descending order of severity, include

- Political mass murder and genocide (high)
- Massacres (high)
- Widespread torture and executions (medium)
- Forcible relocation of group members (medium)
- Number of arrests (low)

Concept 6: External Support for Ethnic Groups

Variable property: extent of external support. As described in the previous section, the concept of external support refers to the entire range of active and passive support an ethnic group can receive from outside the country. Military support is, of course, more valuable than verbal support. The more numerous the sources, the larger the volume, and the longer it is provided, the greater the extent of support.

Indicators of external support. Ethnic groups may receive support from other states, from kindred groups in neighboring states, from international movements like the indigenous peoples movement and the Islamic movement, and from international organizations. Major types of support include

- Weaponry and supplies (high)
- Mercenaries and military advisers (high)
- Provision of safe havens for exiles and refugees (high)
- Provision of intelligence information (medium)
- Financial support (medium)
- Verbal encouragement and advice (low)

Concept 7: International Economic Status

Variable property: degree of international economic status. We proposed previously that the international community awards economic status to states according to the number and value of resources they command, such as scarce resources, high level of food production, a well-educated population, and high levels of technology. Resource-rich states are likely to enjoy higher status than resource-poor states and are more likely to deal with ethnic challengers as they wish.

The status accorded to challenging groups depends upon the position accorded to their state by the international community. Thus, movements fighting regimes with low status that are autocratic and have command economies are likely to enjoy higher international status than ethnic challengers fighting capitalist states.

Indicators for degree of international economic status. High economic status is accorded to states that

- Rank high in gross domestic product and gross national product (high)
- Control large reserves of scarce resources (such as gold, uranium, titanium) (medium)
- Control a high percentage of the global trade of valuable commodities (medium)
- Have a high level of per capita income (medium)
- Have a global network of trading partners (medium)
- Proportion of people with advanced degrees (low)

Support from kindred groups in neighboring countries and in a worldwide diaspora may be another key factor; it is not fully operationalized here because it may be irrelevant in a number of cases, yet extremely relevant in others. The concept also includes conflicts between kindred groups and ethnic rivals in adjacent regions—good examples are the conflicts in Burundi and Rwanda, in which Tutsis and Hutus have fought each other repeatedly. Whatever happens to Tutsis and Hutus in Burundi affects their ethnic brethren in Rwanda and vice versa.

OVERVIEW OF THE MODEL

Remember that we want to explain *why* ethnic mobilization and conflict occur. The logical consequence of accurate explanation is to be able to *predict* under what circumstances ethnic conflict will occur. The model illustrated in Figure 5.1 represents our effort to tie our hypotheses together in a systematic fashion. The hypotheses are testable propositions about real-life events. By using a diagram we are able to demonstrate visually the underlying structures of complex relationships.

Scholars have produced many data-based **empirical generalizations** that are the premises upon which we have built our propositions. In other words, we know much about ethnic conflict thanks to the work of many historians and area specialists who are concerned with describing and interpreting particular ethnic conflicts in specific countries. A viable model is one that re-creates the process leading to ethnic conflict, not in one country but in all countries that have experienced ethnic unrest. Of course, there are idiosyncratic factors that are important in one or two particular situations but not others. It is impossible to incorporate literally all factors that lead to ethnic conflict, and, typically, the use of large numbers of specific factors yields no better predictive results. Instead, one should concentrate on key factors. The best models are those that explain the largest number of phenomena based on a small number of hypotheses.

Our model identifies seven key factors we consider important predictors of ethnic mobilization and conflict. Most of these factors are interrelated or interdependent—that is, they influence one another. The factors also differ in importance. Thus, research on a number of cases may show that external support has a greater impact on the extent of ethnic conflict than does group cohesion. This does not mean our model is incorrect; instead, it gives us additional information that may enable us to improve its accuracy.

Our seven key factors are also likely to vary over time. Thus, information about them needs to be updated periodically, especially in ongoing cases of ethnic conflict. When a rapid increase is observed in one or more of the variables in the model, we can infer that conflict is likely to intensify.

This brief review of the key factors emphasizes the way in which they are interrelated: We propose that a people who strongly identify with their ethnic brethren and who live in an autocratic political system with low international economic status, one that has used discrimination and intermittent violence to repress its ethnic peoples, are the most likely to challenge their oppressors. The conflict potential is greatest if the group is cohesive and has traditional (autocratic) leaders who enjoy the widespread support of international organizations and actors.

PROBLEMS AND ISSUES IN MODELING ETHNIC CONFLICT

Most of our indicators are straightforward and should provide reliable measurements of the variable properties of the concepts. But available information is sometimes difficult to assess. Take, for example, our indicator *the extent to which people share and practice the same religion*. One can usually estimate the number of Catholics or Protestants in a group, but how does one determine whether they truly practice their religion? This is possible only if we have access to surveys that report details about people's beliefs and practices. The same is true for all indicators that deal with attitudes—in essence, they are not readily observable and must usually be inferred from other information.

With regard to group identity, innate characteristics such as race are readily observable, but other factors may require judgment calls. Even more difficult are situations in which group identity is superimposed by outside groups on the basis of one or two traits whose significance is not self-evident or even visible to outside observers. The group identity of *Indios* (Indians) in Latin American countries is an example: The label reflects a social judgment by the dominant group about the culture of a number of rural peoples who to the observer may appear indistinguishable from mestizo villagers. In these and other situations, self-identification is the optimum measure of people's sense of belonging to an ethnic group.

Our indicators of discrimination are readily observable, with the possible exception of *public policies that restrict economic activities or roles of group members and that limit the group's participation in politics and access to political office.* Here we should look for widespread official and political practices, such as quotas that limit various groups' access to jobs and institutions of higher learning or that restrict them to token political roles and activities.

More difficult is our scheme that divides polities into four different categories. It is hard to make a neat separation between populist and autocratic states because of the transitional nature of the former. One may end up treating populist states as those that do not fit any of the three other categories. As a rule, democratic states should be classified as such if they possess most of the defining traits listed for institutionalized democracies.

Our indicators for external support include verbal support and intelligence information. We can focus our search for evidence on verbal support by analyzing the content of speeches made by major policy figures, such as officials of international organizations and presidents and foreign ministers of neighboring states and major powers. The sharing of intelligence information can sometimes be observed in the actions that occur during or after episodes of significant conflict. For example, Israel's nonintervention in the first Gulf War was evidently partly a result of its lack of tactical information. Israeli fighters were reportedly discouraged from engaging Iraqi fighters over Iraq because the Allies withheld critical information; thus, Israeli aircraft would have been subject to attack by the coalition forces. Kurdish nationalists fighting Saddam Hussein in Iraq likely had access to intelligence information from the Allies. Unfortunately, we rarely have decisive information on such intelligence issues.

The indicators for a country's degree of economic status include its relative independence of international trade and control of world trade through industrial capacity, two seemingly contradictory indicators. The United States, an economic superpower, provides an example. The United States dominates trade of a number of items and has large reserves of scarce resources but is not self-sufficient in some other scarce resources; it has a surplus in balance of payments but has a negative trade balance; and it trades extensively but receives a small proportion of its national income from trade compared with other industrial nations such as Germany. In times of international instability or civil conflict, the United States is less vulnerable than Germany to economic blackmail or sanctions because of its lower degree of trade dependence, although the U.S. standard of living would undoubtedly suffer if sanctions were imposed over the long run. Therefore, if the United States committed gross human rights violations against some segment of its population, its high status would likely deflect international responses. Significant support for the victims, therefore, would not likely to be forthcoming. High status, however, carries international visibility, and the internal behavior of high-status states is carefully scrutinized. All U.S. internal affairs attract world attention. If a situation of gross human rights violations were to develop in Mali, a country with low economic status, other states would be more likely to provide substantial aid to victims of government abuse.

CONCLUSION

The U.S. example in the previous paragraph is hypothetical: Oppression of ethnic people is much less likely to occur in a democracy than in other political systems. Two concluding observations follow. First, only the combination of indicators of economic status, with their relative weights assessed against each other, provides the necessary information to allow us to generalize about a country's international status. The same principle applies to discrimination against ethnopolitical groups, to group cohesion, and to all of the variables in the model that is summarized in Figure 5.1: Reliable measurement requires us to obtain information on a number of indicators of a variable, not just one or two. Second, the assessment of the conflict potential of an ethnic group and of a country must take into account the combination and interactions of all of the variables included in the model, both domestic and international.

DISCUSSION QUESTIONS

1. To what extent are the various theoretical approaches that attempt to explain why ethnic groups mobilize compatible with one another; to what extent are they mutually exclusive?
2. Evaluate the argument that each ethnic conflict is specific to a particular historical and political context and, thus, that comparative generalizations are impossible.

3. Is it possible in principle to construct a general theory that can account for all aspects of ethnic conflict?
4. Why should social scientists develop and use models?
5. Are historians able to forecast when and under what circumstances ethnic groups will mobilize and fight?

Research Exercise. Use the model to assess the chances that conflict involving an ethnic group in country *x* is likely to increase.

Step 1: Study the historical and political circumstances under which the ethnic group has maintained its separate identity. Identify its objectives, grievances, and recent actions.

Step 2: Begin to collect information on each variable and indicator specified in the model during the past five years. The sources of current political and statistical information for indicators include:

U.S. State Departments Human Rights Reports
National Trade DataBank
World Bank data
Minorities at Risk dataset www.minoritiesatrisk.com
Polity dataset www.cidcm.umd.edu/inscr/polity
State Failure dataset www.cidcm.umd.edu/inscr/stfail
The Europa World Year Book (London: Europa Publications, annual).

Arthur S. Banks, ed., *Political Handbook of the World* (Binghamton, NY: CSA Publications, State University of New York, annual).

Appendices to T. R. Gurr, *Peoples Versus States: Minorities at Risk in the New Century* (Washington, DC: U.S. Institute of Peace Press, 2000).

Political Risk Year Book (New York: Frost and Sullivan, annual volumes for all world regions).

*   *   *

If no statistical data can be found, make informed judgments based on substantive information gathered in Step 1.

Step 3: Having collected information, evaluate how the group ranks on each variable in the model. On which indicators and variables does it have high rankings or scores? Are there variables that are not included in the model that seem especially important to gaining an understanding of the group's political actions?

Step 4: Assess the chances that conflict will increase by determining whether the group's rankings or scores on the independent variables and indicators have been increasing or decreasing.

6

The Internal Processes of Ethnic Mobilization and Conflict: Four Cases

This chapter uses the theoretical framework developed in Chapter 5 to interpret and compare the domestic processes of ethnopolitical conflict in the four cases described in Chapters 3 and 4. First we analyze and compare the Kurds in Iraq and the Miskitos in Nicaragua, for whom the essential issue of conflict is greater autonomy from state control. We then examine the Chinese in Malaysia and the Turks in Germany. Like other communal contenders and ethnoclasses, they are in conflict with dominant groups over protecting and improving their status within existing social and political institutions. In each pair of cases we begin with variables that refer to characteristics of the group, then move to the government level of analysis. The concept of *levels of analysis* is explained more fully in Chapter 7, which analyzes the international context of these four conflicts. Most information is taken from Chapters 3 and 4; some additional information on specific variables is also used.

We make one other preliminary observation: The framework developed in Chapter 5 is designed to help us understand the extent of ethnic mobilization and conflict. It also highlights an important related issue, which is how the policies and responses of governments and international actors affect the extent of conflict and its outcomes. This chapter gives special attention to the ways in which changes in government policies shape the internal processes of ethnic mobilization and conflict; we examine international responses in Chapter 7.

CONFLICT PROCESSES: THE KURDS IN IRAQ AND MISKITOS IN NICARAGUA

Group Sources of Mobilization

The framework identifies three variables at the group level of analysis: the degree of political and economic discrimination that affects an ethnic group (hypothesis 1), the strength of group identity (hypothesis 2), and the degree of cohesion among leaders and followers (hypothesis 3). We assess each in turn and then suggest how their interactions have contributed to mobilization for political action. Our assessments are summarized in Table 6.1 near the end of the chapter.

Political Discrimination. The Kurds experienced one specific and serious form of political discrimination throughout the Saddam Hussein years, from the 1970s to early 2003. They were subject to arbitrary relocation. In some instances relocations were a reprisal for supporting rebellion, which we treat analytically as an aspect of government coercion. In other instances the relocations were part of a long-term government policy to dilute the Kurdish population of oil-rich and strategically important areas by evicting Kurdish families and replacing them with Arabs from the south. Tens of thousands of Kurds were forced out of the traditionally Kurdish cities of Kirkuk, Mosul, and nearby villages.

None of the Iraqi or Nicaraguan governments during the 1970s and 1980s deliberately restricted the political participation of *individual* members of communal groups. This is not to say Kurds or Miskitos enjoyed Western–style civil and political rights: No one enjoyed such rights in Saddam Hussein's Iraq or the Somozas' Nicaragua.

Kurds had more opportunities than Miskitos for political advancement. The Iraqi government recruited many assimilated Kurds into the lower and middle ranks of the army, the **Baath Party,** and the bureaucracy. Some advanced to high levels, but not to the highest levels; those were reserved for the Sunni Arab clique from the town of Tikrit, who formed Hussein's inner circle.

The Somozas made no effort to encourage or discourage the participation of people from the Atlantic Coast in public life, although, except in local affairs, virtually none of them did participate. The Sandinistas, however, actively sought to recruit Miskitos into the governing party and decision-making bodies. The price was the same as it was for Kurds in Iraq: The Miskitos had to accept the dominant group's means and ends. The Miskitos who initially joined the Sandinista organizations used their positions to advocate Miskito communal interests; therefore, most were expelled or arrested or fled into exile.

The most serious political grievance of Kurds and Miskitos is not discrimination in the usual sense but, rather, involves restrictions on their efforts to express and pursue their group interests. Three such interests are common to both groups and to most other national and indigenous peoples: the right to exercise political control over the internal affairs of their own region and communities, the ability to control and benefit from the development of the region's resources, and the freedom to protect and promote their own culture and language. The immediate antecedent of mobilization by both Kurds and Miskitos was their resentment of failures to reach satisfactory agreements on these issues.

It is important to recognize that the governments of the two countries did not reject outright the validity of group claims. On several occasions from 1961 to the 1980s, the Baathist regimes in Iraq offered significant concessions to Kurds, as pointed out in Chapter 3. In each instance the offers were rejected as inadequate by some Kurdish leaders, who then began a new round of mobilization, which quickly led to armed conflict and repression. In the case of the Miskitos, at first the Sandinistas brought indigenous leaders into state organizations, but rejected Miskito leaders' insistent pursuit of communal interests and instituted new policies that created the conditions for mobilization. By arresting the leaders and taking direct control of economic and political life in the Atlantic Coast region, the Sandinistas created resentments and stimulated organized opposition where little had existed previously.

Economic Discrimination. All Kurdish and Miskito villagers live in relative poverty compared with dominant groups, but their poverty is mainly the result of ecological circumstances rather than of deliberate economic discrimination by dominant groups. Kurds living in Iraqi towns and cities have long participated in the economic life of modern Iraq. There have been no formal barriers to Miskitos' economic participation, but few are fluent in Spanish, and most have not had access to technical or higher education; thus, in practical terms, they can only pursue the limited economic opportunities available in the coastal region.

The economic development policies of the Iraqi and Nicaraguan governments have adversely affected the economic interests of local peoples. The Mosul oil fields are located in a predominantly Kurdish region, but Iraqi governments before 1991 refused to allocate a share of oil revenues for Kurdish regional governments and development. The Somoza regime promoted economic development along Nicaragua's Atlantic Coast by giving outsiders—companies from "Spanish" Nicaragua and North America—concessions to exploit the agricultural, timber, and mineral resources on land to which Miskitos had traditional claims. Development did provide employment opportunities for some Kurds and Miskitos; however, the process was controlled by and designed mainly for the economic benefit of dominant groups rather than the people whose traditional lands and resources were being exploited.

During the 1980s the regimes of both Saddam Hussein and the Sandinistas initiated policies that harmed the economic interests of both communal groups. The Iraqi government devastated the rural Kurdish economy by destroying thousands of villages and forcibly relocating their residents, as described above. The Sandinista government, motivated by socialist ideology, evicted foreign concessionaires from the Atlantic Coast region and sought to induce Miskitos to join fishing and farming collectives. The end of the concessions meant loss of employment, and the collectives were regarded as an infringement on Miskitos' freedom of economic action. The net impact of these policies on the Miskitos was modest compared with the hardship inflicted on the Iraqi Kurds, but it sharpened their sense of grievance against the new government.

Strength of Group Identity. The Miskitos should have a somewhat stronger sense of group identity than do the Iraqi Kurds, based on the five indicators identified in Chapter 3. Each group has at least four centuries of common history, but the unity of Kurdish culture has begun to be eroded by urbanization and modernization. Most Miskitos, however, continue to live in their traditional villages and a few coastal towns and to share a common, gradually evolving culture that incorporates both traditional and modern elements.

With regard to religion, the third indicator of group identity, most Kurds in Iraq are Sunni Muslims, as are the dominant Sunni Arabs. Some are Shi'is; others are Alevis or Yazidis, sects whose members have been persecuted in the past. These religious differences may contain the seeds of future divisions within an autonomous Kurdish society. Almost all Miskitos, by contrast, are Moravians and are acutely aware of the differences between their faith and that of the Roman Catholic "Spaniards."

Language, the fourth indicator, points in the same direction. There are different dialects of Kurdish, and many Iraqi Kurds—our sources do not specify proportions—speak the Arabic language of the dominant group as well as Kurdish. Most Miskitos, by contrast, speak two languages— Miskito dialects and English—which differentiates them sharply from the "Spaniards," who speak neither.

The final indicator of strength of group identity is the presence of visible racial or ethnic traits. Outsiders would probably find it impossible to distinguish Kurds from Arabs or Miskitos from "Spaniards" solely on the basis of physiological characteristics. The visible markers people use to determine ethnic identity in these and many other cases are culturally prescribed—manner of dress, speech, and social behavior. Men in rural Kurdistan, for example, wear distinctive headgear that makes them instantly recognizable even to outsiders. Our sources do not give us enough information to allow us to judge whether urban Iraqis or Nicaraguans can make reliable distinctions between "us" and "them" based on other markers of this sort.

Consideration of the two groups' geopolitical situations suggests a background factor that affects strength of group identity. Both groups live in terrain that is inhospitable to outsiders—humid and swampy lowlands for the Miskitos, rugged mountain valleys for rural Kurds—yet that permits its residents to move freely. The separate identities of both groups have been nurtured and protected by these conditions. Of course, the mountains that separate areas of Kurdish settlement surely have played a major role in the emergence and persistence of tribal divisions within rural Kurdish society. Modern national identity seems strongest in cities, even among Kurdish migrants in Europe, where Kurds of different origins interact on a regular basis.

Group Cohesion and Leadership.   This variable refers to the degree of cohesion among members of an ethnopolitical group. Cohesion is likely to be higher in groups that share a number of common traits, as discussed previously, but cohesion per se depends on whether group members accept a common authority structure, share a common ideology, and are in close communication with one another. A related factor is how fragmented or unified their political organizations are.

The political histories of the Kurds and the Miskitos provide strong clues about their potential for cohesion in the modern political era. Throughout their history, Kurds have been divided among a number of contending principalities, tribes, and clans. Past and present, each Kurdish political movement and rebellion has been supported by some of these segments and opposed by others. This generalization applies equally to all of Kurdistan and to the Kurds in Iraq. The Miskitos, by contrast, have recognized the local authority of village chiefs and for three centuries also recognized a line of kings who nominally ruled them all. Our sources do not mention serious rivalries or warfare among different segments of the Miskitos, although we cannot rule out the possibility that they occurred.

Ideology has played a major role for both peoples. The idea of a Kurdish nation is a century old but, though all modern Kurdish leaders pay lip service to Kurdish nationalism, the ideology has rarely been strong enough to overcome regional and political rivalries among competing Kurdish leaders. The ideology of indigenous rights had a more powerful and unifying effect among the Miskitos. It captured the imagination of a new generation of leaders who used it to identify common goals and lay out a strategy of action that attracted very widespread support.

We have little information on communication networks within the two groups. Interesting research could be done on the use of newspapers and legal and clandestine radio stations to build solidarity among ethnic peoples and on the use of radiotelephone facilities for organizational work by bodies like the Moravian church.

The Kurds of Iraq had one widely respected traditional leader, Mustafa Barzani, and a dominant political movement, the Kurdish Democratic

Party (KDP), from the 1940s to 1975. Barzani returned from his long residence in the USSR in 1958 and for seventeen years was the Kurds' preeminent leader in negotiations and conflict with the government. From the 1950s onward there were two competing tendencies within the movement, however. Barzani represented more traditional and rural interests; Jalal Talabani, a member of the KDP politburo (governing council), led a more modern, socialist, and pro-Arab faction. Barzani's 1975 unilateral decision to end the rebellion after the Iranians cut off support provoked a political split. Talabani's faction broke away and established the Patriotic Union of Kurdistan (PUK). Barzani died soon, and the KDP has since been led by his son, Masoud Barzani. After 1975 the two organizations alternated between cooperation and conflict. They collaborated in the Kurdish Regional Government from 1992 to 1994, then fought a deadly civil war, but patched up their differences in 2002, anticipating the collapse of the Saddam Hussein regime.

The Miskito political movement, MISURASATA, which was founded in 1979, divided in May 1981 over disputes about whether to continue to cooperate with the Sandinistas. Steadman Fagoth led the breakaway MISURA into exile in Honduras, where his followers formed an army the U.S. Central Intelligence Agency (CIA) funded as part of its support for the Contras. Within a year Brooklyn Rivera, disillusioned with Sandinista policies, led the rest of MISURASATA into exile in Costa Rica. The Sandinistas' 1985 policy shift toward offering regional autonomy to the Miskitos prompted further splits and realignments. For example, one MISURA leader, Eduardo Pantin, broke with Fagoth, participated in peace talks with the Sandinistas, then was assassinated. In 1987 Fagoth, Rivera, and other leaders joined in a new organization called YATAMA, but it was not cohesive enough to overcome persisting splits between CIA-supported Miskito groups, which continued to fight the Contras, and the growing numbers of leaders and field commanders who participated in the peace process. The conclusion of the peace agreement in 1989 and steps toward implementing regional autonomy were accompanied by a decline in factionalism. The rivalries that continue among Miskito leaders are similar to those of competing politicians in democratic societies rather than being deep-rooted sources of violent factionalism.

Getting It Together, or the Mobilization of Ethnic Groups

Cohesive groups, as described previously, have a unifying ideology, dense networks of communication and interactions between leaders and followers, and are largely free of factionalism. Cohesion makes mobilization easier, but is not the same thing. Mobilization refers specifically to how much of a group's resources are being committed to political action against other groups and the government. It depends on decisions of leaders combined with their followers' willingness to make the commitments and take the risks necessary for protest and rebellion.

The general proposition is that mobilization is likely to be highest and most sustained among groups whose members (1) share a strong sense of grievance about discrimination, (2) have a strong common identity, and (3) are highly cohesive. Comparison of the Iraqi Kurds with the Nicaraguan Miskitos suggests that both had strong grievances against their governments. Both sought greater cultural autonomy and had economic grievances, but their political grievances were far more important. For the Miskitos, political grievances were the result of new government policies; in Iraq, repressive government policies made existing political grievances worse. Group identity was relatively strong in both groups and was undoubtedly strengthened by heavy-handed government policies. At the beginning of open conflict each group was represented by one political movement. The cohesion of the Iraqi Kurds in the 1960s resulted from the charismatic leadership of Mustafa Barzani; the evidence reviewed earlier points to many underlying cleavages. The doctrine of indigenous rights helped build cohesion among the Miskitos in 1979 and 1980. In both cases, however, rivalries within the political leadership came to a head over differences about strategies of rebellion; as a result, both the KDP and MISURASATA split into two major factions (in 1975 and 1981, respectively). This reduced effective mobilization and made it easier for governments to contain rebellion. The Iraqi government played the two Kurdish groups against one another and continued to do so, even after 1991. The Nicaraguan government was able to draw less-militant factions into negotiations, which eventually paved the way for a settlement.

Political Context and Responses

Ethnic groups' political environment affects the ways in which they formulate and pursue their objectives. Democratic principles and practices encourage ethnically based political movements to use conventional politics and protest in the pursuit of limited demands (hypothesis 4 in Chapter 5). Most leaders of democratic states respect the civil and political rights of opposition groups and accept the principle that democracy requires that competing interests be accommodated. Politically, persistent demands from a large group need some kind of positive response, because to ignore them is to risk losing elections.

The leaders of authoritarian and populist states have different principles and political concerns. They are less likely to feel a moral or political obligation to reach accommodation with challengers and more likely rely on force to deal with threats to their positions and policies. If they do decide to accommodate demands from ethnic or other groups outside the power structure, it is usually because they have calculated that the costs of compromise are lower than the costs of protracted conflict. Ethnopolitical leaders in this type of political environment are likely to mobilize their followers for rebellion with far-reaching objectives—seeking independence rather than limited autonomy, revolution rather than reform (see hypothesis 5 in Chapter 5). First, their chances of achieving any success depend on their mobilizing strongly committed followers for high-risk conflict with high potential gain. Second, by thus raising the stakes, they may convince autocratic leaders that compromise is cheaper than fighting.

The responses of governments to the beginnings of ethnopolitical activism decisively influence later stages of conflict. They may do nothing in the hope that activism will simply go away. If activism is based on serious grievances and a strong sense of identity, however, it is likely to continue until officials are provoked into some kind of response. The mix of policies of repression and of accommodation chosen at this stage is critical. The use of force, we argue, is a two-edged sword: It may dissuade some ethnic activists but is likely to encourage others to greater resistance, up to the point at which the costs and risks become prohibitively high. Accommodation poses lesser risks: The regime that responds to ethnic demands with prompt reforms may encourage some activists to escalate their demands, but it usually satisfies moderates and minimizes the chances of rebellion. The optimum response from the perspective of a government that wants to limit escalation of ethnopolitical conflict is usually a mix of concessions that meet some grievances combined with a show or threat of force to discourage militants from escalation.

Ethnopolitical conflicts escalate for many reasons, despite the best intentions of people on both sides. The accumulated grievances may be so great that activists cannot be satisfied with limited concessions; outside supporters may encourage leaders to fight rather than compromise; governments may decide not to implement promised reforms and, thus, frustrate ethnic expectations that were raised by earlier promises. The longer self-determination wars drag on, the more resistant they are to either containment or settlement.

The Iraqi Kurds and the Nicaraguan Miskitos operated in contrasting political environments and encountered different sequences of responses. All Iraqi regimes since the 1950s to 2003 have had authoritarian leaders who gained their positions through popularly supported coups or internal power struggles and who relied on force to control opposition. The Baathist regime, which first came to power in 1968, was motivated by ideals of Arab socialism and nationalism and was prepared to accommodate Kurds who accepted those principles. But the concessions it offered at various times never satisfied the most militant Kurdish leaders, especially the Barzanis. As a result, proposals for limited autonomy were never fully implemented, and each phase of negotiation and concession was followed by renewed fighting in which the Kurds suffered increasingly costly defeats.

The revolutionary Sandinista regime was not a purely Marxist authoritarian regime, despite its portrayal as such by the Reagan administration. Its leaders were motivated by a mixture of socialist and democratic ideals, and they pursued them by populist means—by attempting to mobilize mass support for the new government among all social groups. When the Sandinistas tried to incorporate the Miskito leaders into the regime, however, the Miskitos pursued their own objectives rather than those of the revolutionaries. The consequences were summarized previously: The Sandinistas abandoned policies of incorporation in 1981 and decided to rely on their own (and Cuban) personnel to implement revolutionary policies on the Atlantic Coast. When the Miskitos protested and began to arm for rebellion, the revolutionary government responded with force. The Sandinista decision to shift from incorporation to the use of force was paralleled by shifts in Miskito tactics from conventional politics to protest and then rebellion.

In 1984 and 1985 the Sandinistas shifted again, this time toward accommodation based on recognition of the Miskitos' demands for autonomy (for reasons analyzed in Chapter 7). Cease-fires, regional self-government, and the return of refugees and guerrilla fighters were negotiated, but it took five years for accommodation to bring peace to the region.

The outcomes of the two conflicts differ. From 1960 to the 1990s Iraqi governments responded to a series of Kurdish rebellions with escalating force. The 1988 Al-Anfal campaign was genocidal in intent and effect. As the model in Chapter 5 postulates, this extreme level of force led the Kurds to suspend hostilities. But when the regime was weakened by its defeat in the 1990–1991 Gulf War, the Kurds who remained immediately rose again in rebellion. Thus, each military defeat succeeded only in contributing to the conditions—intensified grievances, stronger sense of common identity—that prepared the way for future rebellions whenever the strategic balance shifted. Such a pattern is characteristic of most protracted communal conflicts.

Conflict between the Sandinistas and the Miskitos, by contrast, never escalated to the highest levels. Once it became clear that forcible relocation intensified rather than reduced rebellion, the Sandinistas drew back from armed confrontation and shifted decisively toward negotiation. The Sandinista leader Tomás Borge was personally committed to ending the rebellion by dealing with its root causes. Even in this case, though, the negotiations were long and difficult.

This case illustrates another general principle: It is always difficult and sometimes impossible to bring ethnic conflicts to a peaceful conclusion once they have escalated to rebellion. First, as a result of the fighting, the opponents are intensely hostile toward one another and are suspicious of each other's motives, usually for good reason. Second, some factions on both sides usually think they have more to gain from continued fighting than from accepting compromises. Half of the twenty-two armed conflicts for ethnic autonomy or independence being fought at the beginning of 2003 had been under way for more than twenty-five years. Participation of outside parties—foreign governments, international organizations, private mediators—and promises of outside assistance may help to overcome these problems, but only with great difficulty—as is evident in the Palestinian-Israeli conflict.[1]

Ending an ethnic war and gaining autonomy is not an end in itself, not for the people who fight such wars. Neither the Kurds nor the Miskitos have gained all they hoped for. The Kurdish Regional Government has provided security and basic government services for most of its 3.4 million inhabitants. Infrastructure has been rebuilt, Kurdish-language schools and even a university have been established, the economy has been renewed. But the future of the KRG and its people depend on international factors beyond its control, as analyzed in Chapter 7. Regional autonomy for the Miskitos and Creoles has fallen far short of expectations, first for lack of funds, second because the central government continues to make inroads on the region's lands and natural resources without consultation or compensation.

CONFLICT PROCESSES:
MALAYSIAN CHINESE AND TURKS IN GERMANY

These two minorities have similar origins and face similar problems: Both are descended from economic immigrants, both live with political restrictions imposed by governments acting in the interest of dominant groups. And both groups have responded in similar ways: Rather than mobilizing for collective action, almost all of their members are pursuing their interests through conventional political and economic means—community associations, labor unions, and political parties. One important reason for considering these groups is to explain why they have *not* been politically more assertive.

Analysis of the contemporary situation of these two groups should also help us to understand the situation of many similar groups. Other Southeast Asian societies—Indonesia, the Philippines, Thailand, Vietnam, and Cambodia—contain Chinese minorities who are or have been

Classroom at Sulaymaniyeh University, 2001, housed in a former Iraqi prison. Photo by Michael Rubin, reproduced by permission.

subjected to discriminatory treatment. The Turks in Germany are among many recent migrants from less-developed societies to Western industrial societies, minorities that are often the targets of public hostility and the objects of both positive and restrictive government policies. Peaceful relations among groups in all such multiethnic societies depend upon delicate, government-managed balancing of the interests of minorities and majorities. Our two cases offer examples of how the potential for violent ethnic conflict has been contained in two democratic societies; a summary of our assessments is found in Table 6.1 at the end of the chapter.

Group Sources of Mobilization: Discrimination

Most Chinese in Malaysia are economically advantaged compared with the politically dominant Malays, and economic discrimination takes the form of "reverse discrimination" that gives preferences to Malays. Many Chinese fear their languages and culture are also threatened by pro-Malay policies in the area of education. One specific policy that vexes the Chinese is the use of quotas in university admissions that exclude many otherwise qualified Chinese youth, a policy that has both cultural and economic implications. As an alternative, many prosperous Chinese send their children to foreign universities. For less affluent Chinese, this imposes economic hardship because tuition at overseas universities is often too costly. This often means that only one child receives university education and equally qualified siblings have to settle for less.

In the 1960s the Turkish immigrants to Germany began at or near the bottom of the economic ladder, as did the first generations of Chinese immigrants in Malaya. At first the Turks encountered informal discrimination in access to better-paying jobs and good housing. By the 1990s, however, they had substantially improved their economic position, in ways similar to the Chinese, by establishing many small businesses. Moreover, by law their individual economic and social rights are guaranteed to the same degree as those of German citizens.

The most salient grievances of the Turkish community at present concern threats to their personal safety, which is a form of political discrimination. They still are perceived by some Germans as constituting an economic threat, because they hold jobs when many citizens are unemployed. Some Germans also see them as an affront to German society because some still speak Turkish rather than German in public and some Turkish women still wear traditional clothing. These beliefs are used to rationalize anti-Turkish attacks and rhetoric.

A persistent source of political grievance for both groups has been restrictions on their citizenship rights. This was not an issue for the first wave of Turkish immigrants, because most expected to return to Turkey; it was also not an issue for those Chinese who came to Malaya in the 1930s and 1940s with plans to return to Mainland China when the fighting ended. For immigrants and their descendants who have come to think of themselves as permanent residents, however, the citizenship issue becomes more important: It is both a passport to participation in democratic politics and a protection against deportation. In Malaya this issue was largely resolved through liberalization of the citizenship laws during the 1950s: By 1957 more than two-thirds of Chinese residents of Malaya were citizens, and, because of the rules in effect since that time, virtually all are now citizens.

By contrast, German law has made it very difficult for Turkish residents to obtain citizenship. Reforms in the 1990s have eased the process, but noncitizen Turks still outnumber those with citizenship by 6 to 1, and it will be decades before all Turks who want to remain in Germany choose to apply for citizenship. Germany was slow to respond because it has long followed the principle that German citizenship should be restricted to people of German descent; therefore, returning descendants of Germans who immigrated to Eastern Europe and Russia two centuries or more ago are virtually assured of citizenship. In this respect Germany is out of phase with most other European countries, in which citizenship is determined by birth and residence, not by descent. Some countries, including the Netherlands and Sweden, routinely grant citizenship to immigrants after a few years' residence.

In summary, the Malaysian Chinese experience political restrictions on some economic activities and educational opportunities that are supposedly justifiable on grounds of reducing inequalities between Chinese and Malays. The Chinese are very sensitive to local and national policies that are seen as a threat to the teaching and use of Chinese languages. At the same time, they and all other communal groups are barred from making ethnic claims or criticisms that threaten the Malay-dominated balance among communal groups. A more recent problem is that of increasing religious intolerance among Malays. Attempts to convert young Chinese Buddhists to Islam (sometimes without prior knowledge of their parents) and the introduction of mandatory classes on Islamic religion and culture in all publicly supported schools reinforces the resentment of minority Chinese about their treatment as second-class citizens.

The Turks encounter some day-to-day social and economic discrimination, but many are taking advantage of the new citizenship law even though it requires them to give up Turkish citizenship as the price of German citizenship. They also are concerned about right-wing attacks that threaten their personal security. Another and potentially more divisive issue has emerged in recent years, which is public resentment and official suspicion about the presence of large numbers of Islamic militants in Germany, including some Turks. Islamists are under close scrutiny and can expect more arrests and deportations, especially in the aftermath of the 9/11 attacks.

The Chinese grievances at the beginning of the twenty-first century thus are different in both degree and kind than those of the Turks, but both appear much less intense and widespread than were the grievances of the Kurds and Miskitos in the 1980s.

Sources of Group Mobilization: Group Identity

The bases of group identity were weak during the early stages of both groups' immigration, especially for the Chinese. They came to Malaya over a long period of time from different regions of China speaking different languages or dialects. The Turkish immigrants arrived in Germany within a shorter period of time but included a mix of Turkish-speaking and Kurdish-speaking people from urban and rural areas. In each instance the group's identity was, in effect, defined and reinforced by dominant groups who labeled them as a distinct category of people and practiced discriminatory treatment toward all members of the category. Interactions with dominant groups also made minorities more self-consciously aware of defining differences: They were Buddhists or Confucianists in an Islamic society or Muslims in a Christian society; they dressed and acted differently in social situations than did Malays or British or Germans; and they were physically distinct, which meant Malays and British and Germans could recognize them and treat them according to their assigned status.

We also concluded, above, that the degree of discrimination against Chinese and Turks is relatively low. Members of both groups continue to be reminded that they are "different," but not at great personal cost. This may be changing in a negative direction for the Malaysian Chinese, who are under increased pressure to assimilate. Some recently converted Chinese have spoken in mosques in favor of abandoning their ethnicity to facilitate entry into Malay/Muslim society. Although uncommon, this provokes uncomfortable comparisons to the status of Jews in medieval Europe, who could achieve acceptance and freedom from persecution only through conversion.

For such immigrant groups, we think discrimination is the main negative source of group identity. In the absence of deliberate discrimination, their sense of cultural identity is likely to be benign and is not a source of social conflict; it may eventually weaken or disappear entirely as successive generations are absorbed into growing economies and an evolving social order. The greatest threats to ethnic harmony in such situations are economic decline and the resultant intensified competition among groups for shares of the shrinking pie. As we point out in Chapter 7, the economies of Malaysia and Germany are both vulnerable to international economic changes.

Group Cohesion and Mobilization

An attempt to explain the Chinese-based insurgency of the period 1948–1960 raises an important theoretical question, because the conditions for mobilization specified in our theoretical model seem to be missing. Group identity was weak and fragmented, as we suggested previously. Discrimination against the Chinese was widespread but minor, and it was no greater than that experienced by other communal groups under colonial rule. The Malayan Chinese also lacked the cohesion that would have been provided by a common authority structure, by leaders, or by a large-scale political organization. Secret societies were important forms of social organization for Chinese immigrant communities, but they were local rather than countrywide. Trade unions were concerned mainly with economic issues, not ethnic issues. The Communist Party of Malaya (CPM), founded in 1930, was not established as an ethnic political movement, nor did it pursue exclusively Chinese interests. It attracted little external support from either the USSR or the Chinese Communists.

These conditions help to explain why few Chinese in Malaya openly supported the CPM's rebellion; they do not explain why the CPM's leaders initiated it. The most plausible answer begins with the fact that the CPM was already mobilized and had credibility because it had led armed resistance to the discriminatory and repressive policies of the Japanese occupiers during World War II. Its leaders feared the postwar British policy of decolonization would lead to a decline in their political status in an independent, Malay-dominated society, so they made a strategic decision to direct the energies of an already armed and mobilized organization into a nationalist, anticolonial uprising.

The CPM example leads us to an important general conclusion: Once militant communal organizations have mobilized for rebellion, they may decide to continue or resume fighting for strategic or tactical reasons, even in the absence of some of the conditions that prompted their initial mobilization. This may help to explain why the leaders of the Kurdish Democratic Party, for example, so quickly rejected Iraqi government concessions and resumed fighting in 1970 and at other times.

In Malaysia in 2002 the principal organizations that promote Chinese interests are legal political parties. The Malaysian Chinese Association (MCA) has been part of the Malay-dominated government coalition since the early 1950s. It is a politically acceptable channel through which Chinese can pursue their interests and ambitions, albeit within Malay-dictated limits. The principal alternative for Chinese who are dissatisfied with the probusiness, procoalition stance of the MCA is the Democratic Action Party, which has taken more assertive pro-Chinese positions and, for most of the past four decades, has been the principal opposition party at the national level, although it usually holds only a handful of seats in the Malaysian parliament.

In summary, the Malaysian political system gives the Chinese (and other communal minorities) a limited but guaranteed role in the political process but also restricts some freedoms by not allowing what the government considers the divisive pursuit of communal interest. Thus, it encourages participation in conventional politics and discourages any efforts to mobilize Chinese for ethnic protest or rebellion. In the absence of very serious grievances or threats to their status, the Chinese are unlikely to embrace more militant actions.

The Turkish community in Germany has few of the conditions for political mobilization. Divisions between ethnic Kurds and Turks, and between secular and militant Muslims, inhibit the development of an integrating sense of collective identity and interest. Group identity also has been diluted by the partial assimilation of second-generation Turks into German society. Citizenship restrictions alone are not sufficient to create serious grievances. And, like the Chinese in Malaysia, the Turks have established an economic niche. These factors help to explain why the Turks have not developed political associations that command widespread support or promote political action. Now that citizenship is easier to attain, Turks who are interested in German politics—rather than

Turkish or Islamic politics—are most likely to act through existing political parties and community organizations in the cities in which most live.

Political Context and Responses

The Chinese in postindependence Malaysia and the Turks in Germany both illustrate the argument, made previously, that minorities in democracies are likely to pursue their collective interests by conventional means. There are two important reasons for this—one specific to immigrant groups like these, the other a general trait of democracies. The group-specific explanation is that both minorities are descendants of economic migrants who have prospered—the Chinese more than the Turks—in their adoptive countries. In other words, they have been preoccupied mainly with material concerns and have been more accepting—or realistic—about the political restrictions placed on them by the dominant society. The second reason is that the governments of both host societies have sought to accommodate the immigrants, within limits. The Chinese have maintained their leading economic role in rapidly developing Malaysia and have more than token political participation. The Turks are eligible for the full, substantial range of social and economic benefits provided to German citizens; citizenship is now easier to attain; and they mainly lack physical security. The Malaysian limits on communal politics are sometimes criticized as being undemocratic. The Malaysian response is likely that in a divided society, a perfectly egalitarian democracy is at risk of destructive communal conflict that would have to be controlled by instituting authoritarian rule.

Both governments have also used coercive means to counter minority political militancy. The British and Malays' successful counterinsurgency tactics against the Communist Party in the 1950s are discussed in Chapter 4 in "The Chinese in Malaysia." The resurgence of guerrilla activity in the far north of Malaysia in the 1970s was also met with force, which was sweetened by offers of amnesty for fighters who were willing to come in from the jungle. Furthermore, Malaysian authorities have invoked national security considerations to justify the arrest and detention of political opponents; in October 1987, for example, 119 political members of legal political and religious movements were detained.

During the 1970s and 1980s a widely feared policy of both governments was deportation, which was used by Malay and German authorities to deport political activists as well as immigrants who violated various regulations. For example, Turkish Kurds who have organized support for the Kurdish Worker's Party (PKK; see Chapter 3) and other radical causes are regularly deported. In a well-publicized 1975 case, a

Malaysian Chinese citizen was deported for temporarily residing and pursuing university studies in the People's Republic of China. The threat of deportation is one of the reasons citizenship, or the lack of it, has been an important concern of immigrants. Without the protection of citizenship they have little or no recourse against administrative decisions to deport them.[2] And there is little doubt that some specific deportation cases have been decided arbitrarily. The effect of deportation policies did not increase opposition; since it was a policy aimed at a few individuals rather than entire groups, it seems to have encouraged political caution and conformity.

CONCLUSION

Ethnopolitical conflicts usually center on one of three general issues: the desire for "exit" or independence from the state (the Iraqi Kurds), the demand for greater autonomy within the state (the Miskitos), or the recognition and protection of minority interests within a plural society (the Malaysian Chinese and Turks in Germany). Observers sometimes argue that such conflicts are likely to be long and deadly and are difficult or impossible to resolve. Resolution is difficult but not impossible, as our cases illustrate. We conclude this chapter with a brief analysis of the ways in which each of these three issues of ethnopolitical conflict can be accommodated.[3]

Ethnonationalist demands for independence imply the breakup of existing states. States usually counter secessionist movements with all of the political and military means at their disposal, as exemplified by the responses of Turkish, Iranian, and Iraqi governments to the episodic nationalist rebellions by Kurds. Autonomy of the kind negotiated with the Miskitos in Nicaragua is potentially a less costly alternative to protracted civil wars for all parties concerned. State officials who are prepared to consider this approach can usually find some leaders in virtually all ethnonationalist and indigenous movements who are open to compromises that guarantee regional autonomy within a federal framework.

The Miskitos are one of twenty peoples whose armed conflicts over self-determination between 1970 and 2000 led to agreements by which they gained some combination of greater autonomy and power-sharing. Examples of the others include the Basques of Spain, the Nagas and Tripura in India, the Gagauz of post-Communist Moldova, Tuaregs in Niger and Mali, the people of Bangladesh's Chittagong Hill region, the Moros of the Philippines, and the Catholics of Northern Ireland. Other separatist peoples who neared or reached agreements in 2001–2002 include the Bougainvilleans in Papua New Guinea, Tamils in Sri Lanka, Albanians in Macedonia, and the southern Sudanese.[4] The autonomy gained through negotiations is generally more limited than that sought by ethnonationalist leaders, which is the main reason that some factions often try to spoil agreements by continuing to fight. The failure to implement agreements also may prompt renewed fighting. Nonetheless, both sides may conclude that agreements regarding autonomy are preferable to starting or continuing destructive wars that cannot be won.

The interests of communal contenders like the Chinese Malaysians and the Turkish ethnoclass in Germany are not likely to be pursued or satisfied by open rebellion. The strategy of rebellion failed badly for the Chinese who supported the Malay Communist Party in the period 1948–1960. We can distinguish four patterns of accommodation that have been attempted in multiethnic societies in the last half of the twentieth century.

Containment is a strategy of keeping minorities "separate and unequal," as was done to African-Americans until the 1950s and to Black South Africans under apartheid. Such policies are usually forced on minorities by dominant groups and are accepted only for as long as the groups have no opportunity to pursue alternatives. The German government's policies toward the Turks from the 1960s through the 1980s were a relatively benign form of containment.

Assimilation was long the preferred liberal alternative to containment. Assimilation is an individualistic strategy that gives minorities incentives and opportunities to forsake their old communal identities and adopt the language, values, and behaviors of the dominant society. Until the 1960s assimilation was the preferred strategy for dealing with ethnoclasses and indigenous peoples in most Western societies. In practice, the Turks in Germany are moving slowly toward assimilation, and Chinese in Malaysia are being nudged in that direction. Assimilation is also widely used by Third World states to complement strategies of containment. We pointed out that the Baathist government of Iraq actively recruited Kurds and members of the Shi'i religious majority into the Baath Party, the officer corps, and the bureaucracy. The Turkish government has sought to assimilate Kurds by similar means. The strategy of encouraging national minorities to assimilate is attractive to dominant groups, because it diverts the talents of potential opponents into the service of the state. In the long run a stream of individual choices to identify with the dominant society causes a politically assertive ethnic group to lose much of its cohesion and human resources.

Pluralism is an approach to regulating intergroup relations that gives greater weight to the collective rights and interests of minorities. If containment means "separate and unequal," then pluralism means "equal but separate": equal individual and collective rights, including the right to separate identities and cultural institutions. In the United States and Canada the advocates of multiculturalism, which is another name for pluralism, seek recognition and promotion of the history, culture, language or dialect, and religions that define the separate identities of Hispanics and Hawaiians, French-Canadians and indigenous "First Nations," and many others.

The growing emphasis on pluralism in Western societies is a reaction to the limitations of assimilation. For Turks in Germany, assimilation is a potential solution to the discrimination most have encountered. But they are also aware that complete assimilation implies the loss of their distinctive identity as Turks and Muslims, which most want to preserve. Furthermore, policies of assimilation in other Western societies have not meant an end to inequalities or informal discrimination, as the experiences of visible minorities in the United States and France show. So why, ask ethnic activists, give up our identity for incomplete integration? Pluralism has growing appeal for many minorities in this situation and can be expected to be favored by the next generation of Turkish activists in Germany.

Communal power-sharing is an alternative way of regulating group relations in multiethnic societies. It assumes that communal identities and organizations are the basic building blocks of society, as they are in the segmented societies described in Chapter 2's discussion of communal contenders. State power is exercised through collaboration among the ethnic communities, each of which is proportionally represented in government and all of which have mutual veto power over policies that affect their communal interests. This kind of institutionalized power-sharing evolved historically between the Protestant and Roman Catholic communities in the Netherlands and has been extended in modified form to new visible minorities who have emigrated to the Netherlands from Indonesia, the Caribbean, and elsewhere. Power-sharing has intrinsic appeal to some ethnic activists because it seems to guarantee that a communal group can possess both status and access to power without compromising its social or cultural integrity.

One problem is that power-sharing arrangements are not easily constructed, especially when the groups begin from an unequal footing. Attempts to improve the status of disadvantaged minorities often trigger a backlash from advantaged groups that fear the loss of some of their own privileges. Ethnophobic political movements motivated by this kind of concern became increasingly common in multiethnic Western societies during the 1980s and 1990s.

Malaysia illustrates the liabilities of power-sharing arrangements in Asian, African, and Middle Eastern countries. The main flaw has been the fact that Malays have used their advantaged position to selectively benefit the Malays. The Malaysian version of power-sharing has helped to maintain stability and the observance of most democratic principles, but it has worked mainly because the Chinese and Indian communities have been willing to accept their subordinate roles. If the Malay-dominated government were to impose more restrictions on the communal minorities—which is possible, and more likely in present circumstances—a situation like that described here as containment would result. The general point is that power-sharing among unequal partners can lead to exploitation and repression of the weaker parties. The less advantaged groups may be tempted to defect, even to rebel. Lebanon's power-sharing political system degenerated into civil war in this kind of circumstance.

In conclusion, the policies of regional autonomy, assimilation, pluralism, and power-sharing can be used in creative combination to accommodate the essential interests of most disadvantaged and politically active communal groups. To make such policies work, however, compromises among groups and an enduring commitment by leaders of all groups to adhere to agreements reached are necessary. If policies of accommodation are to be effective in any type of political system, they must be pursued cautiously but persistently over the long run—slowly enough that they do not stimulate a political backlash from other groups, persistently enough so disadvantaged minorities do not become disillusioned and mobilize for rebellion.

DISCUSSION QUESTIONS

Review the comparisons in Table 6.1 as the first step in answering these questions.

1. Which kinds of discrimination seem to have the strongest and most consistent effects on the intensity of ethnic conflict?
2. Does conflict between an ethnic group and a government lead to stronger group identity and greater cohesion, as was proposed in Chapter 5? Are there circumstances in which these propositions do not hold?
3. We argued in Chapter 5 that increasing the severity of government force directed against an ethnic group is likely to increase the group's resistance, up to some threshold beyond which extreme force inhibits further opposition. Is the evidence from all four cases consistent with this proposition? Does it seem to hold in both democratic and autocratic political environments?

TABLE 6.1 Summary of internal factors in ethnic mobilization for four groups

Variables	Kurds in Iraq (2002)	Miskitos (1970s)	Chinese in Malaysia (2002)	Turks in Germany (2002)
Discrimination				
Economic	Deliberate destruction of rural economy	Some loss of opportunities	Restrictions on corporate ownership, education	Minor discrimination because of social practices
Political	Denial of autonomy demands, forcible relocation	Denial of autonomy demands, forcible relocation	Minor restrictions on civil service recruitment	Citizenship restraints eased but xenophobic attacks continue
Group identity	Medium to strong, strengthened by conflict with regime	Strong, strengthened by conflict with regime	Low to medium, weakened by partisan political divisions	Weakened by assimilation strengthened by attacks
Group cohesion	Weakened by clan and political divisions	High, but weakened by political divisions during war	Low to medium, weakened by partisan political divisions	Weak to none because of political and ethnic rivalries
Type of political environment	Authoritarian	Socialist	Democratic with restrictions	Democratic
Severity of governmental force	Escalating from severe to genocidal	Escalating from arrests to forcible relocation	Occasional arrests	Deportation of Kurdish and Islamic militants, revolutionaries
Effects on ethnic mobilization and conflict	Recurring rebellions	Protest escalating to rebellion	Conventional political participation since 1960s, limited protest	Growing participation, growing protest

4. Do you think the Turks in Germany have more to gain from increased protest than the Chinese in Malaysia? Than other immigrant minorities in Western societies?

Research Exercise. The Kurds have been less successful than the Miskitos in gaining regional autonomy. Identify half a dozen general factors that explain the difference. Concentrate on factors that are strong or present in one case and weak or absent in the other: For example, there have been deep and persisting divisions among the Kurds but not among the Miskitos. Take into account international as well as internal factors.

7

The International Dimensions of Ethnopolitical Conflict: Four Cases

The connection between ethnic conflict and the international system is a two-way street. The international system shapes the process and outcome of ethnic conflicts in several ways: Its member states may support the warring factions, promote negotiations, impose sanctions to slow down a conflict, or intervene militarily. In the other direction, protracted ethnic conflict often spills over boundaries, devastates economies, and contributes to environmental catastrophes. Ethnic wars sometimes lead to massive human rights abuses and frequently result in large refugee flows. Refugees usually flee to neighboring states, which reluctantly provide temporary sanctuary in the expectation that international organizations will support and resettle the refugees.

We have focused thus far on the reasons ethnic groups challenge state authorities. In Chapters 5 and 6, we analyzed the internal sources of challenges; here we examine their international linkages. Thus, what follows builds upon and extends recent commentaries on the international dimensions of ethnic conflict.[1]

More specifically, we look at international factors that affect the mobilization of ethnic groups and at aspects of ethnic mobilization that prompt international responses. We focus on three questions: How did the international environment affect the regime and challenging minorities in each of the four cases? Which regimes and challengers had high status, why, and with what consequences? And how does regime status affect external support for minorities?

THE EMERGING ETHNIC DIMENSION IN GLOBAL POLITICS

Students of international relations are taught that the international system consists primarily of nation-states, regional organizations like the Organization of African Unity (whose members are also states), and supranational organizations such as the United Nations. The modern state system that emerged after the Treaty of Westphalia in 1648 replaced one central authority—namely, the church in Rome—with a system of absolute rulers competing for space, power, and influence. Although the democratic state is apparently slowly replacing autocratic or absolute rule, other forms of political organization may yet be the answer to current ethnic unrest. In the European Union, for example, minority regions have greater freedom of action than they did in most of its member states before the union was founded.

In the last half-century other kinds of groups have been recognized as important independent actors. They include functional organizations such as the International Committee of the Red Cross; national groups such as the Palestinians, a dispersed national people who do not control their own territory; and multinational corporations—organizations that are not tightly connected to specific state interests. Typically, in municipal and international law individuals and groups are treated as an extension or an integral part of the state in which they reside rather than as independent actors, as we show in Chapter 8. This, however, is slowly changing. During the last decades of the twentieth century, individuals and groups achieved greater recognition as independent actors in international law. For example, the Genocide Convention specifically mentions groups and individuals as enjoying the protection of the international community. The International Covenant on Economic, Social, and Cultural Rights states that "All peoples have the right of self-determination. By virtue of that right they freely determine their political status and freely pursue their economic, social, and cultural development." This covenant was drafted with the colonial subjects of European states in mind, but other subordinate peoples—Palestinians, Tibetans, Kurds, Miskitos, and many others—argue that it should apply to them as well.

The emerging ethnic dimension of global politics challenges our perception that the primary identity of people coincides with the territorial state, or, conversely, that people see themselves as members of larger regional units like the European Union. Arguably, the reassertion of communal identity may be the result of the alienation and frustration that accompany the decline of artificial states. The increasing fluidity of international borders is evident not only in the increase in ethnic strife and separatist movements but also in the ever-increasing flow of labor migrants from the global south to the north, and within the now–borderless European Union. Foreign capital penetration and global environmental concerns further diminish the importance of national borders. As borders become less significant, functional, corporate, ethnic, and religious groups may become a main focus of the study of international relations.

COMMUNAL IDENTITIES AND
THE FORMATION OF NEW STATES

The imagery of the state still dominates international and ethnic discourse. The primary objective of groups identified here as ethnonationalists is a territorial state of their own, or if that is not possible, some form of autonomy on territory within an existing state. Ethnonational self-determination is sometimes achieved peacefully, for example, the secession of fourteen non-Russian republics from the Soviet Union at the end of the Cold War. More typical are attempts to secede through rebellion, as is seen in the ongoing struggle of the Kurds and in the historical example of the Biafrans (Ibos and other peoples of eastern Nigeria) who fought a deadly and unsuccessful war to secede from Nigeria from 1967 until early 1970.

Regimes that are unwilling to accommodate or negotiate in such situations often respond violently to ethnic protests. Ethnic challengers may then organize, seek arms, and respond in kind, which in the worst cases leads to a spiral of violence that may include political massacres and genocide. The more intense these conflicts become, the greater the likelihood of substantial international responses—in regions of strategic interest to the major powers. But in some instances the international community has done little or nothing to prevent intense and protracted violence. Recent examples include the Chechens' bloodily suppressed rebellion against Russia (1995 to present), Rwanda during the 1994 genocide, and the twenty-year secessionist war in Southern Sudan—though there has been a recent flurry of diplomatic activities in the latter. In Chechnya no international actor has the inclination or capability to challenge Russian actions. In other such conflicts diplomatic efforts have been hampered by diffuse national objectives on the side of potential intervenors, lack of interest and political will, and sometimes lack of resources.

Ethnic challengers rarely are able to compete on an equal footing with the well-equipped armies of states. To do so they usually have to seek external support. To the novice outside observer the cohesion of ethnic groups may appear largely symbolic, derived from the cultural, social, and psychological symbols that tie the group together. But some groups are politically very well organized, have sympathetic kindred and emigre communities abroad, and have waged international publicity campaigns—all of which help them get external political and material support. Having achieved that kind of visibility and support, they improve their chances of attaining some of their objectives by political means—or by a two-track strategy of negotiating and fighting. Of course, the type and level of external support they receive depend, in turn, on the varied sympathies and ideological dispositions of international actors, and on the **legitimacy** accorded to the group's demands. Ironically, the legitimacy of groups sometimes depends directly on the level of agreement reached and accommodation offered by their respective governments.

States are usually less dependent on external support in the face of ethnic challenges, but their leaders may also find it necessary or useful to seek foreign recognition and support, especially for efforts to contain secessionist rebellions. Challenged states also play symbolic games. In the aftermath of the 9/11 attacks, as the U.S. mounted a global campaign against jihadist terrorism, China, Russia, India, Israel, and other states facing insurgencies found it useful to label their opponents as terrorists. This helps shield them from international criticism and potential sanctions against human rights violations.

THE THEORETICAL MODEL REVISITED

Our analysis of each of the four cases traces the linkages between international and internal factors as they affect ethnic conflict. We use the language of **levels of analysis** to do so. International relations theory typically organizes the multitude of actors, influences, and processes into different levels of analysis. At the international level our aim is to assess the interactions of states based on such factors as their geographical or power position within the world system of states. Closely related is the global focus, in which researchers analyze global trends that shape events and outcomes. Thus, for example, one can ask how democratization and the growth of the global economy, or demographic and environmental changes, affect the world at large. One cannot always neatly separate one level from another because we also know that even on the lowest level of analysis (the individual), citizens matter in domestic politics and through their representatives influence foreign policy and, by their collective actions (the group level), can determine both the nature of government and its foreign policies. Also, and more typical in autocracies, individual politicians like Saddam Hussein often single-handedly decide on foreign policy matters. Students may be skeptical about the utility of the levels of analysis distinctions and suspect it is another ploy by professors to mystify the study of international relations. Think instead of the approach as a framework or organizing device that makes it easier to do systematic analysis that covers all the relevant bases.

Here is an example of a levels-of-analysis approach. Given our focus on ethnic conflict we know, for example, that in the Iraqi Kurdish situation their leaders, Talibani and Barzani, play extremely important roles in unifying or dividing their people. Thus we may study their personal backgrounds and rivalries, but quickly will recognize that it is mistaken to assess Kurdish politics by the acts of their leaders alone. We also need to take into consideration the nature of the Iraqi regime, international support from the U.S. and Britain, and the conflicted motives of Turkish, Iranian, and Arab leaders vis-à-vis Kurdish nationalism. At present we also need to consider how closely Muslims in Kurdistan are tied to Islamic fundamentalist or terrorist groups, which surely affects potential outside hostility and support. Thus, to understand the actions and prospects of Iraqi Kurds we need to systematically sort through the motives, roles, and actions of a great many actors.

The following analysis begins at the international level, by looking at the international political environment and sketching how it affects the actions of states and ethnic challengers. To a lesser degree we also look at the groups and their leaders, to see how their actions affect international support.

Extent of External Support

We asserted in Chapter 5 that the types of actions ethnic groups take are determined in part by the resources of the group and by outside support and encouragement (hypothesis 6). Outside support may take the form of provision of supplies, training of combatants, and, in rare cases, aggressive intervention on behalf of the ethnic group. These material kinds of external support translate into group resources for protest and especially for rebellion.

Outside encouragement may come in intangible forms. Successful ethnic contenders may inspire their brethren, in adjacent territories or elsewhere, to mobilize for action. This may occur in two different forms: *contagion*—that is, the intentional transmittal of strategies of communal activism from abroad—or *imitation,* in which group leaders find inspiration and guidance in the successes of similar groups elsewhere.

International Economic Status of Regimes

We argued (hypothesis 7 in Chapter 5) that high international status is accorded to states that control large numbers of scarce resources, control a high percentage of the market trade of valuable commodities, have a high level of per-capita income, rank high in gross domestic product and gross national product, have a global network of trading partners, and have a significant number of people with advanced degrees. Of course, all of these figures are only meaningful if compared to other states either in the region or on a global scale. We assume that high status allows states to deal with internal challengers as they wish. International responses also vary with the status of the challenging group, its demands, and the legitimacy of the dominant authority.

The model presented in Chapter 5 does not explicitly explore the linkages between the status and support of regimes and those of the challengers. We suggest that the status of the challengers is not independently determined but, rather, depends on their status in comparison with that of the regime with which they are in conflict. For example, the international status of, and support for, the Kurds has increased relative to the declining international stature of Iraq in the decade since the Gulf War. Previously, the Kurds had little international clout and more typically were pawns of Turkey, Iraq, and Iran. The changing statuses of both regimes and ethnic challengers are examined below.

THE INTERNATIONAL CONTEXT OF THE KURDISH CONFLICT

Here we assess the international dimensions of the conflict between the Kurds and Saddam Hussein's regime. Since shifting international and regional alliances affect the status of regimes and challengers, we begin by analyzing international alignments within the region. The analysis is summarized in Table 7.1 near the end of the chapter.

International and Regional Players in the Mideast During Baathist Rule in Iraq

The traditional Arab governments in the Gulf—such as the United Arab Emirates, Bahrain, Qatar, Saudi Arabia, and especially Kuwait—viewed Saddam Hussein's regime with great suspicion even before Iraq's 1990 invasion of Kuwait. From one perspective, he was thought to help secure the Gulf states against Iranian encouragement of Shi'i minorities and military adventurism in the Persian Gulf, especially in the Strait of Hormuz, where Iran had territorial claims to some islands. From another perspective, Saddam Hussein's socialist Baath Party ideology was an anathema to the autocratic leadership of the Gulf states. Moreover, his secular tendencies were threatening to both Shi'i and Sunni fundamentalist aspirations in the Arab world, especially in Iran.

Through Israeli eyes Iraq was potentially a major threat. Iraqi anti-Israel rhetoric, combined with the largest and best-equipped army in the Arab world, and Iraq's program to acquire weapons of mass destruction were seen as ever-increasing threats to Israel's survival.

The United States, although it had condemned Iraq for using chemical weapons as early as 1984, had not imposed sanctions on Iraq nor seriously interrupted heavy trading prior to the beginning of the Kuwait crisis. After the Iranian revolution of 1979 Iraq's status increased relative to the declining status of the Iranian regime. The United States officially changed its anti-Iraq position by reestablishing formal relations with Baghdad in 1984 and assisted Iraq's war with Iran by buying more oil. After the Iran-Contra affair in 1986, the United States actively sought to stem weapons sales to Iran.

Despite Britain's role in drafting UN Resolution 620 (1988) "condemning the use of chemical weapons and calling for 'appropriate and effective measures' if they were used again," Britain only "reprimanded Iraq verbally" and simultaneously doubled "the amount of its export credit facility to Iraq."[2] The other European states, especially West Germany and France, continued trade as usual. Later inquiries revealed that German and Russian manufacturers and exporters were heavily involved in developing Iraq's nuclear program.

Soviet relations with Iran were cool during the regime of the shah, who was seen by the United States as a bulwark against Soviet expansionism in the region. After the fall of the shah, the Soviets tried to exploit the volatile situation by improving economic relations, but the Khomeini regime had little interest in pursuing closer relations. The Soviet invasion of Afghanistan in 1979 had convinced him that Soviet objectives were expansionist, anti-Islam, and hegemonic.

Regime Status

Iraq is potentially prosperous given its crude oil reserves—fifth largest in the world—but the Baathist regime devoted most of its resources to military purposes. Iraq in the years 1987–1989 had the highest military to social spending imbalance in the Third World; its policy priorities clearly favored a massive military build up.[3] Iraq also had severe economic problems after its war with Iran. Hussein's gamble to make Iraq the dominant regional power in the wake of the Iranian revolution had failed. The war instead left Iraq with a large debt burden, with few gains vis-à-vis Iran, with fewer sympathizers within the Arab world, and with greater Kurdish and Shi'i unrest.

Despite its potential economic strength, its staunch anti-Khomeini posturing, and its large armies, Iraq's international stature was lower than its leader had envisioned. Iraq, after all, had attacked Iran in September 1980 to secure a preeminent position in the Mideast, to resettle the boundaries of the Shatt-al-Arab waterway in its favor, and to cut off any potential Iranian support for the Kurds. Saddam Hussein's abominable human rights record made him a less than ideal candidate for Western support. In 1988, when Baghdad attacked Kurdish villages with chemical weapons, the international community formally condemned Iraq and launched a UN-sponsored investigation. Although Iraq was eventually found guilty of repeatedly using chemical weapons against

Kurdish fighters and civilians, no sanctions were imposed against the Iraqi regime.

The Status of the Challengers: The Kurds

Kurdish internal divisions along clan, religious, urban-rural, and political lines have not helped them to secure external support nor enhanced their international status. The division among Kurds is also evident at the leadership level. Mustafa Barzani, the traditional leader who commanded the largest amount of support from tribal leaders, was frequently at odds with Jalal Talibani, whose ideological position was much closer to the Baathist ideas of socialism and Arab unity. Moreover, over the years, Baathist regimes have tried to meet Kurdish demands by offering limited autonomy and equality in treatment of Arabs and Kurds; thus, the Kurds' demands were largely ignored by outside powers.

Gamal Abdel Nasser emerged as the undisputed leader of the Arab world in the mid-1950s by emphasizing pan-Arabism. This strategy also worked against Kurdish demands for recognition as a distinct ethnic group and their quest for special rights in predominantly Arab lands. Pan-Arabism stresses the unity of Arabs and favors social reforms but does not recognize special ethnic group rights. The union of Syria and Egypt in 1958 led to Kurdish repression in Syria. Thousands of Kurds were stripped of their citizenship, and some Kurds were expelled.

Until the 1990s the Talibani faction dealt more easily with Iraq and other regimes that were favorably inclined toward Arab unity. His ideological left leanings and his willingness to accept Arab Kurdish brotherhood put him at odds with many of Barzani's followers but ingratiated him to the Baathist regime. After 1991 external alliances shifted, as detailed in Chapter 3. Barzani's KDP sought Baghdad's military support to oust Talibani from the Kurdish Regional Government's capital, while Talibani's PUK sought Iranian support. The point seems to be that, where political survival is at stake, power trumps ideology.

Some Kurdish groups have been adversely affected by the revival of Islamic fundamentalism. Although most are Sunnis, who adhere to the Shafi'i school of jurisprudence, some are mainstream Shi'is. About 100,000, most of whom live in Iraq, are adherents of Yazidism, which is not recognized by Islamic religious authorities as part of the umma (community of believers). Others are Alevis (living largely in Turkey), an offshoot of Shi'ism that is also rejected by many pious Muslims. Although among themselves Kurds consider their Kurdishness to be the cornerstone of their identity, Arab regimes have sometimes persecuted Yazidis because of their unorthodox practices and beliefs. With the emergence of more radical factions among Sunni and Shi'i fundamentalists, religious identity may prove to be a greater issue for Kurds and Arabs than has previously been the case and may lead to future command conflict between them.

External Support for Iraq

The Soviet Union was the main weapons supplier for Iraq prior to the Iran-Iraq War; France was a secondary source. The Soviets disapproved of Iraq's invasion of Iran and briefly interrupted arms deliveries but soon once again became Iraq's main supplier of weapons.

Iraq had seen itself as part of the Arab rejection front, which consisted of the Arab countries determined to settle Arab claims against Israel through military means. In the past this hostility had added to Iraq's status in the eyes of many Arab states, and this had often translated into tangible support in the form of hard currency and increased trade. After the collapse of the Soviet Union and the Iraqi invasion of Kuwait, however, Iraq became the pariah state of the Mideast. The Islamic Conference—the international organization that represents all states with significant Islamic populations—indirectly supported the international coalition forces by discrediting Saddam, who tried to declare his war a religious war against the West and their Arab supporters. NATO's logistical support and the UN legitimization of the use of force clearly marked a turning point in Iraqi's position in the world.

The Current Climate

Iraqis pariah status after Desert Storm was crystal clear. Sanctions against Iraq remained in place until 2003. Iraqi aircraft were prohibited from flying in large zones in the north and south, a prohibition enforced through almost daily flyovers by U.S. and British aircraft and frequent attacks on Iraqi air defense systems. UN weapons inspectors who verified the destruction of Iraq's nuclear, biological, and chemical weapon systems remained in the country until they were ousted in 1998. The regime countered sanctions by seeking international political support. By the mid-1990s some states and public opinion in the Middle East and Europe challenged the legitimacy of keeping sanctions in place. The country's per capita income had declined sharply and its reported infant mortality rate was the highest in the Arab world. In 1996, as a result, the United Nations authorized the "oil for food program," which allowed Iraq to export a significant amount of oil for humanitarian purposes. These exports, plus earnings from the sale of oil that was already being exported clandestinely, gave the regime ample resources to import food, medical supplies, and other necessities, but it had different priorities. Much of the proceeds were used to rebuild its military capabilities and to provide luxury goods for the elite.[4] In fall 2002 the United States began a diplomatic campaign against the Saddam Hussein regime, prompted by the suspicion that he supported Islamist terrorism against the West and was again developing weapons of mass destruction. A UN Security Council resolution backed the return of weapons inspectors who, in the short time they were present, found no smoking gun to confirm U.S. suspicions. Nonetheless the United States and Britain pushed ahead with plans for an invasion that began in March 2003, ousted the Baathist regime, and ended all significant military resistance within three weeks.

The status of all actors in the conflict changed as a result of the war. Since the invasion was opposed by the French, German, and Russian governments—among others—and not sanctioned by the UN Security Council, the U.S. and British governments are being sharply criticized by their longtime allies. A diplomatic fight is under way in which the UN, and continental European powers are trying to assert their right to play a major role in reconstructing Iraq, and to continue controlling sales of Iraqi oil under the "oil for food" program or its successor. Islamic countries in the region are secure from future Iraqi attacks, but also have a deep sense of disappointment and humiliation about what they see as a Western assault on Islam and a return to colonial rule. This may inspire new recruits for militant Islamist movements and provoke internal uprisings against Muslim rulers, for example, in Saudi Arabia and the Gulf states, whom many Arabs view as pawns of the West.[5]

Iraq's future status, as well as the status of the U.S. and Britain, will depend on the political reconstruction of Iraq. Some requisites for success are already clear. A representative, federal system is needed with sufficient powers and resources in the hands of the Baghdad government to keep the Kurdish minority from seceding and the Shi'i majority from aligning too closely with Iran. The new institutions should be devised and run by Iraqis, with the U.S. giving up its tutelary role within a year or two. The oil industry should be seen to be managed in the interests of the new Iraqi government and people. The UN and regional powers such as Turkey should play a substantial role in the process of national reconstruction. And, elsewhere in the region, it is essential that substantial progress be made toward a permanent settlement of the Palestinian-Israeli conflict. As a result Israel is under renewed international pressure to negotiate a final settlement with the Palestinian Authority, first, because the United States and Britain need to defuse criticism from Arab countries and, second, because the Palestinian Authority has a new prime minister, Mahmoud Abbas, also know as Abu Mazin, who is widely seen as a more acceptable negotiating partner than President Yasser Arafat.

External Support for the Kurds

The shah of Iran, the United States, and Israel began to give tangible support to Barzani's Kurdish Democratic Party (KDP) during the 1960s as a way of maintaining pressure on the Iraqi regime. In the wake of the nationalization of the British-owned Iraq Petroleum Company in 1972, the U.S. government promised greater support to the Barzani forces that would be channeled through Iran.

Despite a formal agreement in 1970 that gave the Kurds some control over their own affairs in Iraq's northern Kurdish-dominated provinces, Barzani thought he could gain more by fighting. He was undoubtedly encouraged by what he perceived as continuing strong foreign interest in, and support for, his goals of internal autonomy and eventual independence, and he greatly overestimated these states' willingness to supply him with sophisticated weapons to fight the Baathist regime in Baghdad. Although Barzani had secured some heavy guns and missiles, he was unable to secure victory. Reports that Barzani accepted help from Israel seem well-founded but were never acknowledged because any support that could be traced to Israel would have discredited the Kurds in the eyes of Arab and Muslim states.[6]

Soviet prompting and Arab mediation led to a meeting between the shah and Saddam Hussein (then vice president of Iraq) in Algiers in 1975 to settle officially Iraq's claim to the Shatt-al-Arab waterway. Iraq eventually accepted the Thalweg line (that is, the middle of the river) partition.[7] The more important consequence of the conference was a tacit understanding that Iran would immediately cease supporting Barzani forces and would ask its allies, especially the United States, to follow suit. The immediate termination of support led to the collapse of the Kurdish rebellion.

During the Iran-Iraq War, the Kurds intermittently launched their own revolts in border areas. In the later stages of the war, the Kurds, supplied by Iran with heavy guns and missiles, held their own against the Iraqi forces but were unable to secure victory. At times KDP forces supported Iranian efforts in Iraqi provinces, whereas Talibani's forces actively cooperated with regular Iraqi forces to supply Kurdish fighters inside Iran. The infighting between Kurdish pro-Talibani and pro-Barzani forces, combined with the raids by members of the Kurdish Worker's Party (PKK), who were fighting for independence from Turkey, did little to promote the cause of an autonomous Kurdish region. KDP support for Iran was especially costly for the Kurds. Internally, the Baghdad regime responded by razing thousands of villages, forcefully relocating tens of thousands of Kurds to the south of Iraq, and eventually using chemical weapons. Internationally, the Kurds' pro-Iranian stance probably reduced sympathy for their plight.

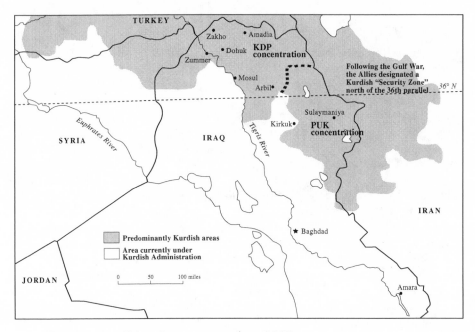

MAP 7.1   Kurdish autonomous region, 2003.

Only after Iraq invaded and then was forced out of Kuwait in 1990 and 1991 did the fortunes of the Kurds change. Encouraged by what they perceived as signs of imminent support, Kurds of all factions openly rebelled in March 1991. Early successes turned into defeat when the coalition forces failed to support Kurdish fighters. Hundreds of thousands of Kurds fled into the border areas of Turkey and Iran; thousands died along the way. In response to this immense human suffering the United Nations passed Resolution 688, which provided a safe haven for Kurdish refugees north of the 36th parallel (see Map 7.1). The Iraqi government very reluctantly agreed to the positioning of UN personnel in this zone.

THE KURDISH SITUATION IN SPRING 2003

In the aftermath of the U.S. and British invasion the Kurds have a higher status and enjoy greater international support than at perhaps any time in the past. The Kurdish Regional Government has a well-established civil administration, military, schools, and health services, all financed by oil revenues and taxes on trade. It has a democratically elected parliament that could serve as a model for the rest of Iraq. During the invasion

Kurdish fighters cooperated with U.S. Special Forces in taking control of Kirkuk, Mosul, and other northern cities abandoned by Iraqi troops. Kurdish authorities moved quickly to put an end to most looting and intimidation that began in the immediate aftermath of the Iraqi collapse. The leaders of the two main Kurdish factions, the PDK and PUK, have hammered out a common position on the future of Iraq that emphasizes their commitment to remaining in a democratic, federal state. Their show of moderation, along with U.S. political pressure, has thus far dissuaded the Turkish government from sending large numbers of troops into northern Iraq.

International views about the Iraqi Kurds remain ambivalent. The U.S. needs them as active participants in a reconstructed Iraq but has long been worried that post-Saddam Iraq may fragment into three parts, adding to long-term instability in the region. Turkey is even more deeply concerned that de facto independence for Iraqi Kurdistan will encourage Turkish Kurds to renew their secessionist rebellion. Much of the international support for the Kurds will disappear if any of three things happen: (1) resumption of divisive rivalry between the PUK and PDK; (2) unilateral moves by Kurds to extend the authority of their regional government to Kirkuk, Mosul, and nearby oil fields; or (3) Kurdish moves toward complete autonomy from Iraq.

INTERNATIONAL CONTEXT OF THE MISKITO CONFLICT

The International Environment

The conflict between the Miskitos and the Sandinistas was, at the highest level of abstraction, one between two global movements: a new movement that advocated indigenous rights to land and respect for the environment and an older one that sought rapid modernization within a classless society. Miskitos were among the charter members of the new indigenous rights movement; the Sandinistas were perhaps the last political movement anywhere in the world to win a revolution inspired by nineteenth-century Marxist ideals. From the Miskitos' point of view, the Sandinista program implied that revolutionaries would determine how their land and resources were developed and for whose benefit; it also foreshadowed pressures for assimilation into a homogeneous national society. From the Sandinistas' perspective, Miskito claims were an obstacle to their economic plans and their vision of a classless society. There were grounds for political compromise between the two: The Sandinistas were sympathetic to people who claimed a history of exploitation by outsiders; the Miskitos wanted the benefits of some revolutionary social and economic programs.

But the fundamental values of the two groups were antithetical. Recognition of the underlying conflict of values by leaders on both sides contributed to the breakdown of initial efforts at cooperation.

At the political level, the Miskitos were unintentionally caught up in the last stages of superpower competition between the United States and the Soviet bloc. Two general principles shaped U.S. policy in the Caribbean during the Cold War. The first was the 1823 Monroe Doctrine, a presidential message to Congress, which included the principle that U.S. foreign policy was directed toward minimizing European intervention in the Western Hemisphere. The second principle was the 1947 Truman Doctrine, another presidential message, which stated that it was U.S. policy to contain the expansion of Communist influence anywhere in the world. The existence of a Soviet-supported Communist regime in Cuba after 1959 was a widely feared threat to U.S. security interests during the 1960s and 1970s. The Cubans fueled U.S. concerns by providing political support, military training, arms, and advisers to Marxist revolutionary movements throughout Latin America and the Caribbean. The Cuban threat was used to justify extensive U.S. military and economic assistance to regimes throughout Latin America and the Caribbean that were thought to be susceptible to Communist insurgencies.

The Nicaraguan Regime's Status and Support

Between 1960 and 1979 no Marxist- or Cuban-supported insurgency came close to toppling a non-Communist government in the Western Hemisphere. Then came the Sandinista revolution in Nicaragua, which overthrew one of the most blatantly corrupt regimes in the region. The Sandinista revolution was homegrown and was supported by a broad spectrum of Nicaraguan society, including much of the middle class and the business community, but many Sandinista leaders were sympathetic to Marxist ideals. During their first year in power the Sandinistas had the cautious support of the Carter administration, which, along with Mexico, Canada, and a number of Western European states, began to supply aid. They also received medical, educational, and technical advisers from Cuba plus increasing amounts of economic and military assistance from the USSR.

The international attention given to Nicaragua was a consequence of its revolution, not of its economic status. Nicaragua was one of the poorest and most heavily indebted countries in Central America. Agricultural goods such as coffee, cotton, sugar, bananas, seafood, and meats accounted for over 80 percent of Nicaragua's export earnings. At the outset the regime attracted the support of both Western and Marxist governments, which sympathized with its populist policies. But Western and especially U.S. support declined in proportion to increased support from the Soviet bloc.

When the Reagan administration took office in January 1981, its senior officials were convinced that the Sandinistas had become the instrument of Communist expansion in the Western Hemisphere. Sandinista support from Cuba and the USSR, expropriation of large landholdings, and cancellation of foreign concessions—many held by North American firms—were seen as steps toward turning Nicaragua into another Cuba. The new administration almost immediately began to use the CIA to channel support to the Contras, opponents of the Sandinistas who included members of the defeated Somoza National Guard plus disillusioned former supporters of the Sandinistas. The Reagan administration also imposed a trade embargo against Nicaragua and used U.S. influence to block international development aid. In 1983 and 1984 the United States clandestinely mined Nicaraguan ports to discourage ships that ignored the embargo. In 1984 the Sandinista government brought a suit against the United States because of the mining to the International Court of Justice, which first ordered the United States to stop the mining and later ruled that Nicaragua could sue for damages. However, the Reagan administration rejected the decisions on grounds that the court had no jurisdiction in this case and that the U.S. Congress had determined that the Nicaraguan government was supplying military support to groups attempting to overthrow other governments in the region.[8]

The Miskitos' International Status and Support

By early 1982 it was widely known that the United States was organizing and supporting a substantial and expanding guerrilla war against the Sandinistas from bases in Honduras. The cooperation of the Honduran government and military in this effort was secured by substantial U.S. aid. Some of the 25,000 Miskitos who fled to Honduras were resettled there with assistance from the UN High Commission for Refugees; others were recruited into CIA-supported Indian armies that soon were fighting a widespread guerrilla campaign in eastern Nicaragua.

From the perspective of the Reagan administration, support for the Miskitos was justified by the larger objective of crippling the Sandinista regime rather than by any sympathy for the indigenous rights movement. Brooklyn Rivera, leader of the Costa Rican–based MISURASATA faction, sought out individuals and organizations sympathetic to the movement in Ottawa, Geneva, and Washington, where he gained the attention of Senator Edward Kennedy and other members of Congress and the support of advocacy organizations like the Indian Law Resource Center. Later, when Rivera began MISURASATA's 1984–1985 round of negotiations with Sandinista officials, he was accompanied by interested observers from indigenous peoples' organizations.

Effects of International Linkages

International pressures contributed directly and materially to the negotiated settlement of the Miskitos' war with the Sandinistas. By 1984 the Nicaraguan economy was beginning to be badly hurt by the effects of U.S. economic pressure and the costs of fighting the Contras and their Indian allies. It was estimated that the total economic cost of U.S. actions against Nicaragua during this period was $3.7 billion, an enormous burden for a poor country. From 1983 on the Sandinistas were also under diplomatic and political pressures from other Central American states, known as the Contadora group, who sought to initiate a regional peace process that would bridge the gap between the U.S. and Nicaraguan governments. The Sandinistas and the Reagan administration both rejected these regional efforts at first, but they were revived in 1987 by Costa Rica's president, Oscar Arias. This time the efforts led to negotiations in 1988 between the Sandinistas and Contra representatives and to a peace agreement, grudgingly accepted by the Bush administration, that culminated in the 1990 elections, which the Sandinistas unexpectedly lost.[9]

By the time of the Arias initiative, the Miskito-Sandinista conflict was well on its way to settlement, because the Miskitos wanted to return to their villages and the Sandinistas wanted to reduce U.S.-supported military pressures. When negotiations reached a stalemate, both sides accepted the mediation of a respected outsider, Jimmy Carter, to overcome the final obstacles to agreement. It is also important to call attention to what did *not* happen. Despite U.S. encouragement of the faction led by Steadman Fagoth to continue fighting, all Miskito leaders eventually accepted the terms of the agreement.

THE INTERNATIONAL CONTEXT OF
THE CHINESE COMMUNIST INSURGENCY IN MALAYA

In Chapter 4 we observed that the Chinese uprising that became known as the Emergency was one of many insurrections that swept Southeast Asia after World War II. One can argue that the movement, although Communist-inspired, was part of the worldwide struggle of colonial peoples to drive out colonial powers.

Characteristics of the International System During the Malay Emergency: The Players

Under President Harry Truman's leadership the United States eagerly supported British efforts to contain civil war in Greece in 1946 and 1947 and later backed the French in the first Vietnam War on the perception that the Communist states were actively pursuing hegemonic interests in the Far East and in Europe. The Truman Doctrine, which was prompted by the civil war in Greece, provided the rationale for future Western interventions. It was now U.S. policy "to support free people who are resisting attempted subjugation by armed minorities or outside pressures." Unfortunately, the "freedom fighters" in Greece, who were actively supported by Britain, with U.S. encouragement, consisted largely of reactionary forces—including former supporters of the Nazis—who were fighting an indigenous Communist movement that received no encouragement from Stalin.

The Soviet Union under Stalin's leadership had its own hegemonic agenda. Stalin's aspirations clearly went far beyond the Soviet Union's borders, as is shown by the Soviet involvement in the Berlin crises, the use of Soviet forces to suppress a popular uprising in East Germany (1953), and indirect Soviet involvement in the Communist coup in Czechoslovakia (1948). The USSR already had a presence in Mainland China (Port Arthur), had bases on former Japanese islands (the Kurile Islands and South Sakhalin), and effectively controlled Outer Mongolia. This presence eventually came to be seen in the same light as U.S. imperialism.

Tangible Soviet involvement in Third World politics was limited to Korea, where during the Korean War the Soviets supplied North Korea with aircraft and weapons, and to China, where support was provided to the Communists in the last phases of civil war. The effect of Soviet support during Israel's war of independence was diminished by its simultaneous support of Syria. Ho Chi Minh received little support during Vietnam's war for independence. Tangible support was seldom given, partly because the Soviets were unable to provide it but also because they were ambivalent about the nationalist-Communist struggles of colonial peoples in the Far East. Thus, support was usually limited to advice and encouragement.

At the onset of the insurgency in Malaya, the Chinese Communists were in the midst of a civil war that was not won until 1949. Moreover, they had few hegemonic interests. Traditionally, China has taken its preeminent role in Asia for granted, and it did not forcefully colonize adjacent territories. It only took or attempted to take what it considered to be the ancestral lands of the Chinese people, broadly understood, including Tibet in 1959. It also claimed territory acquired by czarist Russia through a series of unequal treaties from the mid-eighteenth century onward. The Chinese did provide material support to the Vietnamese nationalists against the French but not to the Malay Communist Party.

Regime Status: Britain After World War II

When the Cold War began, Britain tried to maintain its prominent status within the emerging Western alliance. Becoming embroiled in colonial wars was not popular with its U.S. supporters; Britain also lacked the ability and the interest to engage in protracted struggles in the hinterlands of the British Empire.

As we have argued previously, mainland Malaya was never fully colonized as India or Singapore had been, and Britain was committed to granting Malaya its independence. For the British, the Communists were just one more obstacle in their plan to introduce democracy, power-sharing, and a parliamentary form of government into Malaya. Progressive British policies, such as opening European clubs for Asians, encouraging non-Malays to join the civil service, and creating federation regiments that included all races, increased public sympathy for the British. In the early 1950s communal tensions were further mitigated through the able leadership of Tunku Abdul Rahman, who, with Indian and Chinese cooperation and British prompting, worked out a formula that provided the base for political stability. Under the agreement Chinese economic leadership and Malay political predominance were implicitly recognized.

The Status of the Challengers: Chinese Communists

The Chinese community in post–World War II Malaya was far from cohesive. A large number of Chinese in Malaya were relatively recent arrivals, and many did not envision Malaya becoming their permanent home. During the civil war in China in the 1940s, many had fled to await a Kuomintang victory or at least an end to the struggle. With the impending Communist victory in the late 1940s, however, most chose to stay in Malaya or, if they were prosperous enough, to emigrate to the West.

In contrast, Malaya was home for the Straits Chinese and for most second-generation and third-generation Chinese, who were descendants of laborers recruited to Malaya with the promise of a better life. Fighting colonial authorities made little sense to Chinese who were recuperating from an oppressive Japanese occupation. In their eyes the returning British authorities brought order, a limited sense of security, and a commitment to democratic principles. In 1946 talks were under way to establish a parliamentary form of government, which soon became independent.

The Communists, ironically, had been the backbone of the anti-Japanese resistance and, thus, were respected by the larger Chinese community and returning British authorities. Because of their British training and guerrilla activities during the war, they were the only fighting force capable of resisting the Japanese occupier and, later, the British colonizers. Emboldened by the emerging Communist victory in China and facing an uncertain future as an ethnic minority among Malay Muslims and their autocratic leaders, the Malayan Communists refused to surrender their arms when the British returned. Instead they chose to follow the Chinese Communist model by fighting for national liberation and an end to feudal rule. The party followed shifting political strategies. In the eyes of the rebels the emerging federation of Malayan states gave the sultans unequal shares of power, granted few citizen rights to the Chinese, and ignored Chinese sacrifices during the war. In 1947, after the British authorities had outlawed them, they embraced armed struggle, but their struggles were far from displaying the militancy of Communist movements elsewhere.

The Communists were part of a larger nationalist-socialist-Communist movement that made anticolonial slogans part of its ideological arsenal without necessarily advocating the violent overthrow of colonial regimes. Most Chinese viewed anticolonial struggles with anxiety, despite their sometimes discriminatory treatment by the British authorities. Thus, the Communist insurgents had little support among the Chinese community in Malaya, but they nonetheless chose to fight the British and Malayan authorities for both ideological and political reasons.

External Support for the Regime

Britain's status as one of the World War II victors was secure. Although the United States tacitly disapproved of the preservation of colonial empires, it nevertheless actively supported colonial powers fighting insurgents, such as the French during the first phase of the Vietnam War. In Malaya, however, Britain did not need, nor did it ask, for outside support. Instead it relied on the cooperation of Malays and of some Chinese to design and carry out an effective counterinsurgency campaign, some of the elements of which—like the hamlet resettlement policy—influenced U.S. policy during its phase of the Vietnam War.

External Support for Chinese Communists

The Malayan Communists evidently received little support from China, despite Chinese Communist meetings with their Chinese Malayan counterparts. As was typical, the Chinese Communists rarely offered more than verbal support, in part because of their inability to do so at a stage when they were busy building their own base. Moscow's role was even more uncertain. The Soviet Union, taken by surprise by revolutionary activities in colonial dependencies, verbally supported the so-called national liberation struggles against imperialism but did little else immediately following World War II.

Because of British policy, lack of support among fellow Chinese, and lack of external support, the Communists had to rely exclusively on their own resources to support their campaign. The high status they initially held with Chinese Malay peasants quickly dissipated because of their harsh treatment of Chinese suspected of collaborating with the British. Lacking clear ideological commitments and fighting ability, they attracted little support from either the emerging People's Republic of China or the Soviet Union. In the late 1950s the remnants of the movement, lacking external support and internal credibility, retreated toward the border areas of Thailand. Their campaign wound down, becoming little more than armed banditry.

MALAYSIA FROM INDEPENDENCE TO THE PRESENT

What we know now is Malaysia emerged in 1966. It included Sabah and Sarawak on the island of Borneo, separated from the peninsula by 400 miles of ocean. For two years the new state also included Singapore, which withdrew with the blessing of the Malaysian regime two years later. Malay leaders were relieved at its departure, because in the absence of Chinese-dominated Singapore the Malays were a clear majority. Malaysia's richness in raw materials (tin, copper, petroleum, natural gas, bauxite, and iron ore) led to a boom economy with an average growth rate of 5–8 percent per year after 1970. When the Asian currency crisis hit Malaysia in 1998, its economy recovered faster than expected, thanks to its export-oriented strategy. However, gaps remain between urban and rural development, income is unevenly distributed among ethnic groups—Malays and Indians are typically poorer than Chinese—and environmental neglect plus corruption in the federal government have led to increasing unrest among the people. In 2000 Prime Minister Mahathir's deputy prime minister, Ibrahim, was arrested, accused of dubious moral conduct, beaten and imprisoned, reducing the government's popularity to an all-time low. Because it restricts the formation of labor unions for blue-collar workers and limits the free flow of information, Malaysia's reputation abroad as an up-and-coming democracy has equally suffered. However, its commitment to the region as an active member of the Association of Southeast Asian Nations (ASEAN), its openness to foreign investment, and moderate position on Islamic issues, may compensate for its decline in political legitimacy in Western eyes.

The Chinese Challengers

Now as in the past ethnic Chinese are politically underrepresented and economically advantaged. How long this pattern will persist is difficult to say. Declining Chinese birthrates and rising birthrates among Muslim

Malays are likely to reduce further the political clout of the Chinese. The basic problem is the so-called birthright of Malays. Before independence the Chinese leadership supposedly accepted, in exchange for citizenship, the predominance of ethnic Malays in the future state. It is only rational to assume that no leadership would agree to accept permanent second-class citizenship, and surely the bargain was off as soon as Malays had achieved some measure of economic parity. At present, however, Malay political leaders have erected political barriers to negotiating a "New Deal" for the Chinese. The reasons may lie in the fact that Malays are still somewhat worse off than their Chinese counterparts, and that Malays by and large are unwilling to give up their birthright advantages. A contributing factor may be the growing threat to the democratic state posed by Islamic parties; one example is the Party Islam Malaysia (PAS), which wants to build an Islamic state based on Shari'a (Islamic law) with few or no special rights for non-Muslims.

External support varies for the Chinese. On the one hand the People's Republic of China (PRC) has always regarded its overseas ethnic brethren as part of the larger community of Chinese, yet in times of crisis has not always supported them. The Cambodian regime of Pol Pot had strong support from the PRC despite killing many ethnic Chinese. On the other hand the PRC supported its ethnic brethren when they were persecuted by the Communist regime in Vietnam. At present the PRC actively establishes cultural ties with its overseas community and encourages prosperous Chinese to retire in the PRC. Taiwan and Singapore, the other two predominantly Chinese states in the region, have kept a watchful eye on the treatment of ethnic Chinese in Malaysia. Given that both are important trading partners for Malaysia, this may strengthen the Chinese in their relations with Malays. On the other hand neighboring Indonesia, the largest Muslim country in the world, has consistently discriminated against its Chinese community, targeting them with genocidal killings after a failed Communist-led coup in 1965, and with urban riots and killings in 2000.

We think that the situation of the Chinese in Malaysia is precarious. Economic uncertainty, the risks of further Islamization, and undemocratic practices point to an uncertain future for ethnic Chinese in Malaysia.

THE INTERNATIONAL CONTEXT OF MINORITY ISSUES IN GERMANY

The influx of refugees in the early 1990s was not just a German problem, but it had a greater impact on Germany than on other countries in the European Union. The number of refugees and asylum seekers entering the ten principal host countries in Europe more than tripled between 1987 and 1991. By 1991 Germany was receiving more than double the numbers going to France and the United Kingdom combined. Asylum seekers in Germany reached a peak of 400,000 in 1992.

As a result of its economic interdependence and residual concerns about its pariah status at the end of World War II, Germany was highly vulnerable to international pressures and criticisms concerning domestic political issues, especially regarding the status of immigrants and refugees. In fact, much of the crisis in Germany in the early 1990s over refugees and immigrants was a consequence of laws and policy that guaranteed temporary asylum to anyone claiming to be a political refugee. This policy, which was among the most liberal in the world, was a legacy of Germany's attempt to atone for its past.

German sensitivity concerning the status of immigrants and refugees is reinforced by international scrutiny—by other European states, by the media, and by nongovernmental organizations (NGOs) that monitor human rights performance and political extremism. Thus, neo-Nazi and skinhead attacks on refugees and Turks have been widely and thoroughly reported and criticized outside Germany. In early 1993 Chancellor Helmut Kohl's office took the unusual step of distributing to all German embassies and foreign correspondents a thick handbook that acknowledged the problem of antiforeigner attacks and summarized the government's efforts to deal with them. It also recognized Germany's special obligation in the statement that "there's no injustice in judging Germany more harshly and more emotionally than other states when it comes to the protection of democracy and human rights."[10]

Nonetheless Germany amended its Basic Law in 1993 to slow the influx of refugees. The impact was substantial. By 1995 the number of new asylum seekers reaching Germany had declined to 95,000, and, in subsequent years, far more requests for asylum were denied than accepted. Criticism from other European states has been muted, first because they themselves face domestic pressures to reduce entry of refugees and other immigrants from outside the European Union, second because all members of the union actively cooperate in efforts to regulate migration. Thus Germany was able to move toward more restrictive policies by coordinating its policies with those of other European states. At the same time, German government and society are committed to principles of equal treatment of minorities already resident in Germany. The most substantial evidence of this was the new Nationality Code of 2000, which has made it easier for Turks and other longtime non-German residents to gain citizenship.

Regime Status and External Support

Germany has high international economic status; it ranks in the top 5 percent on all indicators of development, including per capita gross national product, capital formation, value of trade, levels of education, and so forth. Its political status, however, is lower than would be predicted based on economic status alone. Burdened by its Nazi past, the German government avoids involvement in international conflicts, especially those that might lead to military action. Its Basic Law, the equivalent of a constitution, has prohibited German participation in military or peace-keeping actions, except to defend itself and its allies. The first clear break from this prohibition occurred in 1999, when German forces joined NATO's campaign to end the Serbian campaign of ethnic cleansing targeted against ethnic Albanians in Kosovo. Germany's political stature is clearly increasing.

The Status of the Turkish Minority and External Support

The Turkish minority, by contrast, has little intrinsic international status. Since relatively few of its members intend to resettle in Turkey, the Turkish government has less reason to be concerned with their welfare than it had in the past. Moreover, the Turkish government hopes to gain full membership in the EU and, thus, is reluctant to take positions that might antagonize one of that organization's leading members. On the other hand representatives of the German and Turkish labor ministries hold regular consultations aimed at improving the status of Turks in Germany.

As observed above, the status of refugees and foreigners in Germany is widely recognized as one specific instance of a common European problem. In 1993 the last restrictions were lifted on the movement of citizens of European Union countries within the community; foreigners are still subject to checks, but many can and do take advantage of open borders. Hostility toward refugees and visible minorities has increased simultaneously throughout Europe. The greater the proportion of visible minorities and refugees in a country, the more antiforeign sentiment is likely to be a serious issue. Most European governments are moving on tracks parallel to Germany's: They are restricting new immigration and asylum seekers from outside Europe and are accelerating efforts to incorporate those who are already residents. But if these policies are not fully coordinated, one European country's solution can add to its neighbors' problems.

CONCLUSION

In conclusion, we summarize briefly how the international system affects each of the four groups and assess their current status with respect to governing regimes. It is evident that over time the Kurds were drawn into the superpower contest in the Middle East, became pawns in regional realignments, participated indirectly in the Arab-Israeli conflict, played a part in the pan-Arab movement, and were subject to divisions among themselves. At present the Kurds enjoy significant support from the international community, but their future status depends on how constructively they participate in U.S.-led efforts to develop a new Iraqi polity. They are welcome allies only as long as they avoid seizing contested areas in northern Iraq and remain loyal to the Iraqi state.

What are the prospects for communal tensions in Malaysia in the 1990s? The anti-Chinese riots of 1969, in which a number of Chinese and Malays were killed, were an aberration in an otherwise relatively stable semi democracy. At times the Malaysian quest for stability undermines the preservation of civil rights. Freedom of information is curtailed, and harsh punishments are meted out for those who advocate controversial views. The political formula that guarantees preferential treatment to Malays in all government jobs, the military, and universities amounts to discrimination. However, the formula, which is commonly referred to as "positive discrimination," helps to hold the nation together. In Western states, this formula exists in the form of quota systems for minorities, women, the handicapped, and other disadvantaged groups—for better or worse, it is a widely used strategy for improving the lot of those who have traditionally been disenfranchised and disadvantaged.

Because of Malaysia's relatively high level of economic development the country enjoys high international status, though its political legitimacy has been undercut by the authoritarian practices of its prime minister. Typically, high-status countries are watched closely by the outside world and are scrutinized for impending internal troubles, if only to ensure stable economic relationships. The Chinese still control a large share of Malaysia's finance and trade. But susceptibility to world opinion and economic influence may not be enough to deter Malay politicians from further restricting Chinese rights, especially in light of growing Islamist influence.

The Miskitos' armed conflict with the Nicaraguan state ended with a political settlement that was not fully implemented. The regional council of autonomous Yapti Tasba remains at odds with the Nicaraguan government over the control of resource development. What the peoples of the Atlantic Coast need most is money. The flood of international support that was supplied to the government, the Contras, and the Miskitos during the 1980s has virtually dried up. Neither the Managua government nor the Yapti Tasba councils have attracted sufficient public or private aid to meet the needs of the region.

The German government is constrained in how it deals with its Turkish and other immigrant minorities. The country's high economic performance is dependent upon a dense network of commercial and financial ties with other states; it has a high volume of foreign trade with a multitude of customers, and its economy is closely linked to the economies of

TABLE 7.1 Summary of international factors in ethnic mobilization for four groups.

Variables	Kurds in Iraq (2002)	Miskitos (1970s)	Chinese in Malaysia (2002)	Turks in Germany (2002)
External support for group	Limited and dependent upon shifts in regional and international alignments	Limited to political support from indigenous movement, U.S. support for insurgency	Very limited during 1950s insurgency, none since	Minor diplomatic support from Turkish government, some symbolic support from human rights NGOs
Status of regime Economic	Medium but badly weakened by Iran-Iraq War and Gulf War	Very low	Medium because of resources, strong economic performance	Very high but subject to European Union constraits
Political	Low to medium before Gulf War, a pariah state after the war	Low because U.S. opposition outweighed support from socialist states	Strategic and economic importance is weakened by autocratic tendencies and Islamization	High and increasing
Status of ethnic challengers	Low before Gulf War, higher after the war because of strategic and humanitarian concerns	Very low before and after the Contra war, higher during the war because of U.S. support	None because they are not recognized as challenges outside Malaysia	Low to medium because of European Union and international concerns

the other European Union states. Moreover, Germany depends heavily on imports of oil and other raw materials, which means it must maintain good relations with the oil-producing countries of the Middle East and with Third World sources of other primary products. Evidence of this sensitivity is seen in the fact that Germany ranks third among the world's foreign aid donors and allots a quarter of its aid to the least developed countries.

We documented in Chapter 4 the existence in Germany of negative attitudes toward immigrants and refugees. If these attitudes were translated directly into public policy, the status and prospects of the Turks and other visible minorities would not be good. There are two main guarantees of improved status for minorities in Germany. First are the political and civil rights provided for all citizens in Germany's Basic Law. Germany's mainstream politicians are strongly committed to protecting and promoting these rights. Second are the international scrutiny and pressures focused on Germany, to which its policymakers remain highly susceptible. Germany's rising political status in European and world affairs depends in part on domestic politics toward its minorities that are beyond reproach.

DISCUSSION QUESTIONS

Review the comparisons in Table 7.1 as the first step in answering these questions.

1. What factors determine changing patterns of international support for the Iraqi Kurds?
2. What political institutions would you recommend for a post-Baathist Iraq to balance the interests of the Kurds, other communal groups in the country, and the international actors that have a stake in Iraq's future?
3. How important was the U.S.-supported Contra war against the Sandinistas in helping the Miskitos achieve autonomy?
4. Can you foresee any circumstances, however unlikely, in which the Chinese Malaysians might attract more external support or concern?
5. Since Germany's international economic and political status is high, why should its policymakers be concerned about international reactions to attacks on Turks and other foreigners?

8

Ethnic Groups in the International System: State Sovereignty Versus Individual and Group Rights

Ethnic groups have become recognized independent actors in international politics, yet their legal status in international law is dubious. The status of group rights is further complicated or diminished when groups make claims that negate other groups' rights. These tensions may lead to communal conflict or, worse yet, to state repression or genocide. In some cases ethnic conflicts spill over to adjacent territories or contenders become embroiled in hegemonic struggles between external powers. Protracted communal conflicts pose a real threat to international security, as we have seen in Kosovo. Yet despite these dangers, ethnic groups have received only scant attention in international law.

We argue that legal recognition of ethnic groups allows for disputes to be settled in an orderly and civilized fashion. Mechanisms at the disposal of mediators in crisis situations between states could also be applied in dealing with ethnic strife.

Since 1648 states have been the traditional subjects of international law, but in the post-Holocaust era the focus has shifted somewhat to allow for the protection of individual rights vis-à-vis the omnipotent state. In this chapter we argue that it is also necessary to recognize groups as a distinct subject of international law, rather than as an extension of an individual's status as a subject of international law.

LEGAL IMPLICATIONS OF ETHNIC DIVERSITY

Ethnic groups can be divided into several categories, based on distinctions made in Chapter 2. **Ethnonationalists** include all groups that aspire to separate nationhood, in the form of either autonomy within existing states or independence. **Indigenous peoples** also seek autonomy, including control over their traditional lands, resources, and protection of their cultures. **Communal contenders** are minorities who seek greater collective access to

165

power under the law of an existing state. Ethnoclasses and communal contenders peoples share concerns about protecting their cultural traditions as well as fighting for greater economic opportunities and equal political rights. Moreover, some groups define themselves primarily in religious terms and thus may further challenge our conception of what constitutes a group in need of international legal recognition.

Ethnoclasses and communal contenders rarely threaten internal or international security, nor do they mobilize for rebellion to the extent of ethnonationalists or religiously defined groups. Their demands usually can more easily be satisfied by local or national authorities. Group membership is somewhat fluid, members may withdraw support and often do so when their demands are met or conversely when leadership fails to get results. Such groups may not require extensive international legal attention. Existing conventions, protocols, and treaties allow for some if not most of their claims to be dealt with in an equitable fashion, provided a state is signatory to the convention and is willing to abide by the rules. Of course the distances between the rule of law, compliance, and self-enforcement are enormous and constitute a problem inherent in international law, not easily overcome but not an absolute obstacle to peaceful settlement of group claims.

In contrast, ethnonationalists, indigenous peoples, and possibly mobilized religious groups require special status under international law as well as special protection under municipal law (the domestic variant of law). The reasons are complex. On the one side, ethnonationalists and indigenous peoples are a real threat to the continued existence of the territorial state, because they aspire to establish their own state, or demand some form of self-governance within territories of existing states. Mobilized religious groups also may challenge the political system, sometimes aiming to overthrow existing governments and replace them with theocracies. Islamic traditionalists by and large envision governments adhering to shari'a traditions (Islamic law), which poses a threat or at least a challenge to fledgling democracies.

Why have groups been largely overlooked as important and independent actors in international relations? And what accounts for their neglect in international law?

Persons belonging to national, ethnic, religious, and linguistic minorities who reside within sovereign states have always been subjects of municipal law. Thus, when communal groups fought each other without crossing state boundaries, they were engaged by definition in internal conflicts not subject to international law. Once conflict spilled over boundaries, however, the rules of war and peace could be applied to the warring factions. Only with the emergence of laws that granted individuals rights vis-à-vis their states (discussed in subsequent sections) has this invisible threshold of inviolable national boundaries been crossed to allow for third-party intervention. Simultaneously, the emergence of these laws has given rise to claims that groups seeking independence from existing states should be given special legal recognition.

Traditional international principles that deal with the right of secession or self-determination are inadequate to address the avalanche of new group claims to self-rule. In the past new states have come into existence through many routes: **formal recognition** (one of several indicators of statehood), the granting of independence from colonial powers, the dissolution of an empire, mutual consent of two independent states, seizure of independence, or de facto control of a territory. Self-declaration of independence does not automatically carry the right to statehood. One may argue that in such cases rebels could have been offered combatant or belligerent status, but, as Alexis Heraclides pointed out in 1991, "even though a number of insurgents have met the test, none have been accorded such status during the present century." Thus, in situations in which groups have ambitions to secede or to establish internal autonomy, few legal principles exist that could help them bolster their claims vis-à-vis a legally recognized state or, in the case of civil war, bolster one group's claim against that of another.[1]

In civil wars the situation is complicated by the absence of effective, legitimate authorities. These situations require outside observers to seek solutions that resolve competing group claims. The situations in Somalia and the former Yugoslavia may help to illustrate the emerging issues. In both cases the former state ceased to exist as a functioning, effective, legitimate, and legally recognized political entity.

Ethnic groups that we define as communal contenders typically advance claims that do not include autonomy but that include the right to exercise their communal right to share political power as a collectivity. Such requests are habitually treated in international and municipal law as claims of individuals vis-à-vis the state; thus, group rights are not separately recognized.

Collective rights are dealt with summarily as part of the principles that address self-determination of peoples and in the human rights **conventions,** which also stipulate obligations for states. These conventions give states the responsibility to uphold principles of equal treatment under the law and to guarantee bodily integrity, human dignity, freedom from persecution, and similar rights. Violations of such norms enable the international community to punish offenders.

However, at the forty-eighth session of the United Nations Commission on Human Rights on February 21, 1992, the commission approved a draft declaration on the "Rights of Persons Belonging to National or Ethnic, Religious and Linguistic Minorities," which for the first time attempted to give special status to groups under international law. The problem, however, is that the declaration only strengthens the role of the state, insofar as the state is the legal "person" responsible for protecting the rights of minorities. The declaration urges states to fulfill "the obligations and commitments they have assumed under international treaties and agreements to which they are parties." The treaties specifically named are the Universal Declaration of Human Rights, the Convention on the Prevention and Punishment of the Crime of Genocide, the International Convention on the Elimination of All Forms of Racial Discrimination, the International Covenant on Civil and Political Rights, the International Covenant on Economic, Social and Cultural Rights, the Declaration on the Elimination of All Forms of Intolerance and Discrimination Based on Religion or Belief, and the Convention on the Rights of the Child. States that are not signatories to these conventions theoretically could treat their citizens as they wish without fear of outside intervention.

Thus, ethnic groups have few international avenues by which to seek redress of their claims and can do so primarily as individuals seeking protection under existing human rights conventions.

THEORETICAL CONSIDERATIONS: INDIVIDUALS, GROUPS, AND THE STATE

From a theoretical perspective one may argue that states have no independent existence beyond that of individuals; states exist for the express purpose of safeguarding the rights of individuals who have united under the banner of a common heritage, namely, the nation, their ethnicity, or their religion. Such reasoning ignores the role of the modern state, which, through an elaborate network of groups, institutions, and roles, protects its continued existence regardless of the wishes of individual citizens or a national people.

The Treaty of Westphalia, which ended the Thirty Years' War in 1648, marks the beginning of the modern sovereign state and the end of the dominance of the Holy Roman Empire and papal authority. Prior to 1648 individuals typically had multiple allegiances. This could be to a local duke or landgrave, a bishop, the pope, or an emperor. Individual loyalty was rarely bound to a territorial unit, but more often was personalized. However, one can argue that albeit underdeveloped, spatial identity coexisted with personal loyalty to emperor, duke, or pope. After all, prior to 1648 European kingdoms and city states did exist and the Hanseatic League (an organization of city states) could count on the allegiance of its citizenry. With increasing international trade, it became a necessity to regulate commerce and enforce rules, which could only be achieved with local cooperation. The new entrepeneurs did not necessarily rely on personal bonds but instead counted on formal/rational procedures. Thus, with the emergence of the modern state we witness the growth of international law, renewed interests in property laws, and the building of local institutions to accommodate competing political and economic demands.

Was international trade truly the spark that ignited the war that led to the dominance of the secular state in modern Europe? One needs to consider other factors that may have equally contributed to the demise of the Holy Roman Empire, which was presided over by the pope. Disunity within the Roman Catholic Church, the emergence of Protestantism, competing and threatening non-European empires (for example, the Ottomans), all clearly pointed to the declining inability of a large and loosely organized entity to deal with local and external problems in a satisfactory manner. Local dissatisfaction also contributed to the demise of central authority; after all, local leaders typically fought the church's battles, but rarely reaped local benefits from their sacrifices.

After 1648 the sovereign state became the main actor in international relations and law. Although empires coexisted with the European state system, unity in empires was also slowly eroding in favor of smaller, territorial units based on local culture and awakening of ethnic identity rather than religion or loyalty to the emperor.

For nearly 300 years the state was the indisputed subject of international law, and individuals or collectivities were merely objects of the law. However, since World War I, the international community of states has recognized that some minimal protection of individuals is necessary, partially as a result of the tremendous suffering of civilian populations in the wake of the war that introduced mechanized warfare, which became the scourge of the twentieth century. To maintain peace after World War I the League of Nations was founded. Both former U.S. President William Howard Taft and President Woodrow Wilson were strong supporters of the League's aims. Wilson's famous Fourteen Points, which delineated the war aims of the United States during World War I, eventually became the war aims of the Allied powers and also became part of the guiding principles of the League. Despite the absence of the United States (the U.S. never joined), the League became a formidable institution. It was especially active in establishing principles that are today part of public international law such as respect for and preservation of territorial integrity and political independence, collective responsibility, the peaceful settlement of disputes, the establishments of the International Court of Justice (then known as the Permanent Court of International Justice), and the just treatment of non-governing (that is, colonial) peoples. The League also established a Mandate system that, under the tutelage of the advanced states such as Britain and France, prepared non-governing territories for independence. Significant as this may have been, it was perceived by colonial peoples as just another form of domination, because many of the territories were administered as part of the supervising state's territory. But the League's recognition that non-governing peoples essentially have rights to self-determination laid the groundwork for claims that today's ethnonationalists may have legitimate rights to independence.

After World War II and the Holocaust, concerns about individual rights to life and liberty went beyond the minimum protection of minorities within the sovereign domains of the state. But, with the notable exception of the Genocide Convention, discussed below, ethnic group protection was not an issue after 1945 other than as an extension of individual rights.

It is evident that many contemporary ethnic and religious groups are gaining a higher level of group consciousness. They are less likely to accept assimilation with the dominant group, they seek special status simultaneously with nondiscriminatory treatment under civil or international law, and in some cases they want to secede from the territorial state. Such demands are often incompatible with the civic ideal of the state as a heterogeneous social unit that promises equal protection for all its citizens under the law. This is really the crux of the problem. At issue is that minority rights potentially conflict with the cohesion and continued existence of the multiethnic state.

THE CURRENT STATUS OF GROUPS IN THE INTERNATIONAL SYSTEM

The Genocide Convention (1948) is the oldest international document that specifically addresses group rights, although it specifies their violations largely through reference to individuals. For example, in the original text, genocide includes the following: killing *members* of the group and causing serious bodily harm to *members* of the group. Another example of groups as subjects of international law is seen in the internationally recognized prohibition of terrorism, which identifies terrorists as members of identifiable groups.

Few human rights conventions elaborate on group membership. Part of the problem undoubtedly lies in the identification of groups as a separate entity. Is group membership inherently fluid, and can it be changed at will? Or are groups coherent entities that exist in largely unaltered form for extended time periods? What really constitutes a group?

The Genocide Convention specifies four types of groups—national, racial, ethnic, and religious—but avoids any reference to political or gender groups. The UN draft declaration of 1992 identifies national, ethnic, religious, and linguistic minorities and again avoids reference to gender and political groups. Of course, political groups typically have cross-cutting memberships and are more fluid than any of the other groups; they are of lesser concern here because ethnicity is not their primary identifying trait and because they are protected under the covenant that deals with civil and political rights. Recall that, by our definition, ethnic groups may share language, culture, religion, and race in various combinations.

Let us turn briefly to the major European efforts in the 1990s that have contributed to the growing legal attention given to national minorities. Most important are, first, the July 1990 Copenhagen meeting of the Conference on Security and Cooperation in Europe (CSCE); second the November 1990 CSCE Summit in Paris; and third the October 1993 Vienna Summit. These meetings culminated in the framework Convention for the Protection of National Minorities opened for signature by the **Council of Europe** member states on February 1, 1995.

Progress or lack of progress? The Council of Europe no doubt has progressed beyond the standard treatment of group rights as an extension of the rights of individuals. The Copenhagen document affirms the rights of persons belonging to national minorities to

1. exercise their human rights fully without any discrimination
2. use their mother tongue
3. establish and maintain their own cultural, educational and religious institutions
4. practise their religion
5. establish and maintain contacts across frontiers with those with whom they share a common, ethnic or national origin, cultural or religious belief. . . . (articles 31 and 32).

And the list goes on. Equally significant are the obligations of member states.

In article (33) of the Copenhagen document: ". . . states . . . will protect the ethnic, cultural, and linguistic and religious identity of national minorities on their territory and create conditions for the promotion of that identity."

And, in article (40), ". . . states . . . condemn totalitarianism, racial and ethnic hatred, anti-semitism, xenophobia and discrimination against anyone as well as persecution on religious and ideological grounds. In this context, they also recognize the particular problem of the Roma (gypsies)."

The Council of Europe has made it clear that East Central European countries that aspire to full membership in the council are expected to meet these standards as a precondition. Although it appears that these documents are a giant step toward advancing the rights of national minorities—

at least in Europe—problems remain. For example, in the 1995 framework convention

1. there is no explicit definition of national minorities
2. implementation of principles is to be done through national legislation and appropiate government policies
3. identity is a choice, therefore individuals can decide whether or not they want to belong to an identity group and also whether or not to come under the protection of the Convention (article 3, paragraph 34)
4. however, "individuals can not choose . . . arbitrarily to belong to any national minority . . . the choice is inseparably linked to objective criteria relevant to a person's identity" (article 3, paragraph 35)
5. And lastly, (article 37, Copenhagen document) "these commitments . . . cannot be interpreted as any rights to engage . . . in any action in contravention . . . including the principle of territorial integrity of States."

Given the legal status of collectivities prior to 1995 these documents signify a major advance, but probably fall short of what is needed to deal with the full range of aspirations of ethnic groups. Why? First and foremost groups need to be explicitly defined. Clearly it is no secret which groups define themselves in some combination of ethnic, religious, racial, or cultural elements. Recognition of some indigenous groups, such as the many Native American peoples, may be considered too costly in terms of special rights and obligations for states. However, few such groups exist in Europe. Thus, the reluctance to define groups clearly can best be understood as a concession to states, which may enable them to decide which groups within their borders merit group status. A bright spot is the notion that people have a choice in deciding whether or not they want to belong. This is especially important in cases in which groups are primarily religious and cultural groups, whose members typically have multiple identities and loyalties. Troubling is article 35, which makes reference to objective criteria that seem to exist in regard to a person's national identity. Who best chooses one's identity—the state or the person?

Apparently individual states have no rights to interpret the provisions in the convention, though in practice some member states have done so. As always states are asked to implement and uphold these principles, but there is no enforcement mechanism nor is there any punishment for noncompliance.

The most we can expect is that non-compliant states will be subject to domestic and international pressure to comply.

The most troubling part is that an individual's rights do not translate into legally recognized collective rights—thus group members once again enjoy protection as individuals but the collectivity as such does not.

What does this mean for our groups? We think that communal contenders, ethnoclasses, and most indigenous peoples would accept the protections provided by the various agreements and conventions—if they were universally recognized, implemented, and non-compliance would result in punishment. For ethnonationalists aspiring to self-governance within existing states, the protections also are helpful, but insufficient. Secessionists however have no chance to fulfill their aspirations under existing agreements. Thus, progress has been achieved, but not to the degree necessary to avoid serious future conflicts by groups seeking self-determination.

We conclude that existing conventions and the 1995 draft declaration are inadequate in solving the problem of group rights vis-à-vis the rights of states to conduct their internal affairs without outside interference. The new declarations essentially endorse the sovereign rights of states and leaves it up to the conscience of respective policymakers, and to the political process, to uphold obligations regarding their citizens.

THE CASE OF BOSNIA-HERZEGOVINA: INTERNATIONAL IMPLICATIONS OF A GENOCIDAL COMMUNAL CONFLICT

We have pointed out that states are the traditional subjects of international law and that individuals enjoy some special rights but that, in contrast, groups are largely ignored and are more typically treated as extensions of the individual. Group rights are thus the aggregate of individual rights. There obviously exists a relationship among individual consciousness, group identity, national identity, nationalism, and state-building, which has been explored by anthropologists and other social scientists. But there is a lot to learn about changes in the social organization of ethnic groups over time, which in some instances have led to state-building and in others to ethnic disintegration or assimilation. We may yet learn a lesson from the Bosnian conflict that became a genocide.

The Bosnian conflict, which began in 1992, is an example of ethnonational groups—Serbs and Croats—violating other groups' rights within contested national territories. Here it became painfully clear that lack of international legal provisions dealing with group conflict during civil war made it difficult for the UN and the European powers to respond effectively.

There were unquestionably major violations of human rights in Bosnia that constitute crimes under international law. The perpetrators were neither the legitimate authority nor the governing authority of a clearly specified territory. Essentially, the United Nations was asked to respond to an internal communal conflict that (1) had important international security implications because of its spillover or ripple effects, (2) was morally despicable in that it violated human rights laws, and (3) could be contained only by a resort to military force.

For their part, the Bosnian Serbs who initiated most ethnic cleansing and killings claimed that they could not live in a Muslim-dominated territory for fear of potential discrimination. Cynical nationalists played on that fear to incite groups to commit the murder and ethnic cleansing of those "conspiring" to discriminate against Serbs. Of course, such claims were absurd in the absence of any evidence about discriminatory intentions or potential behavior of the Bosnian Muslim leadership. But UN authorities and U.S. and European policymakers had to deal essentially with one group's *claim rights,* which negate another group's rights: the Serbians' claim that they could only live in a homogeneous territorial unit, and the Muslims' insistence that they were willing to share the national domain.

What we witnessed in the case of Bosnia-Herzegovina was not the only instance of an avalanche of similar claims and counterclaims that were precipitated by the disintegration of the former Soviet Union and Yugoslavia into a multitude of national and subnational units. Given the tendency toward fragmentation of national units in the aftermath of the Cold War, the need to protect ethnic groups and guarantee rights of persons belonging to identifiable groups prompted the conventions discussed above.

THE UNITED NATIONS AS LAWMAKER

Although the United Nations is not officially endowed with the authority to make laws, unlike national legislative authorities, it can convert **customary law** into **statutory law** through its ability to propose **multilateral** treaties that are open to ratification by all member states. Once a majority of member states have ratified a treaty, the provisions of the treaty are likely to be treated as general principles—namely, law. The importance of treaties as a source of international law, and the UN ability to promulgate conventions that specify mutual rights and obligations, has effectively granted the United Nations the role of lawmaker. In this role the United Nations has added significantly to the growing body of international law as it affects states in their relations with one another and has included in its **sphere of obligation** the protection of individual rights vis-à-vis the state. The UN Charter, which is essentially the constitution of the United Nations, has also prompted missions and activities that have set precedents that have added to international law. For example, the charter forbids the use of force as a means by which to settle disputes and emphasizes the obligation to settle disputes through peaceful means, such as negotiation, mediation, and similar methods. Although wars have not been abolished by declaring them to be illegal, warring states are obliged to justify their actions in legal terms.

The United Nations has created new laws regarding the use of outer space, the oceans, and national waters; has made genocide a crime under international law; and has dealt with the rights of individuals vis-à-vis their states in the covenants on human rights cited previously. But UN efforts to promote international standards of human dignity and to define specific categories of rights have been significantly hampered by the existence of different legal systems that emphasize different rights. The cultural and ideological differences among the Communist-socialist states, non-Western states, and Western democracies in particular have blocked UN efforts to establish mutually acceptable human rights categories. For example, under Islamic law, in contrast to the **common law** tradition of the United States and Britain, women are treated differently. Muslim women have been granted extensive property rights at times when women in most Western societies had no such rights, but they have been denied the extensive civil and political rights granted as a matter of course to women in most contemporary democracies. Whereas socialist legal systems gave priority to economic and social rights, democracies have traditionally favored civil and political rights.

We may argue that at present only minimum standards of individual rights exist and are widely accepted—that is, have the character of law. Specific rights and obligations are spelled out in the treaties and covenants cited in the previous sections. Although the language of the treaties is often vague, leaving some room for interpretation, this vagueness does not take away from the essential legal character of the documents. The essence of the treaties has been incorporated into many national legal documents, and violations of rights have prompted court decisions by national and international courts that have further amplified the stated principles. International law commissions and legal authorities have worked to eliminate ambiguities by offering legal opinions; moreover, writings on a variety of precedent-setting actions have helped to clarify the meaning of legal provisions.

What has emerged is a fairly specific body of norms that deal with the rights and obligations of individuals vis-à-vis existing states under international law. The real problem is determining how to deal with rights violations. There is no formal enforcement mechanism, and no punishments are attached to crimes committed against humanity. Recent efforts by UN policymakers have concentrated on addressing and remedying these glaring omissions. Beginning in 1992 UN Secretary-General Boutros Boutros-Ghali sought to extend the organization's traditional role as arbiter and mediator by adding policing and enforcement functions. UN actions in Cambodia, the peacekeeping and peace enforcement actions in Somalia, and the UN-sponsored **collective intervention** in the 1990–1991 Gulf War helped set the precedents necessary to provide the mechanisms by which minimum standards of human dignity can be guaranteed. The current UN Secretary-General Kofi Annan has followed in the footsteps of his predecessor.

THE LEGAL BASES FOR INTERNATIONAL ACTION

We showed in Chapter 1 that violent ethnic conflicts increased steadily in frequency and intensity from the 1960s to the early 1990s, sometimes accompanied by political mass murder and genocide. Episodes of political mass murder and genocides since 1945 have caused greater loss of life than all of the wars fought between states during the period between 1945 and 2002. We think it is essential to demonstrate that such mass abuses violate the moral standards of global society and must lead with some certainty to sanctions that are proportional to the crime. From a strategic perspective, it is clear that the diffusion of future episodes of ethnic hatred, passion, and rebellion calls for more forceful measures as discussed in Chapter 9. We know that serious ethnopolitical conflicts rarely remain internal affairs; they often inflame irredentist passions and may politicize kindred groups. Failure to settle ethnic crises in an equitable manner, thus, may encourage authoritarian rulers to suppress ethnic demands by force.

In some cases international pressures and diplomacy may indeed forestall communal crises at an early stage, but too few diplomats are officially designated ombudsmen for national minority issues. An important and highly successful innovation was the creation in January 1993 of a high commissioner on national minorities for the Conference on Security and Cooperation in Europe (CSCE), later renamed the Organization on Security and Cooperation in Europe, OSCE, which, with the help of a very small staff, was charged with giving "an objective evaluation of brewing strife, as well as constructive recommendations for its resolution" to the European member states. The High Commissioner's office has sent a great many observer missions to troubled regions and its impact both locally and in Council of Europe deliberations has been very substantial.[2]

Under the leadership of Boutros Boutros-Ghali and Kofi Annan, the United Nations has pressured member states for greater commitment in terms of resources and political will to respond to ethnopolitical conflicts and flagrant human rights abuses. Typically, national policymakers have been reluctant to commit resources to crises that have no immediate national consequences; interventions are often costly in terms of material and manpower. The need for a more active UN role and for commitments by member states continues to be hampered by a lack of recognition that communal conflicts can indeed cause *threats to international security.* The Bosnian crisis brought this point home to European and U.S. policymakers. The longer the delay in effective responses, the more difficult and costly peacekeeping and **peacebuilding** will be. Responses to humanitarian crises in Kosovo in 2000 and Macedonia in 2001 were much quicker and more effective, suggesting that at least in Europe lessons had been learned from Bosnia. However, any intervention or preemptive action, sometimes referred to as peace enforcement, comes at a price, because it shifts the legal and moral burden to the potential intervenor.

THE LEGALITY OF HUMANITARIAN INTERVENTION

International involvement in past conflicts typically meant unilateral meddling in the affairs of a sovereign state. Although they have been rare, collective interventions have taken place—for example, in the Korean War and, in 1991, in Operation Desert Storm. The right to intervene in the affairs of a sovereign state has been severely curtailed under international law. Collective intervention, however, is allowed under Chapter VIII of the UN Charter, and article 34 empowers the Security Council to investigate disputes that cause international friction. A lawful government of a state can invite another state to intervene on its behalf; there are at least seven other circumstances under which states have a lawful right to intervene. Humanitarian causes are not included, despite clearly established norms that seek to protect basic rights of individuals vis-à-vis the rights of states. Thus, although intervention per se is illegal in principle, there are many exceptions. We maintain that humanitarian crises should be included among the exceptions that allow intervention in the internal affairs of a sovereign state.

But thorny legal issues remain. States or international organizations that intend to intervene in ethnopolitical conflicts prefer to be on solid legal ground, for some interventions prolong conflicts rather than ending aggression, whereas others have resulted in continued occupation. Virtually any proactive response, such as sending a fact-finding mission and mediators or applying sanctions, can be construed as meddling in the internal affairs of a sovereign state. In the absence of legal norms that set clear standards regarding who should intervene and when and how they should do so, any form of intervention may be deemed illegal or unjust. Some legal authorities continue to claim that nonintervention should be the reigning principle; others argue for superiority of the protection of human rights, allowing for intervention in cases of massive abuses. In addition, past indiscriminate interventions by powerful states have victimized weaker states, increasing the sense among legal scholars, policymakers, and UN officials that humanitarian interventions should be evaluated on a case-by-case basis and as a moral issue but not a legal right. Such interpretations fail to consider that the *rights* to life and security of persons are explicitly protected in the Genocide Convention and the Universal Declaration of Human Rights. The Genocide Convention further forbids governments to take steps to destroy any ethnic, religious, or national group. We argue that *signatories to the convention are obliged to uphold its principles and that violations amount to breaches of contract.*

The current trend in international law is encouraging; the United Nations and the international legal community appear to be moving toward codification of principles and identification of appropriate conditions under which humanitarian imperatives will override national sovereignty.[3] This would mean essentially that when massive human rights violations are at stake, states' practices can be debated and condemned and recommendations to remedy the situation can be adopted by the United Nations. What is lacking, however, are (1) clear parameters identifying situations that warrant humanitarian intervention, (2) new laws that attach sanctions (punishment) to crimes committed, and (3) standards that identify what strategies should be applied to what kinds of violations.

Despite a few instances of unilateral interventions in cases of massive human rights abuses, none has ever been undertaken for the sole purpose of correcting such violations. Motives were mixed in the few unilateral interventions that have been cited as precedent-setting humanitarian interventions. For example, in the case of Cambodia, Vietnam intervened in 1978, and Pol Pot went into exile—the killings stopped, the Vietnamese stayed. Tanzania intervened in Uganda in 1979, and Idi Amin went into exile—the killings stopped, but Tanzania never officially claimed it intervened to preserve lives and instead claimed self-defense. Had the Vietnamese left promptly and Tanzania asserted its right to intervene on humanitarian grounds, both interventions would probably be considered precedent-setting humanitarian interventions.

All unilateral interventions are beset with problems. If we are to allow unilateral intervention on humanitarian grounds, clear standards need to be set that identify which kinds of situations warrant which types of attention; otherwise, states could intervene on fabricated grounds, claiming humanitarian reasons. Although we do not argue for the necessity of extending the principles of humanitarian intervention to include *unilateral* interventions, a case can be made for its necessity, provided legal standards have been set. We are arguing for the provision of *standards* so humanitarian actions are not impeded and the United Nations can enforce its human rights provisions. Intervention should take place under the auspices of the United Nations but can be executed by regional organizations or, in rare cases, by individual states. Clear standards on when and how to intervene would, in principle, enable the United Nations to formulate appropriate responses.

Let us summarize our position. Two contradictory principles coexist under international law—the principles of territorial integrity and sovereignty versus the right to intervene in cases of violations of humanitarian principles. It is now widely accepted that the right to territorial integrity does not include the right to treat one's citizens as one pleases, such as starving people into submission, committing mass murder, or engaging in ethnic cleansing. States that are obliged to follow clearly specified rules in their relations with other states should be equally bound in their behavior toward their citizens. Violations of laws that deal with the external behavior of states often result in the violation of territorial integrity. States' internal behavior should be equally scrutinized, and violation of internationally recognized standards should have serious consequences.[4] The task is to identify the kinds of strategies that are appropriate for specific violations.

CONCLUSION

We have shown that the United Nations and the Council of Europe as lawmakers and supranational entities only implicitly recognize specific group rights. Groups, thus, have no legally recognized independent status apart from individuals or states.

Of course, we know that groups exist and take political actions that can lead to civil wars and humanitarian disasters on the scale of Bosnia-Herzegovina, events that affect the international community. Groups that seek independence or ask for internal autonomy from a sovereign state often come into conflict with other groups or with those who represent the legal authority of a sovereign state. When such groups commit atrocities against members of competing groups, we confront crises that require special legal attention and challenge policymakers. Groups that fight legal or de facto recognized authorities challenge the established world order. They have no legally recognized status apart from the nation-state, but they are responsible for many of the world's most protracted conflicts and are perpetrators and victims of many episodes of genocide and politicide that have occurred in the twentieth century. If such groups could attain legal status that details their rights as well as states' obligations to them, this would provide the objective basis on which consistent policy decisions could be reached by outside actors.

DISCUSSION QUESTIONS

Under what circumstances are ethnic conflicts purely domestic matters of states, and under what circumstances do they have international implications?

1. What are the international legal grounds for UN actions in support of individual rights?
2. What recent developments suggest that a stronger legal basis for international protection of the rights of ethnic groups is evolving?
3. Evaluate the argument that states have no independent existence beyond that of individuals. Does this reasoning ignore the role of the modern state?
4. Under which UN Charter provision is collective intervention allowed? Under what circumstances should regional organizations be allowed to intervene?
5. The right to intervene in cases of violations of humanitarian principles contradicts the principle of territorial integrity and sovereignty in international law. What is the current status of each principle among legal scholars?

9
Responding to Ethnopolitical Challenges: Five Principles of Emerging International Doctrine

In this concluding chapter we are concerned with how societies, states, and the international system can and should respond to ethnopolitical conflicts. We showed in Chapter 1 that violent conflicts between communal groups and states increased from the 1960s to the early 1990s but thereafter turned sharply downward. Ethnicity has not disappeared as a political issue—at least as many communal groups are making ethnopolitical claims at the beginning of the twenty-first century as in the early 1990s. But their leaders are more likely to pursue group interests by conventional political means, often with international support, and are scoring significant gains. Consider a few examples:

Apartheid South Africa at the beginning of the 1990s was transformed into a multiracial democracy—not through bloody race war, as many observers predicted, but by a largely peaceful process of political and constitutional change.

After Indonesia's transition toward democracy in 1998, the new government grudgingly accepted a referendum on East Timor's secession and opened negotiations with representatives of the secessionist Free Aceh movement. Ethnopolitical violence continues in some regions but what was unthinkable under Suharto's authoritarian regime has now become a possible alternative to relying exclusively on force.

The German government, after decades in which citizenship was defined exclusively by descent, began in the late 1990s—as we showed in Chapter 4—to lower the barriers used to deny citizenship to the vast majority of Turkish and other non-German immigrants.

Virtually every news analysis and essay on the future of Afghanistan written since September 2001 has stressed that the country's future stability depends on establishing a power-sharing coalition among leaders of its Pashtun, Tajik, Uzbek, and Hazara communities. This is in marked contrast to the discourse of the 1980s and early 1990s, in which outside observers saw only the conflict between mujahedeen rebels and a Communist regime in Kabul, and ignored the ethnic rivalries that have riven Afghan politics for centuries.

Behind these changes is a new global doctrine, or set of good practices, for managing conflicts in heterogenous societies. The doctrine is based on several premises. First, ethnopolitical conflict about access to the state's power and resources should be restrained by recognizing minority rights and enabling them to participate in decision making. Second, demands for self-determination are best managed by decentralization of power within existing states. Third, the international community has proactive responsibility for promoting these outcomes. Once-common strategies of forced assimilation, racial separation, and ethnic cleansing are condemned. They are still practiced in some corners of the world, but the most influential international actors argue forcefully that pluralism, minority power-sharing, and regional autonomy within existing states are morally and practically better.

The impact of the new doctrine is somewhat obscured by the brutality of recent ethnopolitical conflicts in Central and West Africa, in Kosovo and Chechnya, in Timor and Burma, and the messiness or lack of international responses to them. But the trends are positive, as we show below.

FIVE PRINCIPLES FOR MANAGING ETHNOPOLITICAL CONFLICT

Three kinds of actors share responsibility for attaining security and justice in multiethnic societies: governments, civil society, and the international community. We begin with principles that apply to civil society and the state, then move to the international levels of analysis.

Principle 1: States and civil society should recognize and promote the rights of minorities. The previous chapter traced the history of the international doctrine that members of minority groups should be free from discrimination based on race, national origin, language, or religion. The doctrine also includes the right of minorities to organize and act politically, which implies that they have the right to protect and promote their collective interests.

Implementing this principle requires hard political work—antidiscrimination laws that are enforced, policies that promote minority cultures, and community-based programs in which people from the majority group work with minority representatives on common problems. The second author recently visited Bulgaria, a country more successful at incorporating its minorities in the last decade than any other country in the Balkans. In the spirit of Western human rights doctrine, newly democratic Bulgaria rejected Communist-era policies of forced assimilation of Turks

United Nations notice. By Jeff Danziger in *The Christian Science Monitor*, Oct. 15, 1992. Copyright © 1992 TCSPS. Reprinted by permission.

by 1990. The Turkish minority is represented by a single, moderate political party that participates in the current coalition government. There are growing numbers of Turkish mayors, police officers, and military cadets. The Roma (gypsy) minority is not well-organized nationally, but schools have begun courses in Roma language and culture, and civic organizations are working on such issues as keeping Roma children in school and improving relations between police and Roma. Economic inequalities between minorities and Bulgarians remain large, but minorities are gaining the political means to begin reducing the gap.[1]

Many other countries have implemented principles of nondiscrimination, sometimes from the top down but usually in response to pressures from civil society groups, including minority organizations. We have detailed evidence from the Minorities at Risk project (see Chapter 1, note 1) on the extent to which discrimination against minorities has eased during the last half-century. Changes in public policy and social practices have led to declining political and economic discrimination since the 1980s in Western democracies, in Latin America, in post-Communist states, and in Africa. And there has been a complementary increase in numbers of disadvantaged groups that benefit from remedial policies that promote minority cultures and increase their political and economic opportunities.

There are exceptions to the general trend. In post-Communist Europe some militantly nationalist leaders, like Slobodan Milosovic in Yugoslavia and Vladimir Meciar in Slovakia, manipulated the democratic process to demonize and marginalize minorities. In these countries a combination of democratic opposition forces and diplomatic pressure from European institutions ousted such leaders and reversed discriminatory policies by the end of the 1990s. The Middle East is another exception. It is the only world region in which the severity of discrimination against minorities has remained essentially unchanged for the last half-century. Its targets include nationalists like Kurds and Palestinians plus religious minorities throughout the region. Slight improvements for Copts in Egypt and Shi'i in Saudi Arabia have been offset by increased discrimination against groups such as Ba'hais in Iran and Christians and Shi'i in Pakistan.[2]

Principle 2: Democratic institutions and power-sharing are the best means for protecting group rights. It is inherent in the logic of democratic politics that all peoples in ethnically diverse societies should have equal civil and political rights. Democratic politics means that organized minorities can work through the party system and interest groups to shape decisions about policies that affect them. Democratic governance also implies acceptance of peaceful means for resolving civil conflicts. From the viewpoint of minority leaders, democratic institutions give them incentives to pursue moderate political goals and to rely on nonviolent means.

Some democratic arrangements are better than others for channeling minority interests into conventional politics. Decentralized systems give regionally concentrated minorities a greater voice in state or provincial politics. The United States illustrates three different variants of decentralization: the federal system gives Hispanics growing influence in the politics of states like New Mexico and California; more than 200 organized tribes of Native Americans exercise sovereign political authority in their reservations; and the people of Puerto Rico have special status as a self-governing commonwealth. Equally important, proportional (PR) electoral systems like those of most European democracies are better than single-district, winner-take-all electoral systems like that of the United States. PR systems mean that minority parties gain representation in local and national legislatures in proportion to their votes and are more likely to participate in coalition governments. In general, decentralized and PR systems increase the chances that minority parties will attain some of their policy goals, which in turn reinforces their use of moderate strategies. These principles should help guide the design of new political institutions in post-Hussein Iraq.

The worldwide shift from autocracy toward democracy in recent decades provides the context in which ethnopolitical conflict has been

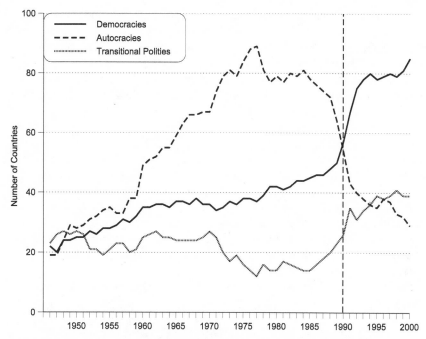

FIGURE 9.1 Global trends in numbers of democratic, autocratic, and transitional regimes, 1946–2001.

tamed. As recently as 1978 autocracies outnumbered democracies by more than 2 to 1. By 2001 the ratio was reversed, with eighty-five full democracies compared to less than forty autocracies plus another forty transitional regimes that incorporated elements of both democracy and autocracy. Figure 9.1 shows the trends. The new democratic states established during the 1990s have a strong record of acknowledging and promoting minority rights. Most quasi-democratic states—such as Russia and Singapore—also have sought to protect minority rights.

There are important exceptions to the democracy-leads-to-ethnic-peace principle. As pointed out above, the democratic transition in the Yugoslav Federation gave rise to militant nationalist parties that polarized ethnic relations and set the stage for new ethnic wars in Bosnia and Croatia. The pacifying effects of democratization in the Yugoslav successor states were delayed and still not achieved in Bosnia. It also is true that in poor states with a history of deep-rooted communal conflict, such as Burundi and Rwanda in the early to mid-1990s, external pressures for democratic power-sharing may contribute to political disasters. Nevertheless, current international norms strongly favor democratic rather than authoritarian approaches to managing ethnic diversity. What is essential is that international actors avoid imposing one particular model of democracy, or associating democracy with a single act such as a national election. The aim of international agencies should be to work with local peoples and authorities in designing democratic institutions appropriate to their specific circumstances.[3]

Principle 3: Conflicts over self-determination are best settled by negotiations for autonomy within existing states. Most ethnic wars of the last half-century have been fought over demands of national peoples like the Kurds for independent statehood. A recent survey shows that seventy territorially concentrated ethnic groups fought armed separatist conflicts—from terrorist campaigns to all–out civil war—between the 1950s and 2000. About a third of them continued to fight for greater self-determination in 2003—for example, some Basques in Spain, Muslims in Kashmir, and Chechens in Russia. Another seventy-six territorially concentrated groups seek greater self-determination by nonviolent political means.[4] The development and current status of international legal thinking about self-determination is traced in Chapter 8; here we are concerned with the political consequences.

Self-determination demands are highly charged. National minorities that make such claims usually provoke a hostile response from governments whose first priority is, almost inevitably, to preserve the integrity of the state and its territory. Based on experience during the 1990s, the optimal outcome of self-determination conflicts is a negotiated agreement between a government and group representatives that acknowledges collective rights and provides institutional means for attaining them. Some separatist groups have gained substantial local or regional autonomy, others have gained better access to decision making in the central government, and of course some agreements include both kinds of reforms.

Self-determination claims can be settled without violent conflict. An example from the early 1990s was the sequence of political shifts and negotiations for regional autonomy that preempted an ethnic rebellion by the Gagauz, a Turkish Christian minority in the post-Communist republic of Moldova. A remarkable achievement of quasi-democratic Russia has been Moscow's successful negotiation of autonomy agreements with Tatarstan, Bashkiria, and some forty other regions in the Russian Federation. These agreements provided models that could and should have been employed to head off ethnic wars in Chechnya and Kosovo.

Democratic and federal political systems are especially open to peaceful accommodation because ethnonational and indigenous group representatives can use the electoral process to gain a decisive voice in municipal or regional councils. But if no autonomy options are open to regionally concentrated minorities, armed conflict may occur. Armed separatist conflicts—including those using low-level terrorism—increased from five in the 1950s to a global maximum of forty-one in 1991, before

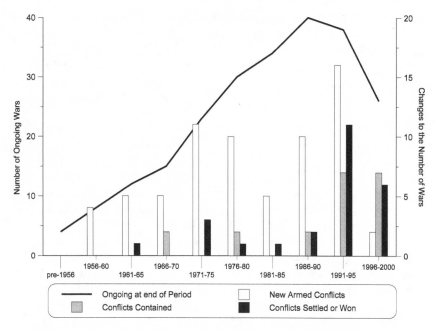

FIGURE 9.2 Global trends in new, contained, and settled armed conflicts for self-determination, 1956–2000.

declining even more abruptly to a low of twenty-two at the beginning of 2003 (see Figure 9.2). The immediate reason for the decline is that many governments and rebels have agreed to cease-fires, peacekeeping forces, and, in a number of cases, have reached autonomy agreements. In the 1990s alone fourteen wars of autonomy were contained, usually as a result of internationally backed negotiations and peacekeeping, and another seventeen led to settlements or—in Slovenia, Croatia, and Eritrea—to internationally recognized independence.

Three factors, in addition to democratization, have contributed to this trend toward settlement. The end of the Cold War gave major powers and international organizations more latitude to contain and promote settlement of conflicts that threaten regional security. States and international organizations—and many ethnonationalists—have come to recognize that secessionist wars are so costly and risky that it is better to seek compromise. And there is a growing number of autonomy agreements, from almost all world regions, that provide positive object lessons. The guerrilla war begun in 2001 by the Albanian minority in Macedonia, led by rebels from neighboring Kosovo, followed a familiar trajectory. Hard-line Macedonian and Albanian nationalists wanted a war, but moderate politicians on both sides recognized that this risked breaking up the

Macedonian state. Heavy European pressure was brought to bear on all parties, and, by the end of 2001, fighting had been contained by an internationally brokered agreement backed up by European peacekeepers who supervised disarmament of the Albanian rebels. The agreement recognized Albanians as a national people within Macedonia, guaranteed their cultural rights, and committed the government to expanding Albanians' participation in security forces and civil administration.

These outcomes provide an answer to observers who feared that the upsurge of self-determination movements in the early 1990s would continue the process of state breakdown signaled by the breakup of the Soviet Union and the Yugoslav Federation. The global lesson learned since then is that self-determination movements need not lead to redrawing of international boundaries, but rather can be settled by the devolution of central power within existing states. Nationalist governments continue to argue that autonomy arrangements are a prelude to all-out wars for independence. This is an unlikely outcome. The more common scenario is that most people accept and work within the framework of autonomy while a few spoilers continue to fight in hopes of greater concession or "total victory." An example is the peace process in Northern Ireland, where fighting was largely ended with the 1998 Good Friday accords. Implementation of the agreement was derailed by hard-liners at least three times in the next four years, though a return to serious violence has thus far been avoided. The greatest risk in autonomy agreements is not the eventual breakup of the state; rather it is that spoilers may block full implementation, thereby dragging out the conflict and wasting resources that might otherwise be used to strengthen new institutions.

Principle 4: International actors should protect minority rights and promote settlement of ethnopolitical wars. The United Nations Agenda for Peace, formulated by Secretary-General Boutros Boutros-Ghali on June 17, 1992, outlined four kinds of responses to serious communal conflicts: preventive diplomacy, peacemaking, peacekeeping, and postconflict peacebuilding. This agenda, subsequently adopted by the UN General Assembly, reflects the widely accepted norm that international and regional organizations, and individual states, have the responsibility to promote peaceful settlement of emerging ethnic conflicts. They may send observer missions to call international attention to ethnic tensions; use diplomacy to encourage governments and their opponents to seek accommodation; provide international mediation and arbitration; and offer incentives to all parties to adopt reforms. Moreover the protagonists in serious ethnic conflicts are very likely to face pressures from neighboring states and international organizations to reach negotiated settlements.

Nongovernmental actors like Amnesty International, Human Rights Watch, and civil society organizations also help implement international norms, especially by publicizing human rights violations and calling for international action on behalf of endangered peoples. Their work, reinforced by the international media—the so-called CNN effect—has been instrumental in building public demands for action on behalf of threatened minorities by North American and European powers.

Some legal dimensions of international engagement in ethnopolitical conflicts are discussed in Chapter 8. The doctrine and practice of international peacekeeping in such conflicts has a long history. The United Nations Security Council has authorized more than fifty peacekeeping operations during the past half-century, fifteen of which were in place in 2002 with a total of 50,000 international military and civilian personnel. Most of them aimed at containing armed conflicts within states, mainly ethnic wars. Current debates within and about the UN responsibility for managing internal wars focus on two issues. One is improving the capacity of the UN to anticipate and respond proactively to emerging crises, the second is improving the effectiveness of UN peace operations.[5]

The UN has often proposed that regional organizations take more responsibility for conflict management. Some have done so with UN Security Council authorization and some have not—most recently and notably NATO's 1999 intervention to halt ethnic cleansing of Albanians in the Serbian province of Kosovo, which received after-the-fact Security Council approval. Regional organizations vary greatly in their willingness and ability to moderate internal conflicts. European organizations—notably the European Union (EU) and the Organization on Security and Cooperation in Europe (OSCE)—have been increasingly effective in identifying and reacting to potential as well as current ethnopolitical conflicts, for example in Macedonia in 2001. The Organization of American States and, especially since the early 1990s, the Organization of African Unity also have sought to prevent and mitigate armed conflicts. No such regional efforts are evident in Asia or the Middle East.

Also at issue is the role of individual states in peacekeeping operations. The U.S. and Russia have engaged in unilateral peacekeeping operations, Nigeria and South Africa have done so through the guise of subregional organizations. The criticism inevitably leveled at such operations is that, whatever their rationale, they aim at advancing the initiating countries' national interests. Nonetheless they can be expected to recur whenever the UN and regional organizations fail to act in threatening situations.

Principle 5: International actors may use coercive means to stop civil wars and mass killing of civilians. It is inevitable that some regimes and rebels do not want their conflicts resolved—they are determined to win, regardless of the costs. The price paid may include the total destruction of a region's economy and infrastructure; vast refugee flows; and genocide. When preventive means and peacekeeping fail to contain conflicts that

threaten such outcomes, it is increasingly accepted that international organizations have the right and responsibility to respond with military
sanctions and peace enforcement operations. This is the newest and still
controversial of the five principles summarized here. The doctrine
emerged in the 1990s out of specific cases. International intervention in
Somalia in the early 1990s originally aimed to ensure the delivery of humanitarian aid. No-fly zones over northern and southern Iraq were established in 1991 to protect Kurds and Shi'i Muslims from government atrocities and continued to be enforced until early 2003. Serbia became a
pariah state and NATO bombing range in 1999 precisely because militant
Serb nationalists blatantly violated principles about human rights in
Kosovo that are widely accepted elsewhere in Europe.

Threats of international use of force and military presence have a critical and expanding role in the process of engagement. Jentleson argues
vigorously for what he calls *coercive prevention*, saying that "while coercion rarely is sufficient for prevention, it often is necessary" and that
without it, "we will continue to do too little too late to prevent ethnic
wars and other deadly conflicts."[6] The doctrine of coercive prevention
means the use of credible threats of military action to deter fighting and
gross human rights violations, as well as to compel an end to them once
underway. Coercive prevention may include preventive deployment of
military forces, as was done in Macedonia in 1993 and, as Jentleson points
out, should have been done in East Timor before an independence referendum in August 1999 that set off an orgy of reprisals by pro-Indonesian
militias, rather than several weeks after the fact.

Doctrine is one thing, consistent practice is another. As noted above,
most UN-authorized peacekeeping forces have been deployed to help
ensure implementation of agreements that had largely ended hostilities.
Blue-helmeted peacekeepers were expected to be neutral and, when
they were targeted, seldom used the limited force at their disposal.
Peace enforcement requires more and better-equipped troops who are
authorized to use force to contain ongoing conflict even in the absence
of, or after breakdown in, agreements by the contenders. A recurring
criticism of the UN Security Council during the 1990s was that it authorized peacekeeping missions in situations where missions should have
been authorized, manned, and equipped for robust peace enforcement
operations, for example in Bosnia (UNPRFOR, 1992–1995), Rwanda
(UNAMIR, 1993–1996), Sierra Leone (UNOMSIL, 1998–1999), and most
recently in eastern Congo.[7]

One further step in the evolution of international doctrine of engagement is acceptance of the principle that, when authority and security
have collapsed, multilateral force can be used to maintain international
protectorates while civil governance is reestablished. In Cambodia, for

example, the UN in 1991 mounted the biggest and most expensive operation in its history, as described in Chapter 1. Similar UN-mandated protectorates were established in Bosnia after the Dayton Peace Accords of 1996, in Kosovo after Serbian forces were forced to withdraw in 1999, and in East Timor in the same year. Only in independent Timor have international forces been able to pull out with their mission accomplished. In Bosnia, despite eight years of massive international engagement, the country's three constituent republics are still dominated by noncooperative nationalist politicians. The United States and its allies have followed a similar program of national reconstruction in Afghanistan since the collapse of the Taliban regime late in 2001, and the Bush administration is planning a similar scenario for post–Saddam Hussein Iraq.[8]

These examples show that a substantial precedent for coercive international engagement in civil conflicts has been established. The important qualification is that international norms require such actions to be authorized by the UN Security Council, or at least by a regional international organization. Otherwise they are likely to be condemned as instances of the kind of big-power bullying that the UN system was designed to contain.

It also is generally recognized that coercive international intervention creates long-term responsibilities. Once settlements have been brokered and civil order reestablished, outside actors have an obligation to provide the material assistance and political guarantees needed to ensure that peace is sustained. If international actors use political and military means to contain ethnic and other internal conflicts, they have a normative obligation to help pick up the pieces afterward. As a practical matter, early withdrawal risks losing all the gains achieved by intervention. The George W. Bush administration seems to have taken this lesson to heart. Candidate Bush said that the United States should get out of the nation building business. President Bush, at war with international terrorism, has committed the United States to nation building on a small budget in Afghanistan and on a much bigger budget in Iraq.

The Bush administration also should remember its initial grounds for skepticism. Long-term intervention and humanitarian assistance can create a host of secondary problems: dependence on aid, a cover for smuggling and racketeering, and a flow of international resources that corrupt local officials, and sometimes international personnel themselves.[9]

THE FUTURE OF ETHNOPOLITICAL CONFLICT

The five principles for managing conflict in heterogeneous societies have taken firm hold in international norms and practice since 1990, but they are not uncontroversial. Some liberal political theorists contend that individual rights but not collective rights deserve international protection. Leaders of new states fear that autonomy arrangements will weaken national identity and contribute to political fragmentation. Many people in the global South reject the right of international actors to judge and intervene in their domestic affairs. Nonetheless the principles are widely asserted and acted on. They are invoked by the United Nations, by major powers, by European and some other regional organizations, by nongovernmental organizations, and by members of civil society in countries divided by political and ethnic cleavages. And, as the evidence suggests, application of the principles has contributed to a substantial improvement in the status of minorities in most parts of the world and a steady diminution of deadly ethnopolitical conflict.

International doctrine and practice for managing conflict in heterogeneous societies remain a work in progress. They have evolved in a trial-and-error process that will continue for the foreseeable future. Each democratic transition in a divided society, each new diplomatic offensive aimed at a crisis situation, each new intervention and peace enforcement operation is in part a political experiment whose success or failure shapes and constrains future engagement. These are some lessons learned thus far.

- Promoting democratic transitions and power-sharing in ethnically diverse societies is risky business. The poorer the country and the deeper its divisions, the less likely are new institutions to take root. If they are to have a chance, they require sustained political and material nurturing by outside actors.
- The most effective strategies of ethnic conflict management are usually those applied early, before the onset of armed conflict or gross violations of human rights, not late. Prevention by political and diplomatic means is less costly than the costs of coercive intervention and reconstruction. The point is widely recognized by policymakers and observers but not yet consistently acted upon. The problem is twofold. One is the lack of reliable and convincing risk assessments about ethnic challenges that lie more than a year or two over the horizon. The second is that policymakers in the United Nations and the major powers focus most of their limited political and material resources on containment of immediate crises.[10]
- The most effective kinds of engagement are both multilateral and multidimensional. The multilateral principle is well-established with regard to peacekeeping and peace enforcement operations. Less widely recognized is the principle that effective engagement in any crisis situation requires collaborative planning among interested states and the United Nations to design meta-strategies that integrate diplomatic, political, economic, and military moves.

- Military options should always be on the table, not as separate strategies but as part of the meta-strategy of engagement. The options range from coercive deterrence, to rescue and training missions, to peacekeeping and peace enforcement, to air and ground warfare. Any threat or use of these actions in specific conflict situations should be linked to a larger political strategy designed to deal with the conflict that incorporates all participating states and international organizations.
- There are no fixed scenarios of political and military engagement in ethnopolitical crises. Eastern Congo requires different strategies than Kosovo or Iraqi Kurdistan or Afghanistan. It is possible to profile high-risk situations, identifying countries and regions where humanitarian crises and ethnic wars are likely.[11] It is much more difficult to design optimum responses except in the context of a given region, country, and conflict situation. There is always the risk that policymakers will learn the wrong lessons from a particular success or failure, using it as a simple guide about what (not) to do next time. "Next time" in fact is likely to differ significantly from "last time."

It is equally important to recognize that the five principles for containing conflicts in ethnically diverse societies cannot be expected to end all ethnic wars. Intense and protracted wars like those in Sudan, Sri Lanka, and Chechnya have a momentum that is very difficult to check. As observed above, antagonists may not want their conflicts settled, rather some are determined to win. Others do not accept the basic principles of power-sharing and democratic governance that are essential to most negotiated settlements. Despite the best efforts of international actors to shore up weak states, failed states will continue to provide both incentives and opportunities for future wars. The Democratic Republic of Congo is an example. Like Somalia and Sierra Leone it is not even a "state"; rather it has become a political arena in which a multiplicity of local and foreign contenders are fighting for control of resources and local power.

It also is the case that some parts of the world are off-limits to the operation of the five principles because regional hegemons like India, Russia, and China reject intervention in their spheres of influence. This does not mean that international engagement is irrelevant in these regions. On the contrary, quiet but persistent diplomatic and political initiatives should be pursued, not because they are likely to succeed in the short run, but because they increase the long-run prospects for proactive peacemaking in places like Kashmir and Tibet, if and when a regime change or regional crisis provides a political opening.

TOWARD AN UNCERTAIN FUTURE

The evolution of international doctrine and practice for promoting peace in heterogenous societies was one of the signal accomplishments of the international community during the first decade after the Cold War ended. It has inspired many sustained and creative efforts to contain and settle serious conflicts that once were thought to be intractable. And it has numerous successes to its credit including recognition of minority rights by new democratic regimes in East Central Europe and Asia, internal wars ended in southern Africa and Central America, humanitarian crises checked in East Timor and Kosovo, serious ethnic conflicts deflected in the Baltic states. These successes should be enough to offset skepticism prompted by failures to end warlord rule in Somalia, or halt genocide in Rwanda, or dissuade Pakistan and India from fighting a proxy war in Kashmir.

But it is naively optimistic to think that communal conflict is no longer an important issue. To the contrary, the assertion of group identities continues to be a major factor in the politics of almost every world region. Examples include visible minorities in Europe and North America, national minorities in the Balkans, indigenous activists in Latin America, Islamists in the Middle East, Tibetans and Uighers in China. Demands that group rights be recognized, self-governance granted, and public resources spent on disadvantaged groups will be major forces in domestic and international politics for decades to come.

Two other factors are likely to reinforce future ethnic challenges: growing inequalities within and among societies, and the rising assertion of religious identities. Minorities almost everywhere resent their material disadvantages and political marginalization, and often blame these conditions on globalization. Religion amplifies the challenge of ethnic conflict because many adherents of embattled faiths are ethnically distinct from those they oppose. Examples are Hindu militants attacking Muslims in India, Islamist terrorists attacking Christians in Pakistan, and Tamils, who are Hindu and Christian, fighting the government of Sri Lanka, which is dominated by Buddhist Sinhalese.

Ethnic and religious identities therefore provide frameworks within which the weapons of the weak are organized—mass mobilization, protest, terrorism, rebellion. The entrepreneurs of ethnopolitical and religious movements will continue to tap into a large reservoir of resentment about material inequalities, political exclusion, and predatory governments and channel it into political movements. Poverty, ethnicity, faith, and hopes for a better future are the main drivers of mass movements at the beginning of the twenty-first century. It is entirely possible that new movements based on creative recombinations of these factors will emerge to tap people's resentments and motivate them to political action. And this in turn will present a new set of challenges for those who promote human rights, democratic governance, and peaceful resolution of disputes in ethnically and religiously diverse societies.

DISCUSSION QUESTIONS

What factors are pushing the international community (the United Nations, regional organizations, major powers) to take greater responsibility for ethnic conflict? What are the sources of resistance to change?

What are the prospects and problems of applying the five principles for managing conflict in heterogenous societies to Iraq or any other country?

Do separatist movements threaten further disintegration of the state system? Where are the risks greatest?

1. Unilateral interventions are beset with problems. Why is this so?
2. Differentiate among peacekeeping and peacemaking in theory, and in practice.
3. What should be the ultimate sanctions against states that engage in genocide, ethnic cleansing, or political mass murder? Who should have the responsibility to act?

Appendix
Serious and Potential
Ethnopolitical Conflicts in 2002

Conflict and Country	Nature of Conflict	Group Type	Conflict Type and Trend, 2002	Lives Affected (in Thousands) Deaths	Refugees
Europe					
1 Azerbaijan	Despite a cease-fire brokered in 1994, Armenians in the Nagorno-Karabakh region continue to clash with Azerbaijanis.	ETHNAT	Low-level violence N	33	767
2 Bosnia	From 1991 to 1994 Bosnia Croats and Serbs fought to partition the country and "cleanse" their region of Muslims. NATO peacekeepers have maintained the cease-fire in the country since 1995. Without the peacekeepers, conflict would likely resume.	ETHNAT	Serious dispute N	200	1,700
3 Georgia	Russian-backed Abkazians won de facto independence in a war that began in 1992 and ended with a cease-fire and the presence of Russian and international peacekeepers in 1995. Many issues remain unresolved and without the peacekeepers, more violence is likely.	ETHNAT	Serious dispute N	3–4	230
4 Russia	Chechen rebels are involved in a war with Russia over the autonomy of the region.	INDIG	War +	20–30	300–450
5 Moldova	Slavic minority established trans-Dniestr republic in 1992 with Russia's help, whose de facto independence is maintained through local peacekeeping forces.	ETHNAT	Serious dispute 0	1	15
6 Macedonia	Albanian rebels fought with Macedonian forces in 2001.	NATMIN	Low-level violence N	0.2	170
7 France	Right-wing attacks on immigrants, particularly from North Africa.	ETHCLAS	Serious dispute +	<0.1	-

8	France	Corsican terrorist groups have carried out periodic bombings and assassination attempts since the 1970s to try to gain independence from France.	ETHNAT	Low-level violence 0	0.2	–
9	Germany	Right-wing attacks on refugees and immigrants, particularly Africans, Turks, and other visible minorities.	ETHCLAS	Serious dispute +	0.2	–
10	Northern Ireland	Catholics and Protestants have fought since 1969 over the Catholics' goal of a union with the Republic of Ireland. Implantation of a 1998 peace accord is on hold.	COMCON	Low-level violence N	3.5	–
11	Spain	Since the 1960s Basque terrorists (ETA) have carried out bombings, assassinations and other activities.	ETHCLAS	Low-level violence A	1	–

Middle East and North Africa

12a	Iraq	Due to government repression, many Iraqi Kurds have fled to Iran. Iraqi Kurds are now protected by the United States and Great Britain's "no-fly zone" and control an autonomous region.	ETHNAT	Serious dispute 0	180–250	530
12b	Turkey	The Kurdish terrorist campaign has largely ended with the demobilization of the Kurdish Workers Party (PKK). Turkey continues to attack PKK base areas in Iraq.	ETHNAT	Serious dispute – –	20–25	400–1000
13	Iraq	Shi'is no longer suffer reprisals for 1991 rebellion. Due to U.S. pressure on Iraq, they have begun to be more vocal in their demands for more autonomy and greater rights.	RELIG	Repression 0	180–250	550
14a	Israel	Arab citizens have protested for greater rights in Israel and have been drawn into the Israeli-Palestinian conflict.	ETHCLAS	Serious dispute 0	< 0.1	–

14b	West Bank and Gaza	Long-running clashes between Palestinians and the Israeli government. Despite attempts at negotiation, Palestinian use of terrorism and Israeli reprisals continue.	ETHNAT	Low-level violence 0	4.4	1,000
15	Lebanon	Without Syrian intervention, armed conflict among Muslims, Druze, and Christians could resume.	COMCON	Serious dispute 0	< 0.1	–
Central and South Asia						
16	Afghanistan	The war between the Taliban government and the other ethnic groups (Tajiks, Uzbeks, and others) ended after U.S. intervention in 2001. Ethnic tensions and the potential for conflict to resume is high.	COMCON	Serious dispute –	?	2,000
17	Bangladesh	A 1998 peace accord ended the Chittagong Hill people's demands for autonomy, but the slow implementation of the accord has led to sporadic violent clashes.	INDIG	Low-level violence A	25	60
18	Burma	Guerrilla wars for autonomy conducted by Karens, Kachin, Shan, Mon, and other hill and tribal people have continued since the 1950s.	INDIG/ ETHNAT	War –	130–150	1,500–2,000
19	India	Hindu nationalists and Muslims have been involved in violent clashes. These clashes intensified in 2002, particularly in the province of Gujarat.	RELIG	Low-level violence +	3–4	?
20	India	Pakistan-supported Kashmir rebels have been fighting for independence since 1990. Both countries now have a strong military presence in the region.	ETHNAT	War 0	65–70	370
21	India	Tripuras, Nagas, Bodos, and others have continued to use violence to try to gain autonomy in the province of Assam.	INDIG	Low-level violence 0	5–7	–

#	Country	Description				
22	Pakistan	Small-scale rebellions and protests in both Sindh and Baluchistan. New groups formed in 2000 and have begun a new phase in the rebellions.	COMCON	Serious dispute 0	11	–
23	Pakistan	Afghan refugees have encountered hostile treatment in Pakistan.	ETHCLAS	Serious dispute 0	–	–
23	Sri Lanka	Liberation Tigers fighting for an independent Tamil state since 1985 finally agreed to a cease-fire in 2002.	ETHNAT	War N	64	200+
Asia Pacific						
24	China	Suppression of Tibetans who seek restoration of autonomy lost in 1951.	ETHNAT	Repression 0	1,000	128
25	China	Sporadic autonomy activity among Muslim Uighurs in Xinjiang.	ETHNAT	Serious dispute 0	1–2	–
26	Fiji	A series of coups and resulting ethnic violence between native Fijians and the minority Indian Fijians have plagued the island.	COMCON	Serious dispute 0	0.1	< 0.7
27	Indonesia	Suppression of Papuan natives resisting Indonesian control since 1970s.	INDIG	Repression 0	0.4	10
28	Indonesia	Escalating conflict between the government and Aceh rebels who have been seeking autonomy since 1970s.	ETHNAT	War +	15–20	10–30
29	Papua-New Guinea	A formal peace accord in 2001 ended a rebellion for independence of Bougainville Island. A referendum on independence is to be held in 2009, but as of 2002 the island had gained a high level of autonomy.	ETHNAT	Serious dispute A	5–20	20+
30	Philippines	While the largest Moros (Muslim) separatist group signed a cease-fire in 2001, smaller groups continue to be engaged in terrorist activities.	ETHNAT	Low-level violence 0	60	200

Africa South of the Sahara

#	Country	Description				
31	Angola	By 2002, civil war between the government and the Ovimbundu-based UNITA had ended, but tensions continue with periodic violence.	COMCON	War N	> 500	2,000–4,000
32a	Burundi	A civil war began in 1993 between the formerly dominant Tutsi and the newly elected Hutu regime. By 2002 political advances had been made, but many rebels continue to fight.	COMCON	War N	200 +	550 +
32b	Rwanda	In 1994 Hutus engaged in genocide against Tutsis. In 2002 Peace and Reconciliation tribunals have begun to operate, but tensions between the two groups remain.	COMCON	Serious dispute 0	800–1,000	3,000
33	Ethiopia	Oromo rebels intensified their campaign against the government. Ethiopia has accused Eritrea of aiding the rebels. In 2002, armed conflict resumed.	COMCON	Low-level violence +	< 1	?
34	Liberia	Opposition to President Charles Taylor has led to resumed civil war by opposition groups from base areas outside of Liberia. Ethnic identities play a secondary role.	COMCON	War +	> 200	1,500
35a	Nigeria	Since 1980s the northern region has seen deadly communal clashes between Muslims and Christians.	RELIG	Low-level violence 0	18	500
35b	Nigeria	Violent clashes between various ethnic groups in the oil-rich Nigerian Delta continue.	COMCON	Low-level violence 0	5	50
36	Senegal	Autonomy rebellion in Casamance region since 1980s.	ETHNAT	Low-level violence 0	1.0	60
37	Sierra Leone	From 1991 to 1999 the country was engaged in a civil war funded by rebel control of the large diamond industry. A tentative cease-fire is in effect and is enforced by peacekeepers. Ethnic identities play a secondary role.	COMCON	War N	50	> 2,000

38	Somalia	The civil war that started in the late 1980s has caused the state to collapse. There is no functioning central government but the level of violence has decreased since 1995.	COMCON	War -	> 500	2,900
39	Sudan	Civil war began in 1983 when the Muslim government broke an agreement with Christian Southerners. Many Southerners and Nubans have fled and remain near starvation as a result of Africa's most severe ethnic conflict.	ETHNAT	War N	2,000	5,600
40	Ivory Coast	Sporadic ethnic conflict and attempted coups since 1999 divide the country along north-south ethnic and Muslim/non-Muslim lines.	COMCON	Serious dispute 0	1	10–15
41	Uganda	Fighting between the army (mostly from Baganda and Banyarwanda) and northern Acholi and Langi rebels (members of the Lord's Resistance Army).	COMCON	Low-level violence -	20	350
The Americas						
42	Ecuador	Countrywide indigenous rights protest throughout 1990s led to government concessions.	INDIG	Serious dispute 0	–	–
43	Guatemala	At the end of 1996 the government recognized greater indigenous rights, ending the persecution of the group for their support of leftist insurgencies that began in the 1960s.	INDIG	Serious dispute N	150	130
44	Nicaragua	Indigenous Miskitos continue to demand full implementation of 1989 autonomy agreement.	INDIG	Serious dispute +	–	–
45	United States	Tensions among urban ethnic groups lead to periodic riots, as in Los Angeles and Cincinnati.	ETHCLAS	Serious dispute 0	< 0.1	–
46	United States	Sporadic terrorism since 1970s by supporters of Puerto Rican independence and the protection of the island from U.S. military training exercises.	ETHNAT	Serious dispute	< 0.1	–

Notes

1. Type of ethnopolitical group(s) involved in conflict (see Chapter 2)

   ETHNAT = ethnonationalists   COMCON = communal contender
   INDIG   = indigenous peoples   NATMIN = national minority
   ETHCLAS = ethnoclass   RELIG   = religious groups

2. Codes for type of conflict in 2002

   War = Major armed conflict
   Low-level violence = low-intensity conflict with significant violence, including armed clashes, terrorism, or deadly rioting
   Serious dispute = serious dispute with little violence but a potential for escalation
   Repression = serious conflict in which most violence is a consequence of state repression

3. Codes for trends in conflict during 2002

   ++ escalating conflict, ethnopolitical group close to military or political victory
   +   escalating conflict, no end in sight
   0   conflict continuing, no significant change in level
   N   conflict low or fluctuating during cease-fires or negotiations
   A   conflict low due to accommodations that satisfied most of the group
   -   deescalating conflict, no end in sight
   -- deescalating conflict, ethnopolitical group close to defeat or annihilation

[1] Estimates of the number of deaths, in thousands, attributed to the conflict, either directly through fighting or indirectly through starvation, disease, and displacement, from the beginning of its current phase through October 2002. Most such estimates are very imprecise and some are show as ranges. The symbol "<" means *less than*. The symbol ">" means *greater than*.

[2] Estimates in thousands of the number of refugees from the conflict in need of international assistance plus the number of internally displaced people within the country as of the end of 2001. International refugees can usually be counted accurately; the number of internally displaced people is more difficult to estimate.

Sources: A variety of sources were used to gather information. The 1993 version of the Appendix was used as a reference point. The majority of information on refugees was acquired from the United States Committee for Refugees reports. Other information was acquired from U. S. State Department country reports, Amnesty International reports, Project Ploughshares reports and a variety of newspaper articles located through Lexis-Nexis.

Notes

CHAPTER 1

1. The study is detailed in Ted Robert Gurr, *Peoples Versus States: Minorities at Risk in the New Century* (Washington, DC: U.S. Institute of Peace Press, 2000). Current information can be accessed on the project's website, www.cidcm.umd.edu/inscr/mar or, alternatively, www.minoritiesatrisk.com. Five rules were used for identifying groups to be included in the study: (1) Only countries with populations greater than 500,000 were analyzed; (2) only groups that numbered 100,000 or exceeded 1 percent of the population of a country were included; (3) ethnic groups that live in several adjoining countries were counted separately within each country; (4) divisions within an ethnic group in a country were not counted separately—for example, Native Americans in the United States were analyzed as one group, not as three hundred plus separate tribes; and (5) twenty-five minorities with political or economic advantages were included, for reasons explained in Chapter 2.

2. Quoted in "Clinton Seeks Foreign Policy Bearings in Post Cold War Fog," *Washington Post,* October 17, 1993, p. A28.

3. Based on conversations with the authors in Kusadasi, Turkey, June 1990.

CHAPTER 2

1. This is based on Donald L. Horowitz's analysis of differences between ranked and unranked ethnic systems in his classic study, *Ethnic Groups in Conflict* (Berkeley: University of California Press, 1985), Chapter 2.

2. In 1730, the Mediterranean island of Corsica rebelled against rule by the Italian Republic of Genoa, which sought assistance from its French allies, which in turn conquered and absorbed Corsica into the kingdom of France in the 1760s. The autonomous dukedom of Brittany was incorporated into revolutionary France in 1789.

3. Most of these "wars" are small-scale terrorist and guerrilla movements. A list of these groups and the status of their conflicts compiled by David Quinn appears in Monty G. Marshall, Ted Robert Gurr, *Peace and Conflict 2003: A Global Survey of Armed Conflicts, Self-Determination Movements, and Democracy* (College Park, MD: Center for International Development and Conflict Management, University of Maryland, 2003), pp. 56–64.

4. Population figures are from the 1989 USSR census. The Soviet data on national peoples are approximately accurate, because all citizens were required to carry internal passports that specified their primary nationality. Estimates of the sizes of national and minority peoples in most Western societies are also relatively reliable. In Africa, the Middle East, and most of Asia and Latin America, the data are seldom more than estimates and are sometimes only guesses.

5. Information on developments in the indigenous peoples' movement is available from many websites. Especially useful is Native Web (www.nativeweb.org) and the website of

the UN High Commission on Human Rights, with links to groups working on indigenous rights. An analysis of the origins of the movement is Franke Wilmer, *The Indigenous Voice in World Politics: Since Time Immemorial* (Newbury Park, CA: Sage Publications, 1993). A new study of Amazonian peoples is Pamela L. Martin, *The Globalization of Contentious Politics: The Amazonian Indigenous Rights Movement* (New York: Routledge, 2002).

6. See International Labor Organization (ILO), *Partial Revision of the Indigenous and Tribal Populations Convention, 1957* (no. 107), Report 6 (1 and 2), 75th Session (Geneva: International Labor Office, 1988). The new convention, no. 169, was adopted in 1989 but, like other ILO conventions, is not binding on member states. Rather, it sets a standard against which states' labor policies toward indigenous peoples are judged by the international community. This summary is based on a research paper prepared by Jean-Carlos Rivera.

7. The Chinese in Malaysia meet our definition of communal contenders; other Chinese communities in Southeast Asia have been largely assimilated (Thailand, the Philippines). Palestinians are by and large a professional and commercial minority throughout the Middle East and also in Central America; on the latter, see Nancie Gonzalez, *Dollar, Dove and Eagle: 100 Years of Palestinian Emigration to Honduras* (Ann Arbor: University of Michigan Press, 1992).

8. Two comparative studies of ethnoreligious conflict in the Islamic world are Jonathan Fox, "Is Islam More Conflict-Prone Than Other Religions? A Cross-Sectional Study of Ethnoreligious Conflict," *Nationalism and Ethnic Politics* vol. 6 (Summer 2000), pp. 1–24; and Jonathan Fox, "Two Civilizations and Ethnic Conflict: Islam and the West," *Journal of Peace Research* vol. 38 (July 2001), pp. 459–472.

CHAPTER 3

1. From "My Life," by Asir Shawkat, a fourteen-year-old Kurdish boy. In 1991 Shawkat was a student at London's Stockwell Park Kurdish School. His and other Kurdish refugee children's autobiographies are included in Rachel Warner, ed., *Voices from Kurdistan* (London: Minority Rights Group, December 1991), pp. 15–17.

2. An overview of Kurdish history and politics is provided by David McDowall, *A Modern History of the Kurds*, rev. ed. (London: I. B. Taurus, 1999). Detailed accounts of the Al-Anfal campaign include P. W. Galbraith and C. Van Hollen, Jr., *Chemical Weapons in Kurdistan: Iraq's Final Offensive, A Staff Report* (Washington, DC: Committee on Foreign Relations, U.S. Senate, 1988); Kanan Makiya, "The Anfal: Uncovering an Iraqi Campaign to Exterminate the Kurds," *Harper's Magazine*, vol. 284, no. 1704 (May 1992): 53–61; *The Anfal Campaign in Iraqi Kurdistan: The Destruction of Koreme* (New York: Middle East Watch and Physicians for Human Rights, 1993); and *Report on the Situation of Human Rights in Iraq*, prepared by Max Van der Stoel, Special Rapporteur of the Commission on Human Rights (New York: United Nations, E/CN.4/1992/31). Al-Anfal is used in the Quran to refer to the spoils of a battle against the unbelievers in Mecca. The implication of the Iraqi government's use of the term is that the Kurds are unbelievers and that their lives and properties are forfeit.

3. Major studies of the Kurds are listed in Suggested Readings, pp. 216–217. Our summaries also make use of chronologies prepared for the Minorities at Risk project by Deina AbdelKader, Hossein Shabazi, Michael Johns, and David Quinn.

4. There are many names for traditional authorities in Kurdish society. Aghas are leaders of clans or extended families; some are very influential. Mirs and begs are the chiefs of tribal communities. Shaikhs were the leaders of Sufi religious brotherhoods who played important roles in resolving disputes among Kurdish clans and tribes in the nineteenth

and early twentieth centuries. Pasha and Bey were titles given to traditional leaders who the Ottomans appointed or confirmed in office as rulers or governors of Kurdish tribes and principalities.

5. The Ottoman and Persian rulers in earlier centuries had also forcibly deported many Kurds to locations as distant as Baluchistan on the Indian Ocean and modern-day Bulgaria. Mehrad R. Izady, *The Kurds: A Concise Handbook* (Washington, DC: Taylor & Francis, 1992), pp. 99–107, provides a detailed summary of historical and contemporary Kurdish deportations and diaspora.

6. Quoted in David McDowall, *The Kurds: A Nation Divided* (London: Minority Rights Group Publications, 1992), p. 32. A strong Armenian nationalist movement was already in existence. Kurdish and Armenian representatives quickly took advantage of the changed international situation and presented a memorandum on their common interest in independence to the 1919 Peace Conference in Paris. The boundaries proposed for the two new states are shown in Izady, *The Kurds*, p. 58.

7. For details on the Lausanne Treaty, see Gerard Chaliand, ed., *People Without a Country: The Kurds and Kurdistan* (London: Zed Press, 1980), pp. 41–44, 58–60, 158–163, 215. The treaty included provisions for the protection of the rights of non-Muslim minorities in the former Ottoman domain (e.g., Greeks and Armenians) but made no separate reference to Kurds. Minority rights were ignored in Turkey after 1924, but the separate status and rights of Kurds were respected in Iraq and French-mandated Syria until their independence in 1930 and 1946, respectively. Iran was not a signatory to the treaty.

8. The Kurdish minority in Syria was the target of discriminatory policies as part of an "Arabization" campaign from 1958 to the late 1970s. This campaign was inspired at first by the intense Arab nationalism of Gamal Abdel Nasser in Egypt; from 1958 to 1961 Syria and Egypt joined in the "United Arab Republic." It was also provoked by the beginning of political activism among Kurds in Syria. The Kurds in the former USSR are a small and widely dispersed minority. Neither group has taken significant political actions since the 1970s.

9. McDowall, *The Kurds*, p. 36.

10. This example comes from the memoirs of a Turkish governor of a Kurdish province, cited in Chaliand, *People Without a Country*, p. 83. Special government officials enforced the ban in urban Kurdish markets; the five-piaster fine was about one-tenth the market value of a sheep.

11. Written by a fourteen-year-old refugee in London; in Warner, *Voices from Kurdistan*, p. 11.

12. The statistics are from M. Hakan Yavuz and Michael M. Gunter, "The Kurdish Nation," *Current History*, January 2001, p. 35. An illustrated account of Kurdish life, politics, and state repression is Jonathan Rugman and Roger Hutchins, *Ataturk's Children: Turkey and the Kurds* (London: Cassell, 1996).

13. A comprehensive analysis of solutions, and obstacles to them, is Henri J. Barkey and Graham E. Fuller, *Turkey's Kurdish Question* (Lanham, MD: Rowman & Littlefield for the Carnegie Commission on Preventing Deadly Conflict, 1998).

14. An overview of the Kurds in Iran is provided by A. R. Ghassemlou in Chapter 3 of Chaliand, *People Without a Country*. An important English-language source on the Republic of Mahabad is William Eagleton, *The Kurdish Republic of 1946* (London: Oxford University Press, 1963). Kurdish resistance to the Islamic republic is reviewed in McDowall, *The Kurds*, Chapter 9. Yavuz and Gunter, "The Kurdish Nation" (see note 12) briefly review recent developments.

15. From documents captured in the 1991 Kurdish uprising; quoted by Aryeh Neier, "Putting Saddam Hussein on Trial," *New York Review*, September 23, 1993, p. 47.

16. This section draws mainly on Chaliand, *People Without a Country*, Chapter 5; Mc-Dowall, *The Kurds*, Chapters 10–12; and Pelletiere, *The Kurds*, Chapters 6–8. A detailed analysis of relations between the Baath governments and the Kurds is Edmund Ghareeb, *The Kurdish Question in Iraq* (Syracuse: Syracuse University Press, 1981).

17. Two good analyses of Kurdish nationalism and its rivalries since 1991 are Hanna Yousif Freij, "Tribal Identity and Alliance Behaviour among Factions of the Kurdish National Movement in Iraq," *Nationalism & Ethnic Politics* vol. 3 (Autumn 1997), pp. 86–110, and Michael M. Gunter, *The Kurdish Predicament in Iraq: A Political Analysis* (London and New York: St. Martin's Press, 1999).

18. For a news account of the agreement see *Washington Post*, September 19, 1989. The text of the agreement is contained in a letter dated September 22, 1989, from Jimmy Carter to Nicaraguan President Daniel Ortega. Copies of this and other documents on negotiations between the government and Miskito leaders were obtained from the files of the Indian Law Resource Center, Washington, DC.

19. Estimates of the Miskito population vary widely, because census information is inadequate and because there are no objective criteria for determining group membership. A 1981 Nicaraguan government report gives an impossibly precise "estimate" of 66,994 Miskitos in the Atlantic Coast region (in Carlos M. Vilas, *State, Class and Ethnicity in Nicaragua: Capitalist Modernization and Revolutionary Change on the Atlantic Coast* [Boulder: Lynne Rienner, 1989, p. 4]). Our 1990 figure, derived from expert estimates, is 126,000 in Nicaragua and 20,000–30,000 in Honduras. Bernard Nietschman proposes higher estimates of 150,000 in Nicaragua and 50,000 in Honduras (in "The Miskito Nation and the Geopolitics of Self-determination," in Bernard Schechterman and Martin Slann, eds., *The Ethnic Dimension in International Relations* (Westport, CT: Praeger, 1993), p. 28.

20. Miskitos and Creoles have continued to intermarry with one another and with European, Chinese, and mestizo immigrants. To be considered an Indian or a Creole in this context, therefore, is mainly determined by where and how one lives and what group one identifies with rather than by one's genetic makeup. Most Creoles live in coastal towns, especially in Bluefields and El Bluff, which are at the southern limit of Miskito lands. Both groups share a broader identity as Costeños, people of the coast, as distinct from the "Spaniards." But their interests are not identical: Armed opposition to the Sandinista government during the 1980s came mainly from the Miskitos, whereas most Creoles resigned themselves to Sandinista rule after a 1980 protest campaign failed.

21. Other frames of reference that have been used to interpret the conflict are sketched by John Paul Lederach, "The Conflict in Nicaragua's Atlantic Coast: An Inside View of War and Peacemaking," in Edmundo G. Garcia, ed., *War and Peacemaking: Essays on Conflicts and Change* (Quezon City, Philippines: Claretian, 1994), pp. 101–122.

22. The principal sources for this section include a chronology prepared by Michael Hartman and Stephen Kurth for the Minorities at Risk project; Vilas, *State, Class and Ethnicity in Nicaragua*, a thoroughly researched account that is sympathetic to the Sandinista government; Roxanne Dunbar Ortiz, *The Miskito Indians of Nicaragua* (London: Minority Rights Group, Report no. 79, 1988); and a series of articles in *Cultural Survival*, a source that favors the indigenous rights movement. Useful analytic accounts are Lederach, "The Conflict in Nicaragua's Atlantic Coast" (note 21) and Martin Diskin, "Revolution and Ethnic Identity: The Nicaraguan Case, in Nancie L. Gonzalez and Carolyn S. McCommon, eds., *Conflict, Migration, and the Expression of Ethnicity* (Boulder: Westview Press, 1989). Another good source is Charles R. Hale, *Resistance and Contradiction: Miskitu Indians and the Nicaraguan State, 1984–1987* (Stanford: Stanford University Press, 1994).

23. Few accounts have been published in English about the status of the Miskitos or about implementation of the autonomy agreement since the rebellion ended. This sum-

mary is based on chronologies compiled from news sources and brief articles in the magazine *Cultural Survival* by Michelle Boomgaard and David Quinn of the Minorities at Risk project. Details of the July 2002 declaration of independence appear in the *Nicaragua News Service*, vol. 10, no. 31 (Washington, DC: Nicaragua Network Education Fund, 2002).

CHAPTER 4

1. A more detailed account of the Emergency is given in the section entitled "The Emergency." Major sources include Richard L. Clutterbuck, *The Long War: Counterinsurgency in Malaya and Vietnam* (New York: Praeger, 1966); Edgar O'Ballance, *Malaya: The Communist Insurgent War, 1948–60* (Hamden, CT: Archon Books, 1966); Sir Robert Thompson, *Defeating Communist Insurgency: The Lessons of Malaya and Vietnam* (New York: Praeger, 1966); Anthony Short, *The Communist Insurrection in Malaya: 1948–1960* (New York: Crane, Russak, 1975); and Richard Stubbs, *Hearts and Minds in Guerrilla Warfare: The Malayan Emergency 1948–1960* (Boulder: Westview Press, 1989).

2. On Malaysian Chinese politics, see, for example, Sumit Ganguly, "Ethnic Policies and Political Quiescence in Malaysia and Singapore," in Michael E. Brown and Sumit Ganguly, eds., *Government Policies and Ethnic Relations in Asia and the Pacific* (Cambridge, MA: MIT Press, 1997); Robert W. Hefner, *The Politics of Multiculturalism: Pluralism and Citizenship in Malaysia, Singapore, and Indonesia* (Honolulu: University of Hawaii Press, 2001); and Heng Pek Koon, *Chinese Politics in Malaysia: A History of the Malaysian Chinese Association* (Singapore: Oxford University Press, 1988).

3. On the historical origins of ethnic divisions in Malaya, see sources in note 1 to this chapter.

4. For general accounts of Malaysian politics, see Zakaria Haji Ahmad, ed., *Government and Politics of Malaysia* (Kuala Lumpur: Oxford University Press, 1987); Karl von Vorys, *Democracy Without Consensus: Communalism and Political Stability in Malaysia* (Princeton: Princeton University Press, 1975); and Lee Hock Guan, "Malay Dominance and Opposition Parties in Malaysia," *Southeast Asian Affairs* (2002): 177–195.

5. Quotation from Robert Klitgaard and Ruth Katz, "Overcoming Ethnic Inequalities: Lessons from Malaysia," *Journal of Policy Analysis and Management,* vol. 2, no. 3 (1983): 337. On post-1969 policies, also see Milton Esman, *Administration and Development in Malaysia* (Ithaca: Cornell University Press, 1972); Donald R. Snodgrass, *Inequality and Economic Development in Malaysia* (Kuala Lumpur: Oxford University Press, 1980); Hing Lee Kam and Tan Chee-Beng, eds., *The Chinese in Malaysia* (New York: Oxford University Press, 1999); and Eugene K. B. Tan. "From Sojourners to Citizens: Managing the Ethnic Chinese Minority in Indonesia and Malaysia," *Ethnic and Racial Studies,* vol. 24, no. 6 (2001): 949–978.

6. Assessments of Malaysian politics include Zakaria Haji Ahmad, "Malaysia: Quasi Democracy in a Divided Society," in Larry Diamond, Juan J. Linz, and Seymour Martin Lipset, eds., *Democracy in Developing Countries: Asia* (Boulder: Lynne Rienner, 1991); Gordon P. Means, *Malaysian Politics: The Second Generation* (Singapore: Oxford University Press, 1991); and references in notes 2 and 5, above.

7. German policies on immigration of guest workers and data on their origins, numbers, and employment are described in Klaus J. Bade, ed., *Population, Labour, and Migration in 19th- and 20th-Century Germany* (New York: St. Martin's Press, 1987), pp. 146–159. A recent analysis is Ruud Koopmans, "Germany and Its Immigrants: An Ambivalent Relationship," *Journal of Ethnic and Migration Studies* 24 (October 1999), pp. 627–647. Current statistical information on foreigners in Germany and other European countries is

reported in annual issues of *Trends in International Migration: Continuous Reporting System on Migration* (Paris: Organization for Economic Co-operation and Development Publication Service).

8. See Stephen Castles, *Here for Good: Western Europe's New Ethnic Minorities* (London: Pluto Press, 1984), pp. 76–85.

9. Quotation from Bade, *Population, Labour and Migration,* p. 149. This and the following discussion of the current status of Turks in Germany use materials from journalistic accounts. The status of Turks is well-covered in the mainstream European press and in the EFE News Service and Turkish Daily News, which focus on immigrant issues. Foreign workers as a group have higher unemployment levels than German citizens. Figures for 1999, a relatively good year economically, showed unemployment among Germans in the former West German states at 8.8 percent compared with 18.4 percent for foreign workers; from *Trends in International Migration* (note 7; 2001 edition).

10. Koopmans analyzes these flows of immigration and their consequences in "Germany and its Immigrants," note 7.

11. A detailed report on the early 1990s is *"Germany for Germans": Xenophobia and Racist Violence in Germany* (New York: Human Rights Watch Report 1495, 1995).

12. On the National Democratic Party see Castles, *Here for Good,* pp. 201–204. On the Republicans, see articles on Germany in Christian Soe, ed., *Comparative Politics 92/93* and *Comparative Politics 93/94* (Guilford, CT: Dushkin, annual editions).

13. Political activism by Turkish immigrants in the 1970s is described by Mark J. Miller, *Foreign Workers in Western Europe: An Emerging Political Force* (New York: Praeger, 1981).

14. Citizenship is readily obtained by immigrants in the Netherlands, Belgium, and the Scandinavian countries, for example. The German rejoinder is that their society has much larger numbers and proportions of immigrants than other European countries.

15. A detailed study that supports this interpretation is Nedim Ögelman, "Organizations, Integration, and the 'Homeland Hangover': The Case of Germany's Turkish-Origin Community," paper presented to the Annual Meeting of the American Political Science Association, Atlanta, September 1999.

16. An excellent analysis of migration pressures, including the 1999 data cited here, is *National Intelligence Estimate: Growing Global Migration and Its Implications for the United States* (Washington, DC: National Intelligence Council, NIE 2001–02D, 2001).

17. See Ronald Koven, "Muslim Immigrants and French Nationalists," *Society* 29 (May–June 1992): 25–33.

CHAPTER 5

1. A critical survey of general theories is James B. Rule, *Theories of Civil Violence* (Berkeley: University of California Press, 1988). Theories of revolution are surveyed by Jack A. Goldstone, T. R. Gurr, and Farrokh Moshiri, eds., *Revolutions of the Late Twentieth Century* (Boulder: Westview Press, 1991), Chapters 2, 3, 14.

2. A classic work is Frederik Barth, ed., *Ethnic Groups and Boundaries: The Social Organization of Culture Difference* (London: Allen and Unwin, 1969). An important recent study is Nancie L. Gonzalez and Carolyn S. McCommon, eds., *Conflict, Migration, and the Expression of Ethnicity* (Boulder: Westview Press, 1989).

3. A recent review and synthesis is Susan Olzak, *The Dynamics of Ethnic Competition and Conflict* (Stanford: Stanford University Press, 1992).

4. The foundation of modernization theory was laid down by Karl Deutsch, *Nationalism and Social Communication* (Cambridge, MA: MIT Press, 1953). A later statement is

David E. Apter, *The Politics of Modernization* (Chicago: University of Chicago Press, 1965). Data on the upward trends in ethnopolitical conflict from 1945 to the early 1990s and its subsequent decline are reported in Ted Robert Gurr, *Peoples Versus States: Minorities at Risk in the New Century* (Washington, DC: United States Institute of Peace Press, 2000), Chapter 2.

5. Influential theorists who assume the fundamental importance of ethnic identity and solidarity include Connor, "Nation-Building"; Donald L. Horowitz, *Ethnic Groups in Conflict* (Berkeley: University of California Press, 1985); Anthony D. Smith, *The Ethnic Revival in the Modern World* (New York: Cambridge University Press, 1981); and Pierre L. van den Berghe, *The Ethnic Phenomenon* (New York: Elsevier, 1981).

6. Charles Tilly interprets all civil conflicts as resulting from the instrumental pursuit of group interests in response to changing opportunities; see *From Mobilization to Revolution* (Reading, MA: Addison-Wesley, 1978). The internal colonialism theory was first developed by Michael Hechter, *Internal Colonialism: The Celtic Fringe in British National Development* (Berkeley: University of California Press, 1975).

7. Many writers analyze how ethnic identities are constructed and how they affect collective action. For anthropological case studies see Nancie L. Gonzalez and Carolyn S. McCommon, eds., *Conflict, Migration, and the Expression of Ethnicity* (Boulder: Westview Press, 1989). On the emergence of Palestinian nationalism see Rashid Khalidi, *Palestinian Identity: The Construction of a Modern National Consciousness* (New York: Columbia University Press, 1998). A theory of the symbolic origins of ethnic violence is Stuart J. Kaufman, *Modern Hatreds: The Symbolic Politics of Ethnic War* (Ithaca, NY: Cornell University Press, 2001).

8. For a review and synthesis of theories of secession, see Alexis Heraclides, *The Self-Determination of Minorities in International Politics* (London: Frank Cass, 1991), Chapter 1, Appendix 2. He tests his arguments with case studies of separatist movements, including the Kurds in Iraq.

9. See Susan Olzak, *The Dynamics of Ethnic Competition and Conflict* (Stanford: Stanford University Press, 1992), Chapters 1 and 2. Her theoretical argument is more complex than this sketch and is concerned mainly with Western societies; on ethnic stratification, competition, and conflict in African and Asian societies see Horowitz, *Ethnic Groups in Conflict*.

10. A review of theories and evidence about genocide is Helen Fein, "Genocide: A Sociological Perspective," *Current Sociology* 38 (Spring 1990): 1–126.

11. This theory is sketched in Barbara Harff, "The Etiology of Genocides," in Isidor Wallimann and Michael N. Dobkowski, eds., *Genocide and the Modern Age: Etiology and Case Studies of Mass Death* (Westport, CT: Greenwood Press, 1987), pp. 41–59. It is refined and tested empirically, using data on all genocides and politicides since 1955, in Barbara Harff, "No Lessons Learned from the Holocaust? Assessing Risks of Genocide and Political Mass Murder since 1955," *American Political Science Review* 97 (February 2003): 57–73.

CHAPTER 6

1. Studies of the settlement of protracted ethnic conflicts include I. William Zartman, *Ripe for Resolution: Conflict and Intervention in Africa* (New Haven: Yale University Press, 1989); Joseph V. Montville, ed., *Conflict and Peacemaking in Multiethnic Societies* (Lexington, MA: Lexington Books, 1990); and Roy Licklider, ed., *Stopping the Killing: How Civil Wars End* (New York: New York University Press, 1993). A survey by David Quinn of the status and outcomes of all self-determination conflicts of the last fifty years appears in Monty G.

Marshall, Ted Robert Gurr, and others, *Peace and Conflict 2003: A Global Survey of Armed Conflicts, Self-Determination Movements, and Democracy* (College Park, MD: Center for International Development and Conflict Management, 2003), pp. 56–64.

2. The uses of detention powers are critically analyzed in Jomo Kwame Sundaram, "Malaysia: Economic Recession, Ethnic Relations and Political Freedom," *Cultural Survival Quarterly* vol. 12, no. 3 (1988): 55–63. On deportation and citizenship status of immigrants in Malaysia, see Minority Rights Group, *The Chinese of South-East Asia* (London: Minority Rights Group, Report 92/6), pp. 6–7; in Germany, see Stephen Castles, *Here for Good: Western Europe's New Ethnic Minorities* (London: Pluto Press, 1984), pp. 82–84.

3. This section is based on a more detailed analysis of the accommodation of ethnopolitical conflicts in Ted Robert Gurr, *Minorities at Risk: A Global View of Ethnopolitical Conflict* (Washington, DC: United States Institute of Peace Press, 1993), Chapter 10.

4. These and other instances are summarized in Marshall, Gurr and others, *Peace and Conflict 2003*, note 3.

CHAPTER 7

1. Recent studies that survey this topic include Michael Brown (ed.), *The International Dimensions of Internal Conflict* (Cambridge: MIT Press, 1997); David Carment and Patrick James (eds.), *Wars in the Midst of Peace: The International Politics of Ethnic Conflict* (Pittsburgh: University of Pittsburgh Press, 1997); and David A. Lake and Donald Rothchild (eds.), *The International Spread of Ethnic Conflict: Fear, Diffusion, and Escalation* (Princeton: Princeton University Press, 1998).

2. David McDowall, *The Kurds: A Nation Denied* (London: Minority Rights Publications, 1992), p. 129.

3. Data for this and similar comparisons can be found in United Nations, *World Development Report* (New York: United Nations, various years).

4. A careful and convincing analysis of what Iraq did and did not do with oil revenues is Milton Leitenberg, "Saddam Is the Cause of Iraqis' Suffering," *The Institute for the Study of Genocide Newsletter* 28 (Winter 2002), pp. 4–14.

5. The potential gains and risks of an invasion of Iraq are reviewed by Kenneth M. Pollack, *The Threatening Storm: The Case for Invading Iraq* (New York: Random House/Council on Foreign Relations, 2002) and Carl Kaysen et al., *War with Iraq: Costs, Consequences, and Alternatives* (Cambridge: American Academy of Arts & Sciences, 2002).

6. CIA assistance probably began in the early 1960s, but the first agreement for significant aid was reached in 1969. On U.S. and other sources of aid for the KDP, see Edmund Ghareeb, *The Kurdish Question in Iraq* (Syracuse: Syracuse University Press, 1981), Chapter 7; and Stephen C. Pelletiere, *The Kurds: An Unstable Element in the Gulf* (Boulder: Westview Press, 1984), Chapter 8.

7. For an elaboration of the reasons for the settlement of Iraq's claim, see McDowall, *The Kurds*, p. 98; and Ghareeb, *The Kurdish Question*, Chapter 8.

8. Two documents on the case are reprinted in Gary E. McCuen, *The Nicaraguan Revolution* (Hudson, WI: GEM Publications, 1986), Chapter 4.

9. The regional peace process was very complex, because it involved other states in the region and aimed at resolving other regional conflicts as well. For accounts of the role of international actors in the Nicaraguan conflict see Carlos M. Vilas, *State, Class and Ethnicity in Nicaragua: Capitalist Modernization and Revolutionary Change on the Atlantic Coast* (Boulder: Lynne Rienner, 1989), Chapter 5; and Cynthia Arnson (ed.), *Comparative Peace Processes in Latin America* (Stanford: Stanford University Press, 1999).

10. "Germany Now Telling Its Officials to Acknowledge Neo-Nazi Problem," *Washington Post*, March 19, 1993, p. A54.

CHAPTER 8

1. For an extended discussion of the etiology of secession see Alexis Heraclides, *The Self-Determination of Minorities in International Politics* (London: Frank Cass, 1991); the quotation is from Heraclides, p. 25. Two other major studies of historical and contemporary cases are Allen Buchanan, *Secession: The Morality of Political Divorce from Fort Sumter to Lithuania and Quebec* (Boulder: Westview Press, 1991); and Ruth Lapidoth, *Autonomy: Flexible Solutions to Ethnic Conflict* (Washington, DC: U.S. Institute of Peace Press, 1997).

2. See P. Terrence Hoppman, *Building Security in Post-Cold War Eurasia: The OSCE and U.S. Foreign Policy* (Washington, DC: U.S. Institute of Peace, Peaceworks, 1999).

3. Thomas G. Weiss and Cindy Collins, *Humanitarian Challenges and Intervention*, 2d ed.(Boulder: Westview Press, 2000), especially chapters 1 and 6.

4. The doctrine of humanitarian intervention is discussed in Barbara Harff, *Genocide and Human Rights International Legal and Political Issues*, (Denver: University of Denver Monograph Series in World Affairs, vol. 20, book 3, 1984) and in Chopra and Weiss, "Sovereignty Is No Longer Sacrosanct: Codifying Humanitarian Intervention," *Ethics and International Affairs* 6 (1992): 95–117. A comprehensive annotated bibliography is Barbara Harff and David Kader, "Bibliography of Law and Genocide," in Israel W. Charny, ed., *Genocide: A Critical Bibliographic Review*, Vol. II (New York: Facts on File, 1990)

CHAPTER 9

1. For details see *The Bulgarian Ethnic Experience* (Princeton, NJ: Project on Ethnic Relations, 2002).

2. Trends in discrimination are reported in Ted Robert Gurr, "Attaining Peace in Divided Societies: Five Principles of Emerging International Doctrine," in Nicholas N. Kittirie, Rodrigo Carazo-Odio, and James R. Mancham (eds.), *The Future of Peace: Responding to the Discontents of a Global Community* (Washington, DC: Eleanor Roosevelt Institute for Justice and Peace, 2003), pp. 418–432.

3. Influential nongovernmental organizations in North America and Europe promote these principles, for example the National Endowment for Democracy in the United States and the International Institute for Democracy and Electoral Assistance (IDEA) in Sweden. A good compendium and evaluation of democratic approaches to managing ethnic diversity is Peter Harris and Ben Reilly (eds.), *Democracy and Deep-Rooted Conflict: Options for Negotiators* (Stockholm: IDEA, 1998). Also see Sammy Smooha, "Types of Democracy and Modes of Conflict Management in Ethnically Divided Societies," *National and Nationalism*, October 2002, pp. 423–432.

4. See chapter 2, note 3.

5. A survey of evidence and proposals is Fen Osler Hampson and David M. Malone (eds.), *From Reaction to Conflict Prevention: Opportunities for the UN System* (Boulder: Lynne Rienner Publishers for the International Peace Academy, 2002).

6. Bruce W. Jentleson, *Coercive Prevention: Normative, Political, and Policy Dilemmas*, Peaceworks No. 35 (Washington, DC: United States Institute of Peace, October 2000), p. 5.

7. Many factors, political as well as military, internal as well as international, shape the outcomes of peacekeeping missions. See, for example, Dennis C. Jett, *Why Peacekeeping*

Fails (New York: St. Martin's Press, 1999); and Michael Bhatia, *War and Intervention: A Global Survey of Peace Operations* (Bloomfield, CT: Kumarian Press, 2003).

8. See Richard Caplan, *A New Trusteeship? The International Administration of War-Torn Territories* (London and New York: Oxford University Press for the International Institute for Strategic Studies, 2002) and Sumantra Bose, *Bosnia After Dayton: Nationalist Partition and International Intervention* (London and New York: Oxford University Press, 2002).

9. See Bose, *Bosnia After Dayton*, and Weiss and Collins, *Humanitarian Challenges and Intervention*, Chapter 5.

10. European institutions are something of an exception to this generalization. They have been relatively effective in anticipating and heading off potentially serious ethnic conflicts in the post-Communist states of East and Central Europe. See Hoppman, *Building Security in Post-Cold War Eurasia,* and Bruce W. Jentleson, ed., *Opportunities Missed, Opportunities Seized: Preventive Diplomacy in the Post-Cold War World* (Lanham, MD: Rowman & Littlefield, 2000).

11. Social scientists have a growing capacity to provide empirically based assessments of the risks and stages of ethnic and political conflict that complement the more conventional expert-based assessments used by foreign policy makers. See the approaches and evidence in John L. Davies and Ted Robert Gurr, eds., *Preventive Measures: Building Risk Assessment and Crisis Early Warning Systems* (Lanham, MD: Rowman & Littlefield, 1998); and Barbara Harff, "No Lessons Learned from the Holocaust? Assessing Risks of Genocide and Political Mass Murder Since 1955," *American Political Science Review*, February 2003, 57–73. On the role of early warning and strategies for conflict transformation, see Janie Leatherman, William DeMars, Patrick Gaffney, and Raimo Väyrynen, *Breaking Cycles of Violence: Conflict Prevention in Intrastate Crises* (Bloomfield, CT: Kumarian Press, 1999).

Suggested Readings and Research Sources

RESEARCH MATERIALS ON ETHNICITY AND ETHNOPOLITICAL CONFLICT

Scholarly books, like the studies listed below, usually provide the most thorough background information on ethnicity and politics. For specialized and current research, though, it is usually necessary to screen journal articles, specialized websites, and media accounts. The most relevant scholarly journals are *Ethnicity* and *Racial and Ethnic Studies,* both published since the 1970s, and two journals founded in the mid-1990s, *Nations and Nationalism* and *Nationalism & Ethnic Politics.* Also especially useful are the reports issued by the Minority Rights Group (London) at www.minorityrights.org and the latest edition of their reference work *World Directory of Minorities.*

Many politically active ethnic groups have websites. A general source of current information is the website of the Minorities at Risk project, which includes sketches, risk assessments, chronologies, and coded data for nearly 300 ethnopolitical groups. The project can be accessed either at www.cidcm.umd.edu/inscr/mar or at www.minoritiesatrisk.com. Excellent in-depth reports on major regional conflicts are prepared by the International Crisis Group, a Brussels-based NGO with field offices throughout the world. See its website at icg@crisisweb.org.

Ahmed, Ishtiaq. 1996. *State, Nation and Ethnicity in Contemporary South Asia.* London and New York: Pinter.

Barth, Frederik. 1969. *Ethnic Groups and Boundaries: The Social Organization of Culture Difference.* London: Allen and Unwin.

Bengio, Ofra, and Gabriel Ben-Dor, eds. 1999. *Minorities and the State in the Arab World.* Boulder: Lynne Rienner.

Braathen, Einar, Morten Boas, and Gjermund Saether, eds. 2000. *Ethnicity Kills? The Politics of War, Peace, and Ethnicity in SubSaharan Africa.* London: Macmillan.

Brass, Paul R., ed. 1985. *Ethnic Groups and the State.* Totowa, NJ: Barnes and Noble.

———. 1991. *Ethnicity and Nationalism: Theory and Comparison.* New Delhi: Sage Publications.

Brown, Michael E., and Sumit Ganguly, eds. 1997. *Government Policies and Ethnic Relations in Asia and the Pacific.* Cambridge, MA: MIT Press.

Esman, Milton J., and Itamar Rabinovich, eds. 1988. *Ethnicity, Pluralism, and the State in the Middle East.* Ithaca, NY: Cornell University Press.

Fein, Helen. 1993. *Genocide: A Sociological Perspective.* London: Sage Publications.

Ganguly, Rajat, and Raymond C. Taras. 1998. *Understanding Ethnic Conflict: The International Dimension.* New York: Longman.

Gonzalez, Nancie L., and Carolyn S. McCommon, eds. 1989. *Conflict, Migration, and the Expression of Ethnicity.* Boulder: Westview Press.

Gurr, Ted Robert. 2000. *Peoples versus States: Minorities at Risk in the New Century.* Washington, DC: United States Institute of Peace Press.

Harff, Barbara. 2003. "No Lessons Learned from the Holocaust? Assessing Risks of Genocide and Political Mass Murder Since 1955." *American Political Science Review* 97 (February): 57–73.

Harris, Peter, and Ben Reilly, eds. 1998. *Democracy and Deep-Rooted Conflicts: Options for Negotiators.* Stockholm: International Institute for Democratic Education and Action.

Horowitz, Donald L. 1985. *Ethnic Groups in Conflict.* Berkeley: University of California Press.

Kaufman, Stuart J. 2001. *Modern Hatreds: The Symbolic Politics of Ethnic War.* Ithaca, NY: Cornell University Press.

Lake, David A., and Donald Rothchild, eds. 1998. *The International Spread of Ethnic Conflict: Fear, Diffusion, and Escalation.* Princeton: Princeton University Press.

McGarry, John, and Brendan O'Leary, eds. 1993. *The Politics of Ethnic Conflict Regulation.* London: Routledge.

Mikesell, Marvin W., and Alexander B. Murphy. 1991. "A Framework for Comparative Study of Minority-Group Aspirations." *Annals of the Association of American Geographers* vol. 81, no. 4: 581–604.

Montville, Joseph V., ed. 1990. *Conflict and Peacemaking in Multiethnic Societies.* Lexington, MA: Lexington Books.

Ringer, Benjamin R., and Elinor R. Lawless. 1989. *Race, Ethnicity and Society.* New York: Routledge.

Rothchild, Donald. 1997. *Managing Ethnic Conflict in Africa: Pressures and Incentives for Cooperation.* Washington, DC: Brookings Institution Press.

Rupesinghe, Kumar, Peter King, and Olga Vorkunova, eds. 1992. *Ethnicity and Conflict in a Post-Communist World.* New York: St. Martin's Press.

Smith, Anthony D. 1986. *The Ethnic Origins of Nations.* Oxford: Basil Blackwell.

_____. 1999. *Myths and Memories of the Nation.* Oxford: Oxford University Press.

Smooha, Sammy. 2002. "Types of Democracy and Modes of Conflict Management in Ethnically Divided Societies." *Nations and Nationalism* 8 (October): 423–432.

Szayna, Thomas S., ed. 2000. *Identifying Potential Ethnic Conflict: Application of a Process Model.* Santa Monica, CA: RAND.

Tiryakian, Edward A., and Ronald Rogowski, eds. 1985. *New Nationalisms of the Developed West: Toward Explanation.* Boston: Allen and Unwin.

Triesman, Daniel A. 1999. *After the Deluge: Regional Crises and Political Consolidation in Russia.* Ann Arbor: University of Michigan Press.

Wilmer, Franke. 1993. *The Indigenous Voice in World Politics: Since Time Immemorial.* Newbury Park: Sage Publications.

ON THE KURDS

Barkey, Henri J., and Graham E. Fuller. 1998. *Turkey's Kurdish Question.* Lanham, MD: Rowman & Littlefield for the Carnegie Commission on Preventing Deadly Conflict.

Chaliand, Gerard, ed. 1980. *People Without a Country: The Kurds and Kurdistan.* London: Zed Press.

Gunter, Michael M. 1990. *The Kurds in Turkey: A Political Dilemma.* Boulder: Westview Press.

_____. 1999. *The Kurdish Predicament in Iraq: A Political Analysis.* New York: St. Martin's Press.

Izady, Mehrdad R. 1992. *The Kurds: A Concise Handbook.* Washington, DC: Taylor and Francis.

Kaysen, Carl, Steven E. Miller, Martin B. Malin, William D. Nordhaus, and John D. Steinbruner. 2002. *War with Iraq: Costs, Consequences, and Alternatives.* Cambridge, MA: American Academy of Arts & Sciences.

Kreyenbroek, Philip G., and Stefan Sperl, eds. 1992. *The Kurds: A Contemporary Overview.* London: Routledge.

Makiya, Kanan. 1992a. "The Anfal: Uncovering an Iraqi Campaign to Exterminate the Kurds." *Harper's Magazine* 284, no. 1704 (May): 53–61.

_____. 1992b. *Cruelty and Silence: War, Tyranny, Uprising, and the Arab World.* New York: Norton.

McDowall, David. 1999a. *A Modern History of the Kurds,* rev. ed. London: I. B. Taurus.

_____. 1992b. *The Kurds: A Nation Denied.* London: Minority Rights Publications.

Middle East Watch. 1990. *Human Rights in Iraq.* New Haven: Yale University Press.

_____. 1993. *The Anfal Campaign in Iraqi Kurdistan: The Destruction of Koreme.* New York: Middle East Watch and Physicians for Human Rights.

Pollack, Kenneth M. 2002. *The Threatening Storm: The Case for Invading Iraq.* New York: Random House/Council on Foreign Relations.

Saatci, Mustafa. 2002. "Nation-states and Ethnic Boundaries: Modern Turkish Identity and Turkish-Kurdish Conflict." *Nations and Nationalism* 8 (October): 549–564.

van Bruinessen, Martin. 1991. *Agha, Shaikh, and State: The Social and Political Structures of Kurdistan* (1st ed. 1978). London: Zed Press.

Yavuz, M. Hakan, and Michael M. Gunther. 2001. "The Kurdish Nation." *Current History,* January 2001.

ON THE MISKITOS AND OTHER INDIGENOUS PEOPLES

Useful websites for researching indigenous peoples throughout the world are www. nativeweb.org and www.treatycouncil.org. Also use the UN High Commission's webpage at www.unchr.ch to access the extensive reports of the UN Working Group on Indigenous Rights.

Americas Watch. 1987. *The Sumus in Nicaragua and Honduras: An Endangered People.* New York: Americas Watch.

Dennis, Philip A. 1981. "The Costeños and the Revolution in Nicaragua." *Journal of Interamerican Studies and World Affairs* vol. 23 (August): 271–296.

Diskin, Martin. 1989. "Revolution and Ethnic Identity: The Nicaraguan Case." In Nancie L. Gonzalez and Carolyn S. McCommon, eds., *Conflict, Migration, and the Expression of Ethnicity.* Boulder: Westview Press.

Dunbar Ortiz, Roxanne. 1988. *The Miskito Indians of Nicaragua.* London: Minority Rights Group, Report no. 79.

Hale, Charles R. 1994. *Resistance and Contradiction: Miskitu Indians and the Nicaraguan State, 1984–1987.* Stanford: Stanford University Press.

Martin, Pamela. 2002. *The Globalization of Contentious Politics: The Amazonian Indigenous Rights Movement.* New York: Routledge.

Nietschmann, Bernard. 1993. "The Miskito Nation and the Geopolitics of Self-determination," in Bernard Schechterman and Martin Slann, eds., *The Ethnic Dimension in International Relations.* Westport, CT: Praeger.

Ohland, Klaudine, and Robin Schneider. 1983. *National Revolution and Indigenous Identity: The Conflict Between Sandinistas and Miskito Indians on Nicaragua's Atlantic Coast.* Copenhagen: International Working Group on Indigenous Affairs, Document no. 47.

Reyes, Reynaldo, and J. K. Wilson. 1993. *Ráfaga: The Life Story of a Nicaraguan Miskito Comandante.* Norman: University of Oklahoma Press.

Vilas, Carlos M. 1989. *State, Class and Ethnicity in Nicaragua: Capitalist Modernization and Revolutionary Change on the Atlantic Coast.* Boulder: Lynne Rienner.

ON THE CHINESE IN MALAYSIA AND OTHER SOUTHEAST ASIAN COUNTRIES

The websites of the two political parties that represent Chinese interests in Malaysia are www.dapmalaysia.org and www.mca.org.my. Also relevant is the site of Suaram, the Malaysian human rights organization, at www.suaram.org.

Ahmad, Zakaria Haji, ed. 1987. *Government and Politics of Malaysia.* Kuala Lumpur: Oxford University Press.

Freedman, Amy L. 2000. *Political Participation and Ethnic Minorities: Chinese Overseas in Malaysia, Indonesia, and the United States.* New York: Routledge.

Ganguly, Sumit. 1997. "Ethnic Politics and Political Quiescence in Malaysia and Singapore," in Michael E. Brown and Sumit Ganguly, eds., *Government Policies and Ethnic Relations in Asia and the Pacific.* Cambridge, MA: MIT Press.

Hefner, Robert W. 2001. *The Politics of Multiculturalism: Pluralism and Citizenship in Malaysia, Singapore, and Indonesia.* Honolulu: University of Hawaii Press.

Hing, Lee Kam, and Tan Chee-Beng, eds. 1999. *The Chinese in Malaysia.* New York: Oxford University Press.

Ho, Chin Ung. 2000. *The Chinese of South-East Asia.* London: Minoritiy Rights Group.

Koon, Heng Pek. 1988. *Chinese Politics in Malaysia: A History of the Malaysian Chinese Association.* Singapore: Oxford University Press.

Means, Gordon P. 1991. *Malaysian Politics: The Second Generation.* Singapore: Oxford University Press.

Mutalib, Hussin. 1990. *Islam and Ethnicity in Malay Politics.* Singapore: Oxford University Press.

O'Ballance, Edgar. 1966. *Malaya: The Communist Insurgent War, 1948–60.* Hamden, CT: Archon Books.

Short, Anthony. 1975. *The Communist Insurrection in Malaya: 1948–1960.* New York: Crane, Russak.

Snodgrass, Donald R. 1980. *Inequality and Economic Development in Malaysia.* Kuala Lumpur: Oxford University Press.

Stubbs, Richard. 1989. *Hearts and Minds in Guerrilla Warfare: The Malayan Emergency 1948–1960.* Boulder: Westview Press.

Tan, Eugene K. B. 2001. "From Sojourners to Citizens: Managing the Ethnic Chinese Minority in Indonesia and Malaysia." *Ethnic and Racial Studies* vol. 24, no. 6 (November): 949–978,

von Vorys, Karl. 1975. *Democracy Without Consensus: Communalism and Political Stability in Malaysia.* Princeton: Princeton University Press.

ON TURKS IN GERMANY AND OTHER IMMIGRANT MINORITIES IN EUROPE

Turks in Germany have recently established a website at www.vaybee.de. It focuses on popular news, however, not politics. For statistical information and commmentary on government policies on migration and noncitizen residents of all European countries see the

Organization for Economic Cooperation and Development (OECD)'s annual publication *Trends in International Migration: Continuous Reporting System on Migration*, Paris: OECD.

Bade, Klaus J., ed. 1987. *Population, Labour and Migration in 19th- and 20th-Century Germany.* New York: St. Martin's Press.

Castles, Stephen. 1984. *Here for Good: Western Europe's New Ethnic Minorities.* London: Pluto Press.

Castles, Stephen, and Godula Kosak. 1985. *Immigrant Workers and Class Structure in Western Europe,* 2d edition. Oxford: Oxford University Press.

Human Rights Watch. 1995. *"Germany for Germans": Xenophobia and Racist Violence in Germany.* New York: Human Rights Watch.

Koopmans, Ruud. 1999. "Germany and Its Immigrants: An Ambivalent Relationship." *Journal of Ethnic and Migration Studies* vol. 24 (October): 627–647.

Miller, Mark J. 1981. *Foreign Workers in Western Europe: An Emerging Political Force.* New York: Praeger.

Power, Jonathan, with Anna Hardman. 1984. *Western Europe's Migrant Workers.* London: Minority Rights Group, Report no. 28, 2d revised edition.

Solomos, John, and John Wrench, eds. 1993. *Racism and Migration in Contemporary Europe.* Oxford: Berg Publishers.

Waever, Ole, Barry Buzan, Morten Kelstrup, Pierre Lemaitre, and others. 1993. *Identity, Migration and the New Security Agenda in Europe.* London: Pinter Publishers.

INTERNATIONAL DIMENSIONS OF ETHNIC CONFLICT

Legal documents on the changing status of minorities in Europe can be accessed on the website of the Organization on Security and Cooperation in Europe (OSCE) at www.osce.org/docs.

Bhatia, Michael. 2003. *War and Intervention: A Global Survey of Peace Operations.* Bloomfield, CT: Kumarian Press.

Bose, Sumantra. 2002. *Bosnia After Dayton: Nationalist Partition and International Intervention.* Oxford: Oxford University Press.

Boutros-Ghali, Boutros. 1992. *An Agenda for Peace: Preventive Diplomacy, Peacemaking, and Peace-Keeping.* New York: United Nations.

Brown, Michael E., ed. 1996. *The International Dimensions of Internal Conflict.* Cambridge, MA: MIT Press.

Buchanan, Allen. 1991. *Secession: The Morality of Political Divorce from Fort Sumter to Lithuania and Quebec.* Boulder: Westview Press.

Caplan, Richard. 2002. *A New Trusteeship? The International Administration of War-Torn Territories.* Oxford: Oxford University Press for the International Institute for Strategic Studies.

Chopra, Jarat, and Thomas G. Weiss. 1992. "Sovereignty Is No Longer Sacrosanct: Codifying Humanitarian Intervention." *Ethics & International Affairs* vol. 6: 95–117.

Damrosch, Lori Fisler, ed. 1993. *Enforcing Restraint: Collective Intervention in Internal Conflicts.* New York: Council on Foreign Relations.

Davies, John L., and Ted Robert Gurr, eds. 1998. *Preventive Measures: Building Risk Assessment and Crisis Early Warning Systems.* Lanham, MD: Rowman & Littlefield.

de Silva, K. M., and R. J. May, eds. 1991. *Internationalization of Ethnic Conflict.* New York: St. Martin's Press.

Doyle, Michael W. 1994. *UN Peacekeeping in Cambodia: UNTAC's Civilian Mandate.* Boulder: Lynne Rienner.

Ehrlich, Thomas, and Mary Ellen O'Connell. 1993. *International Law and the Use of Force.* Boston: Little, Brown.

"Ethnic Conflict and International Security." 1993. Special issue of *Survival: The IISS Quarterly* vol. 35, no. 1 (Spring): 3–170.

Gottlieb, Gidon. 1993. *Nation Against State: A New Approach to Ethnic Conflicts, the Decline of Sovereignty, and the Dilemmas of Collective Security.* New York: Council on Foreign Relations.

Hampson, Fen Osler, and David M. Malone. 2002. *From Reaction to Conflict Prevention: Opportunities for the UN System.* Boulder: Lynne Rienner for the International Peace Academy.

Hannum, Hurst. 1990. *Autonomy, Sovereignty, and Self-Determination: The Accommodation of Conflicting Rights.* Philadelphia: University of Pennsylvania Press.

Harff, Barbara. 1984. *Genocide and Human Rights: International Legal and Political Issues.* Denver: University of Denver Monograph Series in World Affairs, vol. 20, book 3.

_____. 1991. "Humanitarian Intervention in Genocidal Situations." In Israel W. Charny, ed., *Genocide: A Critical Bibliographic Review, Vol. II.* New York: Facts on File.

_____. 1995. "Rescuing Endangered Peoples: Missed Opportunities." *Social Research* vol. 62, no. 1 (Spring): 23–40.

Heraclides, Alexis. 1991. *The Self-Determination of Minorities in International Politics.* London: Frank Cass.

Hoppman, P. Terrence. 1999. *Building Security in Post-Cold War Eurasia: The OSCE and U.S. Foreign Policy.* Washington, DC: U.S. Institute of Peace.

International Commission on Intervention and State Sovereignty. 2001. *The Responsibility to Protect: Research, Bibliography, Background.* Ottawa: International Development Research Centre, www.idrc.ca.

Jentleson, Bruce W. 2000. *Opportunities Missed, Opportunities Seized: Preventive Diplomacy in the Post-Cold War World.* Lanham, MD: Rowman & Littlefield.

Lapidoth, Ruth. 1997. *Autonomy: Flexible Solutions to Ethnic Conflict.* Washington, DC: U.S. Institute of Peace Press.

Leatherman, Janie, William DeMars, Patrick Gaffney, and Raimo Väyrynen. *Breaking Cycles of Violence: Conflict Prevention in Intrastate Crises.* Bloomfield, CT: Kumarian Press.

Licklider, Roy, ed. 1993. *Stopping the Killing: How Civil Wars End.* New York: New York University Press.

Makinda, Samuel M. 1993. *Seeking Peace from Chaos: Humanitarian Intervention in Somalia.* Boulder: Lynne Rienner.

Martin, Ian. 2001. *Self-Determination in East Timor: The United Nations, the Ballot, and International Intervention.* New York: International Peace Academy Occasional Paper.

Peck, Connie. 1998. *Sustainable Peace: The Role of the UN and Regional Organizations in Preventing Conflict.* Lanham, MD: Rowan & Littlefield for the Carnegie Commission on Preventing Deadly Conflict.

Preece, Jennifer Jackson. 1997. "National Minority Rights vs. State Sovereignty in Europe: Changing Norms in International Relations?" *Nations and Nationalism* vol. 3, no. 3: 345–364.

Rupesinghe, Kumar, and Michiko Kuroda, eds. 1992. *Early Warning and Conflict Resolution.* New York: St. Martin's Press.

Weiss, Thomas G., and Cindy Collins. 2000. *Humanitarian Challenges and Intervention,* 2d edition. Boulder: Westview Press.

Zartman, I. William. 1989. *Ripe for Resolution: Conflict and Intervention in Africa.* New Haven: Yale University Press.

Glossary

Assimilation is a strategy for accommodating ethnic minorities that gives individual members incentives and opportunities to subordinate their identities to the language, values, and lifeways of the dominant group. Also see the definitions of **pluralism** and **power-sharing.**

Autocracies sharply restrict civil rights and political participation, concentrate most or all political power in the executive, and distribute and transfer political power within a small political elite.

Autonomy is a political arrangement in which an ethnic group has some control over its own territory, people, and resources but does not have independence as a sovereign state. The specifics of autonomy arrangements vary widely.

Baathists—The Baath Party was founded in the 1940s in Syria. Originally, it combined a secular blend of pan-Arabism with non-Marxist socialism. During the 1970s Baathist power was concentrated within ethnoreligious minorities in Syria (Alawis) and Iraq (Sunnis who were largely from the Tikrit region).

Civil war is violent conflict between roughly equal factions within a state trying to create, or prevent establishment of a new government for the entire state or some part of it.

Collective intervention is the interference by a group of states in another country's internal or territorial affairs.

Communal contenders are culturally distinct peoples, tribes, or clans in heterogeneous societies who seek a larger share of state power. Most African states are made up of numerous communal contenders and are governed by coalitions of these groups.

Constructivism is a theoretical approach that focuses on the ways in which changing perceptions and norms impact on group identities and interests.

Contagion is the intentional transmittal of models of political action from one country to another.

Containment became a major theme in U.S. foreign policy after World War II and refers to policies aimed at halting the spread of communism.

Contras were opponents of the Sandinista government in Nicaragua who included members of the defeated Somoza National Guard plus disillusioned former supporters of the Sandinistas.

A **convention** in international law is a formal written agreement between states that creates legal obligations for the parties involved.

The **Council of Europe** represents all the states of Western Europe and most of the post-Communist states. It is headed by a Committee of Ministers—the foreign ministers of each member state—and an elected assembly. It is especially concerned with drafting and implementing conventions for the protection of human rights in all European countries.

Democracies guarantee political and civil rights for all citizens, have constitutional limitations on the power of the executive, have multiple parties that compete for office, and transfer power by constitutionally prescribed means.

Discrimination refers to deliberately maintained inequalities in ethnic group members' material well-being (**economic discrimination**) or political access (**political discrimination**) in comparison with those of other social groups.

Dominant minorities are numerically small ethnic groups that exercise a preponderance of both political and economic power within a society. Contemporary examples include Tutsis in Rwanda and Burundi and the Alawites of Syria.

Empirical generalizations are conclusions about a substantial number of cases based on observation, experience, and data.

Ethnic cleansing is the systematic elimination of ethnic minorities from a given territory using such means as terror, forced deportation, and murder.

Ethnic groups are composed of people who share a distinctive and enduring collective identity based on shared experiences and cultural traits. They may define themselves, and may be defined by others, in terms of any or all of the following traits: lifeways, religious beliefs, language, physical appearance, region of residence, traditional occupations, and a history of conquest and repression by culturally different peoples. Ethnic groups are also called **communal groups, identity groups,** and **minorities.** The term **minorities** can be misleading, because some people so labeled, like Black South Africans and Shi'i Muslims in Iraq, constitute numerical majorities.

Ethnoclasses are ethnically or culturally distinct peoples, usually descended from slaves or immigrants, who have special economic roles. Examples from Western societies, like the Turks in Germany and African Americans in the United States, are usually of low status. Asian examples, like the Chinese in Malaysia and Indonesia, are often economically advantaged but politically restricted.

Ethnonationalists are large, regionally concentrated groups of people with a history of political independence or autonomy who seek to reestablish their independence or extend their autonomy. Those who want complete independence are called **separatists.**

Ethnopolitical groups are ethnic groups that have organized to pursue political objectives, or that are assigned an inferior political status by authorities.

Formal recognition in international law and practice refers to the establishment of relations between two countries exemplified by the accreditation of ambassadors.

Genocide is mass murder carried out by or with the complicity of political authorities and directed at distinct communally defined groups. See also **politicide.**

Hegemony refers to the domination of the world or of a region by one state and also to the preponderance of a state's power **within** the international system.

Humanitarian intervention (see also **intervention**) is reliance on force for the justifiable purpose of protecting the inhabitants of another state from treatment that is arbitrary and persistently abusive.

A **hypothesis** is a testable proposition (one that includes an if-then statement) that can be verified or disproved.

Indigenous peoples are conquered descendants of original inhabitants of a region who usually live in peripheral areas, practice subsistence agriculture or herding, and have cultures that are clearly distinct from those of dominant groups.

Instrumental explanations of ethnic conflict attribute it mainly to the use or manipulation of ethnic identity in the pursuit of material and political objectives; see also **constructivism** and **primordial.**

Insurgency refers to guerrilla wars fought by revolutionaries. Strategies designed by military planners during the Cold War to fight such challengers were called **counterinsurgency.**

International law refers to the body of rules that govern primarily relations among states; it is derived mostly from custom and treaties. An important distinction is made between **common** or **customary law,** which is based on those practices that through repeated usage have been widely accepted as binding rules by states, and **statutory law,** which is enacted by the legislative branch of governments or by an international body and is intended as a permanent rule.

Intervention means the dictatorial interference by one state in the affairs of another state for the purpose of either maintaining or changing the existing order of things, rather than mere interference per se.

Irredentism is the aspiration by groups or nations to regain lost territory or rejoin their ethnic kindred in a neighboring state.

Islamic fundamentalism is a movement that stresses the literal adherence to basic principles as written in the Quran, the Hadiths, and the Shari'ah (Islamic law), and its five schools of legal interpretation. There are four Sunni schools (Hanafi, Maliki, Shafii, Hanbali) and one Shi'i school (Ja'fari).

Legitimacy refers to the perception that a government, its leaders, and its policies are just and worthy of support.

Levels of analysis refers to the factors thought to influence the decision-making process; they range from individual preferences to roles, societal input, regime characteristics, regional relations, and traits of the world system.

Mestizo is a term used in Latin America to refer to people of mixed Spanish and Indian descent.

Mobilization is the process by which leaders organize the energies and resources of their followers to pursue common political objectives.

A **model** is a simplified image of reality that describes the causes of any given phenomenon.

Modernization refers to the process by which people break away from primordial ties and develop loyalties to larger associations, a nation, or a state. The term was formerly used to refer to the process by which non-Western peoples adopt Western economic and political institutions, but it is now widely recognized that people can modernize without following Western models.

Multiculturalism is a synonym for **pluralism.**

Multilateral means international actions that involve several countries, as distinct from **unilateral,** which describes actions initiated by one country.

Operationalization refers to the process of defining concepts in a hypothesis so they can be measured in observable quantities.

Pan-Arabism is a doctrine that stresses the unity of all Arabs, favors social reform and economic development, and opposes imperialism and Zionism. It was especially influential in Middle Eastern politics during the 1950s and 1960s.

Peacebuilding refers to the ability to anticipate conflict in order to apply proper measures to create the conditions for peace.

Peacekeeping refers to the use of international military personnel in noncombatant roles, such as monitoring cease-fires. Such activities require the consent of the warring parties.

Peacemaking (also called **peace enforcement**) enables peacekeeping forces not only to monitor a cease-fire but also to enforce it if it breaks down. Control over deployment and operation is exercised by the UN Security Council or can be delegated to a regional organization.

Plural societies consist of a number of ethnic groups, each with a distinct collective identity and interests, who are not ranked or **stratified** in relationship to one another. See also **stratified societies.**

Pluralism is a strategy for accommodating ethnic minorities that recognizes their individual and collective right to preserve their language, values, and lifeways in coexistence with those of the dominant group. Also see **assimilation** and **power-sharing.**

Politicide is mass murder carried out by or with the complicity of governing authorities (as in **genocide**), but victims are targeted primarily because of their political affiliation and activities.

Populist states are weakly institutionalized political systems that are in a transitional state to either democracy or increased autocracy. Political power is usually transferred through military coups or popular uprisings short of revolution.

Power-sharing is a strategy for accommodating ethnic minorities based on the assumption that ethnic identities and organizations are the basic elements of society. Political power is exercised jointly by these groups, each of which is represented in government and each of which has veto power over policies that adversely affect group members. Also see **assimilation** and **pluralism.**

Preventive diplomacy refers to nonmilitary options used to prevent escalation of crisis into open conflict, such as sending fact-finding missions, providing for mediation and arbitration, issuing formal warnings of impending sanctions, and offering political or material incentives.

Primordial explanations of ethnic conflict attribute it mainly to the desire to protect a people's deeply rooted identity and culture; see also **constructivism** and **instrumental.**

Probability statements in social science research indicate that there exists a partial or tentative relationship between x (cause) and y (effect). That is, there is a tendency for x to be associated with y, but the relationship is not exact.

Propositions are untested statements or ideas about a specific kind of causal relationship.

Sanctions are agreements among states to stop trade with violators of international law completely or in one particular commodity, such as military goods.

Shi'i Muslims are the minority that follows basic tenets of Islam but that regards Ali and his heirs as the only legitimate successors to the prophet Muhammad.

Socialist states use the doctrines of Marx and Lenin to justify concentration of power in a single party that is used by the elite to mobilize mass support for the regime, encourage political participation only within the party, and transfer power through competition within the party.

The **state system** is the political organization of the world into a set of territorial-based states with governments whose sovereignty is recognized by other states.

In **stratified societies** status, power, and wealth are unequally distributed among groups according to their ethnicity. The socially maintained distinctions among groups in stratified societies are called **cleavages.** Also see **plural societies.**

Sunni Muslims are the orthodox majority of Islam who accept the teachings of the Quran, the Hadith, and the four schools of jurisprudence (identified under **Islamic fundamentalism**), and who also accept the Sunna and the historic succession of caliphs.

Variables are measurable properties of concepts.

Visible minorities is a fairly recent term used in European and North American societies to refer collectively to resident minorities of African, Asian, and indigenous origins. It is replacing the older term *people of color.*

Wars of secession are violent conflicts in which a regionally based ethnic group attempts to secede from an existing state. They are different from **revolutions,** in which rebels who may or may not have a common ethnic identity seek to seize power in an existing state. Also see **civil war.**

About the Book and Authors

New ethnic wars flared up from Bosnia to the Caucasus to the Horn of Africa when the Cold War ended in 1990 but most subsided as new democracies were established and the international community actively sought to promote peaceful solutions to ethnic conflicts within states. This book is an introduction to this new era in which civil society, states, and international actors attempt to channel ethnic challenges to world order and security into conventional politics.

From Africa's post-colonial rebellions in the 1960s and 1970s to anti-immigrant violence in the 1990s, this second edition of *Ethnic Conflict in World Politics* surveys the historical, geographic, and cultural diversity of ethnopolitical conflict. Using an analytical model to elucidate four well-chosen case studies—the Kurds, the Miskitos, the Chinese in Malaysia, and the Turks in Germany—the authors give students tools for analyzing emerging conflicts based on the demands of nationalists, indigenous peoples, and immigrant minorities throughout the world. The international community has begun to respond more quickly and constructively to these conflicts than it did to civil wars in divided Yugoslavia and genocide in Rwanda by using the emerging doctrines of proactive peacemaking and peace enforcement that are detailed in this book.

The text is illustrated with maps, tables, and figures to enhance students' understanding of the quest of unfamiliar peoples for autonomy and rights, putting it into the context of international politics. An appendix surveys nearly fifty serious ethnopolitical conflicts at the beginning of the 21st century-keyed to a global map. The appendix identifies the groups and issues as well as counting the number of lives affected, showing the enormous geopolitical and cultural reach of this issue. The bibliography identifies representative websites plus books, articles, and other sources to guide students' own research.

*   *   *

Barbara Harff is professor of political science at the U.S. Naval Academy in Annapolis. **Ted Robert Gurr** is distinguished university professor and founding director of the Minorities at Risk project at the Center for International Development and Conflict Management, University of Maryland at College Park. Both are senior consultants to the U.S. government's State Failure Task Force.

Index

Africa
  anti-colonialism in, 9
  communal contenders in, 19
  states in, 6
African-Americans, 8, 19
Afrikaaners, 29
Al-Anfal operation, 37, 125
Al-Bakr, Hasan, 51
Albanians, 19, 24, 187–88
Alliance for the Progress of Miskitos and
  Sumus (ALPROMISU), 61
ALPROMISU. *See* Alliance for the
  Progress of Miskitos and Sumus
Amin, Idi, 13–14, 15, 178
Amnesty International, 16, 188
Annan, Kofi, 17, 176–77
Arabs, 9, 38
Arafat, Yasser, 148
Arias, Oscar, 154
Armenians, 4, 44
Arusha Accords, 14, 15
Asia
  anti-colonialism in, 9
  currency crisis in, 158
  indigenous peoples in, 25
  states in, 6
assimilation, 22, 48, 134–35, 182
Ataturk, Mustafa Kemal, 44
autocracies
  ethnic demands and, 8
  ethnopolitical conflicts and, 104–5,
    184–85
  indicators of, 110
autonomy
  communal contenders and, 29
  ethnonationalists and, 8, 23–25, 32
  ethnopolitical conflicts and, 11, 22
  indigenous peoples and, 25
  Kurds and, 35–55, 40–42, 44, 51
  limits of arrangements for, 63–65

  Miskitos and, 56–65
  self-determination and, 186–88

Baathist government, 51, 52, 118, 119,
  144–45
Balkans, 17, 182
Bangladesh, 16, 24, 25
Barzani, Masoud, 53
Barzani, Mustafa, 49, 52, 53, 55, 121–23,
  142–43, 146
Barzanji, Shaikh Mahmud, 51
Bolivia, 4, 25
Borge, Tomás, 56, 125
Borneo, 70, 158
Bosnia, 2, 11–12, 16, 173–74
Boutros-Ghali, Boutros, 17, 176–77, 188
Brazil, 5, 22, 27
Britain. *See* Great Britain
British East India Company, 73
British North Borneo Company, 70
Bulgaria, 11, 182
Burma, 21
Burundi, 2, 5, 7, 14
Bush, George H. W., 37

Cambodia, 15–16, 98, 126, 178
Canada, 3, 22, 96
Carron, Luis, 56
Carter, Jimmy, 56, 63, 152
Central Intelligence Agency (CIA), 52, 62,
  122
Chamorro, Violetta, 56, 63
Chechnya, 11, 141
Chinese Communist Party, 67
Chinese Malays. *See* Malaysian Chinese
CIA. *See* Central Intelligence Agency
citizenship
  discrimination and, 128
  in Germany, 87–88, 181
cleavage, 5, 123

Clinton, Bill, 10
Cold War
    communal contenders and, 29
    end of, 10–11, 84
    ethnopolitical conflicts and, 6, 10–11,
        13, 17, 106
collective intervention, 176
colonialism, 1, 14, 21, 96–97
Comintern (International Communist
        Movement), 68
common law, 175
communal conflicts
    responses to, 188
    U.N. and, 174
communal contenders
    autonomy and, 29
    claims of, 167
    Cold War and, 29
    interests of, 134
    legal recognition of, 165–66
    Malaysian Chinese, 19
    political objectives of, 28–29
    power sharing and, 32–33
    segmented society and, 19
Communist Party of Malaya (CPM),
        130–31
concepts, 107
Conference for Security and Cooperation
        in Europe (CSCE), 171, 176
Congo, 2, 9, 15
contagion, 143
containment, 134
Contras, 122, 154
contra war, 58
Convention for the Protection of National
        Minorities, 171
Convention on the Prevention and
        Punishment of the Crime of
        Genocide, 168
Convention on the Rights of the Child, 168
Council of Europe, 171–72
CPM. See Communist Party of Malaya
CSCE. See Conference for Security and
        Cooperation in Europe
Cuba, 152–53
culture
    ethnic groups and, 5
    group identity and, 120

Kurds and, 38, 39–40, 47
    Malaysian Chinese and, 72–73, 79–80
customary law, 174
Czechoslovakia, 11, 155

Declaration on the Elimination of All
        Forms of Intolerance and
        Discrimination Based on Religion
        or Belief, 168
democracies
    ethnic demands and, 8
    ethnopolitical conflicts and, 104–5
    group rights and, 184–86
    indicators of, 110
    political action and, 123
Democratic Action Party, 69, 131
discrimination
    citizenship and, 128
    degree of, 108
    economic, 108, 119–20
    ethnic groups and, 3, 4–5
    ethnopolitical conflicts and, 103–4, 108,
        117–20
    group identity and, 130
    indicators of, 108
    political, 108, 117–19
    positive, 162
    reverse, 127
    social, 85–86
dominant minorities, 29–30

education
    discrimination and, 127
    Malaysian Chinese and, 73, 78, 79
Egypt, 12, 31, 146
Emancipation Proclamation, 22
Emergency, 67–68, 74–76, 154–58
empirical generalizations, 112–13
England. See Great Britain
Eritrea, 12–13, 24
Ethiopia, 12–13, 20
ethnic cleansing, 12, 16, 174, 182
ethnic conflicts. See ethnopolitical conflicts
ethnic groups
    coexistence of, 3
    common identity and, 35
    communal contenders, 19, 28–29,
        165–66

conflict between, 96
culture and, 5
discrimination and, 3, 4–5
economic status of, 111–12
ethnoclasses, 19, 27–28
ethnonationalists, 19, 23–25, 165
external support for, 111
human rights and, 30
identity and, 3
indigenous peoples, 9, 19, 25–27,
 165
interests and, 3
international implications of, 32–33
international law and, 165–68
international system and, 161–64,
 170–73
mobilization of, 96, 96–98, 122–23
origins of, 3–5
political environment and, 123–26
politically active, 4(fig)
as "psychological communities", 3
religious groups vs., 3
size of, 107
states and, 6–10
types of, 19, 20(fig), 30, 165–66
 See also ethnic identities;
 ethnopolitical conflicts
ethnic identities
colonial rule and, 21
constructivist interpretation of, 97
ethnopolitical conflicts and, 95–98,
 103–4
modernization theory and, 96
 See also ethnic groups; ethnopolitical
 conflicts; group identity
ethnoclasses, 27–28
dominant minorities and, 29–30
international factors and, 28
legal recognition of, 166
origins of, 27
political objectives of, 27–28
stratified societies and, 19
ethnonationalists
autonomy and, 8, 23–25, 32
Kurds, 19
legal recognition of, 165–66
objective of, 141
Palestinians, 19

political demands of, 4
self-determination and, 141
ethnopolitical conflicts
autonomy and, 11, 22
causes of, 11, 35
coercive prevention of, 189–91
Cold War and, 6, 10–11, 13, 17, 106
colonialism and, 1, 14, 21
contemporary examples of, 11–17
discrimination and, 103–4, 108,
 117–20
economic status and, 111–12
effects of, 139
ethnic identities and, 95–98, 103–4
external support for, 141–42, 143
future of, 191–95
government and, 96, 105, 111, 124
group cohesion and, 104, 109
group identity and, 108–9
historical background of, 19–23
internal processes of, 137(t)
international action in, 176–77
international dimensions of, 139–64
international system and, 5–11
management of, 133–36, 181–95
modeling, 95–116
models of, 96
numbers of, 2(fig)
political environment and, 104–5, 110
religion and, 31–32
social science approaches to, 95–116
states and, 8–9, 182
theory of mobilization for, 95
U.N. and, 13, 17, 29, 176–77, 188–91
 See also ethnic groups; ethnic identities;
 mobilization
EU. *See* European Union
European Community. *See* European Union
European Union (EU), 140
 ethnopolitical conflicts and, 16, 189
 Turkish government and, 47

Fagoth, Steadman, 61–62, 63, 122, 154
Federation of Turkish Workers, 89
formal recognition, 167
Fourteen Point Program for World Peace,
 44, 169
France, 3, 23, 90–91, 147

genocide, 8, 96, 98
Genocide Convention, 140, 170, 178
Georgia, 8, 24
Germany
    anti-Semitism in, 9, 86
    citizenship in, 87–88, 91, 181
    economy of, 130
    immigrants in, 3, 11, 91–92
    internal crises in, 92–93
    minority issues in, 159–61
    refugees and, 159–60
    state system of, 6
    status of, 160–61
    Turks in, 3, 81–84
governments
    ethnopolitical conflicts and, 105, 111, 124
    international economic status of,
        143–44
    use of violence by, 105, 111
    See also states
Great Britain
    Greece and, 154–55
    immigrants in, 3
    Kurds and, 50–51
    Malaysia and, 67–68, 73–75
    Malaysian Chinese and, 156–57
    Miskitos and, 58–59
    state system of, 6
Greece, 154–55
group cohesion
    ethnopolitical conflicts and, 104, 109
    indicators of, 109
    indigenous rights and, 123
    mobilization and, 122, 130–32
group identity
    awareness of, 35
    culture and, 120
    discrimination and, 130
    ethnopolitical conflicts and, 108–9
    indicators of, 109
    language and, 120
    political action and, 89–90
    religious groups and, 120
    states and, 43–44
    strength of, 108–9, 120–21
    See also ethnic identities
group rights
    democracies and, 184–86
    international actors and, 188–89

    in plural societies, 67–93
    power sharing and, 184–86
    self-determination and, 167
    states and, 182–84
Guatemala, 25
Gulf War (1990), 8, 16, 37

Habyarimana, Juvenal, 14
HADEP. See People's Democratic
        Party
Hanseatic League, 168
hegemony, 11, 155, 165
Heraclides, Alexis, 167
Ho Chi Minh, 155
Holocaust, 1, 98
Honduras, 56, 59–60
Hosseini, Shaik Izzeddin, 49
humanitarian intervention
    international law and, 177–79
    problems with, 178–79
    U.N. and, 38
human rights
    ethnic groups and, 30
    international law and, 173–74
Human Rights Watch, 16, 188
Hussein, Saddam, 10, 30
    foreign policy and, 142
    Gulf War and, 37
    human rights record of, 145
    Iraqi economy and, 119
    Iraqi government and, 144–50
    Kurds and, 52–53, 144–45
    toppling of regime of, 38
Hutus, 5, 7, 14, 16
hypotheses, 95, 101

Ibrahim, deputy prime minister, 158
identity groups. See ethnic groups
ILO. See International Labor
        Organization
imitation, 143
India, 5, 21, 25
Indian Law Resource Center, 153
indicators, 107
indigenous peoples
    autonomy and, 25
    international law and, 165–66, 172
    political objectives of, 22, 25–26
    rights of, 121, 123

Indonesia, 25, 126, 181
Inter-American Court of Human Rights, 64
interests
    ethnic groups and, 3
    political action and, 3
Internal Security Act of 1960, 69, 79
International Committee of the Red Cross, 140
International Convention on the Elimination of All Forms of Racial Discrimination, 168
International Court of Justice, 169
International Covenant on Civil and Political Rights, 168
International Covenant on Economic, Social, and Cultural Rights, 140, 168
International Crisis Group, 16
International Indian Treaty Council, 26
International Labor Organization (ILO), 27
international law
    ethnic groups and, 26, 165–68
    humanitarian intervention and, 177–79
    states and, 7, 165, 169
    war and, 8
international system
    ethnic groups and, 161–64, 170–73
    ethnopolitical conflicts and, 5–11
    states and, 139–40
Iran
    Kurds in, 37, 38, 48–50
    Soviet Union and, 145
Iran-Contra affair, 145
Iran-Iraq War, 36, 147, 149
Iraq
    current climate in, 147–48
    economy of, 119
    external support for, 147
    France and, 147
    Hussein and, 144–50
    invasion of Kuwait by, 8
    Kurds in, 5, 10, 35–38, 50–55, 117–26, 144–50
    regime status of, 145–46
    Soviet Union and, 147
    U.N. and, 144–45, 147–48

Iraq Petroleum Company, 149
Ireland, 32
Irish-Americans, 3
Israel, 8, 32

Jeremy I, 59

KDP. See Kurdish Democratic Party
KDPI. See Kurdish Democratic Party of Iran
Kennedy, Edward, 153
Khatami, Mohammad, 50
Khmer Rouge, 98
Khomeini, Ayatollah, 49, 145
Khuzistan, 48
Kohl, Helmut, 160
Kosovo, 16, 24, 165
KRG. See Kurdish Regional Government
Kurdish Democratic Party (KDP), 51, 151
    external support for, 149
    leadership of, 121–22
    PUK vs., 53–55
Kurdish Democratic Party of Iran (KDPI), 49–50
Kurdish Regional Government (KRG), 122
    area controlled by, 52
    current situation of, 150–51
    establishment of, 38, 53, 126
Kurdish Worker's Party (PKK), 47–48, 50, 132, 149
Kurdistan, 38, 42, 44, 50, 55
Kurds
    assimilation and, 48
    autonomy and, 35–55, 40–42, 44, 51
    Baathist government and, 51, 52
    culture and, 38, 39–40, 47
    current situation of, 150–51
    discrimination and, 118–20
    dispersion of, 38, 39(map), 40(t), 43
    as ethnic group, 3
    as ethnonationalists, 19, 24
    external support for, 149–50
    group cohesion and, 121–22
    group identity of, 120–21
    historical situation of, 7
    international context of, 144–50
    international system and, 161–62
    in Iran, 37, 38, 48–50

Kurds *(continued)*
　　in Iraq, 10, 35–38, 50–55, 144–50
　　language and, 51
　　language of, 39
　　Miskitos vs., 65, 117–26
　　mobilization and, 123
　　nationalism of, 39–45
　　as people, 38
　　political environment and, 124–25
　　religion and, 147
　　in Soviet Union, 38
　　status of, 146–47, 150
　　in Syria, 38
　　in Turkey, 37, 38, 46–48
　　Turkish government and, 4–5
　　Turks and, 38
　　twentieth-century changes of, 42–43

language
　　group identity and, 120
　　Kurds and, 39, 51
　　Malaysian Chinese and, 72, 129
Latin America, 5, 9
law
　　common, 175
　　customary, 174
　　statutory, 174
　　See also international law
leadership
　　cohesion among, 109
　　of KDP, 121–22
League of Nations, 26, 169–70
Lebanon, 19, 28, 29
legitimacy, 142
Le Pen, Jean-Marie, 91
levels of analysis, 117, 142

Macedonia, 19, 24, 187–88
Mahabad Republic, 48–49, 52
Mahathir, Prime Minister, 158
Malaya. *See* Malaysia
Malaysia, 28
　　Chinese in, 19, 22, 67–81
　　Chinese population in, 68(map)
　　communal riots in, 69
　　Communist party in, 68, 74–76
　　CPM rebellion in, 130–31
　　democracy in, 78–79
　　economy of, 80–81, 130
　　emergence of democratic, 73–74
　　Emergency and, 74–76

　　Emergency in, 67–68
　　ethnic divisions, 69–73
　　Great Britain and, 67–68, 73–75
　　history of, 76–81, 158–59
　　modern, 71(map)
　　New Economic Policy in, 78
　　power sharing in, 135–36
　　regime status of, 156
　　riots in, 76–77
　　social contract of, 76–77
Malaysian Chinese
　　as communal contenders, 19
　　culture of, 72–73, 79–80
　　discrimination and, 79–80, 127–29
　　education and, 73, 78, 79
　　external support for, 157–58
　　group identity and, 129–30
　　history of, 158–59
　　immigration of labor and, 22
　　international context of, 154–58
　　language and, 72, 129
　　mobilization and, 130–31
　　political environment and, 132–33
　　religion and, 72, 80
　　status of, 69, 156–57
　　Turks vs., 126–33
Malaysian Chinese Association (MCA), 131
Mandela, Nelson, 29
Mazen, Mahmoud Abbas, 148
MCA. *See* Malaysian Chinese Association
Meciar, Vladimir, 184
micronationalism, 24
Middle East
　　communal conflicts in, 15
　　ethnopolitical conflicts in, 17
　　Palestinians in, 10
　　states in, 6
Milosevic, Slobodan, 16, 184
Minorities at Risk project, 4, 19, 31, 183
Miskito Council of Elders, 64–65
Miskitos
　　autonomy and, 56–65
　　autonomy of, 26
　　discrimination and, 118–20
　　dispersion of, 57(map)
　　as ethnic group, 3
　　group cohesion and, 121–22
　　group identity of, 120–21
　　history of, 56–63
　　international context of, 151–54
　　international system and, 162

Kurds vs., 65, 117–26
  mobilization and, 123
  as people, 56–58
  political environment and, 124–25
  Sandinistas and, 60–63, 118, 125,151–54
  self-determination and, 56, 133
  status of, 153
  support of, 153
Miskitos, Sumus, and Ramas (MISURA),
    62, 122
Miskitos, Sumus, Ramas, and Sandinistas
    United (MISURASATA), 61–62, 122
MISURA. See Miskitos, Sumus, and Ramas
MISURASATA. See Miskitos, Sumus,
    Ramas, and Sandinistas United
mobilization
  of ethnic groups, 96
  group cohesion and, 122, 130–32
  group sources of, 117–22
  instrumental nature of, 96
  international factors affecting, 139
  international factors in, 163(t)
  in Latin America, 5
  political action and, 122–23
  primordial approach to, 96, 97
  See also ethnopolitical conflicts
models, 98
modernization theory, 96
Moldova, 186
Monroe Doctrine, 152
Mosquito Reserve, 59
Muhammad, Qazi, 48
multiculturalism, 134–35
multilateral treaties, 174
Muslim Brotherhood, 3, 31
Muslim Chams, 98
Muslim Kashmiris, 5
Muslims
  Christians vs., 28
  Hindus vs., 13

National Autonomy Commission, 62
National Union for the Total Independence
    of Angola (UNITA), 29
nation-state. See states
Native Americans, 8, 19, 25
NATO. See North Atlantic Treaty
    Organization
Nazzer, Gamal Abdel, 146
NEP. See New Economic Policy
Netherlands, 3, 128

New Economic Policy (NEP), 78
New Zealand, 25
NGOs. See nongovernmental
    organizations
Nguma, Macias, 13–14, 15
Nicaragua
  Autonomy Statute of, 62–63
  economy of, 119–20
  Honduras vs., 59–60
  Miskitos in, 26, 56–65, 117–26
  regime status of, 152–53
  Sandinistas and, 60–63
  Somoza dictatorship in, 60–61
Nicaraguan Institute for the Development
    of Autonomous Regions, 56
Nigeria, 9, 21
nongovernmental organizations (NGOs),
    16–17, 26, 160
North Atlantic Treaty Organization
    (NATO), 16, 189
Ntaryamira, Cyprien, 14

OAU. See Organization of African Unity
Öcalan, Abdullah, 47–48, 90
Oezdemir, Cem, 87
Organization of African Unity (OAU), 15,
    16, 29, 139, 189
Organization of the Islamic Conference, 15
Organization on Security and Cooperation
    in Europe (OSCE), 176, 189
OSCE. See Organization on Security and
    Cooperation in Europe
Ozal, Turgut, 47

Paasha, Abdurrahman, 42
Pakistan, 21, 28, 32
Palestinians, 5, 8, 10, 19, 32, 140
Pantin, Eduardo, 122
Patriotic Union of Kurdistan (PUK), 51,
    53–55, 122, 151
peacebuilding, 177
Peace of Westphalia, 140
Peng, Chin, 68
People's Democratic Party (HADEP), 46
People's Republic of China (PRC), 159
Philippines, 25, 126
PKK. See Kurdish Worker's Party
pluralism, 134–35
political action
  group identity and, 89–90
  interests and, 3

political action (*continued*)
  mobilization and, 122–23
  occurrences of, 5
  political environment and, 110
  strategies of, 5, 6(fig)
  See also ethnopolitical conflicts
political environment
  ethnic groups and, 123–26
  ethnopolitical conflicts and, 104–5,
    110
  political action and, 110
  types of, 110
  See also states
political mass murder
  etiology of, 98
  models of, 96
Pol Pot, 159, 178
populist states
  ethnopolitical conflicts and, 104–5
  indicators of, 110
  political action and, 123
power sharing, 135–36
  communal contenders and, 32–33,
    165–66
  group rights and, 184–86
PRC. *See* People's Republic of China
primordialism, 96
probability statements, 102
propositions, 100–101
PUK. *See* Patriotic Union of Kurdistan

Qasim, Abdul Karim, 51, 52
Qassemlou, Abdul-Rahman, 50

Rahman, Tunku Abdul, 76
Reagan, Ronald, 125, 153, 154
Regional Council of Indigenous Peoples,
  61
Región Autónoma del Atlántico Norte, 63
Región del Atlántico Sur, 63
religion
  ethnopolitical conflicts and, 31–32
  Kurds and, 147
  Malaysian Chinese and, 80
religious groups
  ethnic groups vs., 3
  group identity and, 120
rights
  group vs. individual, 170–73, 191–92
  indigenous, 121, 123

"Rights of Persons Belonging to National
    or Ethnic, Religious and Linguistic
    Minorities", 167
Rivera, Brooklyn, 56, 62, 63, 122
Rwanda, 141
  ethnic groups in, 2, 5
  ethnopolitical conflict in, 14
  state system of, 7
Rwandan Patriotic Front, 14

sanctions, 100
Sandinistas
  contra war and, 58
  Iraqi economy and, 119–20
  Miskitos and, 60–63, 118, 125,
    151–54
  in Nicaragua, 60–63
Savimbi, Jonas, 29
Selassie, Haile, 12
self-determination
  autonomy and, 186–88
  ethnonationalists and, 141
  group rights and, 167
  Latin America and, 9
  Miskitos and, 56, 133
  wars of, 24
socialist states
  ethnopolitical conflicts and, 104–5
  indicators of, 110
society
  segmented, 19
  stratified, 19, 21
Somalia, 2, 10, 167
Somoza Debalye, Anastasio, 60
Soviet Union
  breakup of, 141
  Cold War and, 10–11
  common interest and identity in, 11
  communism in, 10
  Communist doctrine in, 9
  dissolution of, 4, 17, 24
  Eritrea and, 12
  hegemony and, 155
  Iran and, 145
  Iraq and, 147
  Kurds in, 38
sphere of obligation, 174
states
  communal identities and formation of,
    141–42

creation of, 167
ethnic groups and, 8
ethnopolitical conflicts and, 8–9, 182
group identity and, 43–44
group rights and, 182–84
identity and, 43–44
individual rights and, 165
individuals vs., 168–70
international law and, 7, 165, 169
international system and, 6, 139–40
See also governments; political
environment
statutory law, 174

Taft, William Howard, 169
Talabani, Jalal, 53, 122, 142–43, 146
Thailand, 73, 126
theories, 98, 101
Treaty of Lausanne, 44
Treaty of Sèvres, 44, 45(map)
Treaty of Westphalia, 168
Truman, Harry, 154–55
Truman Doctrine, 152, 155
Turkey, Kurds in, 4–5, 7, 37, 38, 46–48
Turks
discrimination and, 85–86, 127–29
as ethnic group, 3
as ethnoclass, 19
group identity and, 129–30
hostility toward, 81–82
international system and, 162, 164
Kurds and, 38
Malaysian Chinese vs., 126–33
mobilization and, 131–32
organs and status of, 83–84
political action and, 89–90
political environment and, 132–33
political situation of, 86–89
status of, 161
Tutsis, 5, 7, 14, 16, 29–30

UN High Commission for Refugees, 153
Ubaydullah, Shaik, 42
Uganda, 13–14, 15, 178
UMNO. *See* United Malay National
Organization
UNITA. *See* National Union for the Total
Independence of Angola
United Malay National Organization
(UMNO), 76

United Nations
communal conflicts and, 174
creation of, 1
ethnopolitical conflicts and, 13, 15, 17,
29, 176–77, 188–91
humanitarian intervention and, 38,
177–79
ILO and, 27
Iraq and, 144–45, 147–48
as lawmaker, 174–76
as peacekeeper, 15–16, 17
United Nations Agenda for Peace, 188
United Nations Commission on Human
Rights, 167
United States
economic status and, 114–15
ethnopolitical conflicts and, 15–16,
29
Gulf War and, 37
Irish in, 3
Universal Declaration of Human Rights,
168, 178
UN Security Council resolution 620,
145
UN Security Council resolution 688, 37
UN Working Group on Indigenous
Rights, 26
Uwilingiyimana, Agathe, 14

variables, 102, 107
Vietnam, 8, 126, 178
Vietnam War, 157

Wilson, Woodrow, 44, 169
World Bank, 26
World Council of Indigenous Peoples, 26,
61
World Trade Organization, 26

xenophobia, 3, 9, 86

Yapti Tasbaya Masrika (YATAMA), 63, 64,
122
YATAMA. *See* Yapti Tasbaya Masrika
Yugoslavia, 14, 167
breakup of, 24
civil wars in, 11, 13
Serbian nationalism in, 9

Zelaya, 60–62